Dieter Bös · Bernhard Felderer (Eds.)

The Political Economy of Progressive Taxation

With 4 Figures

Springer-Verlag Berlin Heidelberg New York
London Paris Tokyo Hong Kong

Professor Dr. Dr. Dieter Bös, Institute of Economics, University of Bonn,
Adenauerallee 24-42, D-5300 Bonn 1, FRG

Professor Dr. Bernhard Felderer, Department of Economics,
University of Cologne,
Albertus-Magnus-Platz, D-5000 Cologne 41, FRG

ISBN-13:978-3-642-75001-4   e-ISBN-13:978-3-642-74999-5
DOI: 10.1007/978-3-642-74999-5

This work is subject to copyright. All rights are reserved, whether the whole or part of the material is concerned, specifically the rights of translation, reprinting, reuse of illustrations, recitation, broadcasting, re-
production on microfilms or in other ways, and storage in data banks. Duplication of this publication or
parts thereof is only permitted under the provisions of the German Copyright Law of September 9, 1965,
in its version of June 24, 1985, and a copyright fee must always be paid.
Violations fall under the prosecution act of the German Copyright Law.

© Springer-Verlag Berlin · Heidelberg 1989
Softcover reprint of the hardcover 1st edition 1989

The use of registered names, trademarks, etc. in this publication does not imply, even in the absence of a
specific statement, that such names are exempt from the relevant protective laws and regulations and
therefore free for general use.

Typeset: Lydia Danner and Heinz-Dieter Ecker on TEX,
under assistance of Sfb 303 at the University of Bonn

2142/7130-543210

Preface

This volume presents papers which were given at a conference of the Liberty Fund, Washington, co-sponsored by the Carl-Menger Institute, Vienna. The conference took place in Vienna in January 1988. All papers were subject to a refereeing process; some of them had to be revised very extensively.

The economics of progressive taxation have been a research topic ever since economists have dealt with the economic role of the state. Old puzzles are the best: the theoretical underpinning of progressivity still is not fully convincing, even after 200 years of economic research. In the present volume we succeeded in publishing some contributions of outstanding economists which present their visions of the topic.

Niskanen distinguishes two types of contributions of public choice analysis to understanding and evaluating the tax and transfer system in modern economics: the *positive* analysis, which examines the issue of how a tax and transfer system would look if it were established by a government subject to majority rule; and the *normative* analysis, which tries to discern an optimal system of taxes and transfers. In the normative case the author distinguishes between the "libertarian perspective", in which each person has full rights to any property that he has acquired legally and in which transfers are determined entirely by the preferences of the donors, and the so-called "constitutional perspective", in which each person elects the rules affecting taxes without knowledge of his position in the post-constitutional distribution.

Peacock criticizes and comments on the literature on the Laffer curve and suggests new approaches to the subject. The paper starts with a simplified exposition of the Laffer analysis. In reviewing the literature, one comes to the conclusion that, within the strict confines of the Laffer analysis as depicted in many academic journals, the Laffer curve is a highly suspect construction. Most contributions to the literature accept the hypothesis that taxpayers react passively to government action. Consequently, the author proposes a framework for a public choice approach to the Laffer problem.

Streissler, in his contribution, elaborates on the international consequences of less progressive taxation. He argues that, given the worldwide movement towards less progressive income taxation, the decisive factor in international trade is no longer comparative advantage, but comparative taxation. The author is interested in the international aspects of the relation between such factors as labor supply, saving and capital formation, risk taking, etc., when taxation becomes less progressive. In addition, factor movements elicited between countries with less or more progressive taxation is an important topic in this paper. Though the author admits that theoretical answers to many of these questions are ambiguous, he succeeds in finding convincing explanations for most phenomena and questions raised by using empirical results and arguments.

Bös and *Tillmann* look for an income taxation scheme which leads to equitable and fair allocations: can an income tax be defined in such a way that everyone prefers his own position to the position of any other person? If only individual consumption-labor bundles are considered, regardless of the individual abilities, it is impossible to achieve an equitable state by means of an income tax. If, on the other hand, the individual productivities explicitly are taken into account, an income tax always yields an equitable allocation. However, only the laissez-faire state is equitable *and* Pareto optimal. Hence, the Bös–Tillmann paper implies a rather pessimistic view of an equity-based theoretical explanation of progressivity. Consequently, the authors hint at second-best solutions, where the equitability postulate can be re-interpreted as a postulate of self-selection.

Swoboda and *Steiner* integrate various recent branches of the literature on entrepreneurial behavior and taxation. The effects of progressive taxation on the risk-taking of entrepreneurs are very indeterminate. Whether progressive taxation enhances or hinders risk-taking depends essentially on the utility function of the individual. Contrary to widespread intuition, flat (linear) taxes are most efficient only under special assumptions. According to the authors, further developments of the principal-agent theory could solve the open problems mentioned above.

Finally, this volume contains two papers which deal extensively with the shadow economy. *Neck, Schneider,* and *Hofreither* first present a model in the Allingham–Sandmo tradition. The "rational tax evaders" decide on the supply of underground labor and the demand for underground goods. Under particular assumptions the households' supply of underground labor is increased by higher marginal income tax rates. The firms' demand for underground labor and the supply of underground goods depend positively on the indirect tax rate. Whether official sector wage rates have a positive or negative influence on the equilibrium amount of underground labor depends upon whether demand or supply side changes dominate.

In their second paper, *Schneider, Hofreither,* and *Neck* deal with a small macroeconomic model of the Austrian economy. Their estimation of the shadow economy applies the currency-demand approach, which is based on the assumption that shadow transactions are undertaken in the form of cash payments. A hidden

Preface

economy, therefore, generates excess demand for currency which can be used to deduce the size of the shadow transactions. In their econometric model the authors show that easing the direct tax burden effectively reduces the shadow economy. A reduction of indirect tax rates has a more modest influence on the relative size of the shadow economy.

Dieter Bös
Bernhard Felderer

Table of Contents

Preface *(D. Bös and B. Felderer)* v

Progressive Taxation and Demographic Government:
A Public Choice Analysis *(W.A. Niskanen)* 1

Progressive Taxation: Models and Policies *(Ch. Kirchner)* 19

The Rise and Fall of the Laffer Curve *(A. Peacock)* 25

On the Irrelevance of the Laffer Curve *(C.-A. Andreae and Ch. Keuschnigg)* 41

The International Consequences of Less Progressive Taxation *(E. Streissler)* 43

Tax Reforms and International Mobility *(L.B. Yeager)* 71

Equitability and Income Taxation *(D. Bös and G. Tillmann)* 75

A Political Philosopher's View of Equitable Taxation *(J. Gray)* 101

An Economists' View of Equitable Taxation *(D. Bös and G. Tillmann)* 107

Capital Markets, Entrepreneurship and Progressive Taxation
(P. Swoboda and P. Steiner) 111

Taxing Entrepreneurs: Models and Reality *(T.W. Hazlett)* 145

The Consequences of Progressive Income Taxation for the Shadow
Economy: Some Theoretical Considerations *(R. Neck, F. Schneider,
and M.F. Hofreither)* 149

The Consequences of Progressive Income Taxation for the
Shadow Economy *(F.A. Cowell)* 177

The Consequences of a Changing Shadow Economy for the "Official"
Economy: Some Empirical Results for Austria *(F. Schneider,
M.F. Hofreither, and R. Neck)* 181

Notes on Taxes and Tax Evasion in Austria *(G. Lehner)* 213

Addresses of Authors 219

Progressive Taxation and Democratic Government: A Public Choice Analysis

William A. Niskanen, Washington, D.C., USA

Introduction

Public choice analysis provides two important types of contributions to understanding and evaluating the tax and transfer systems in contemporary economies. *Positive* public choice analysis addresses such questions as "What are the characteristics of the tax and transfer system that are likely to be selected by contemporary governments?" *Normative* public choice addresses such questions as "What characteristics of a tax and transfer system would commend unanimous consent, given the conditions and preferences of each person affected?" A comparison of the results of these two types of analyses, in turn, provides interesting insights about the direction of desirable changes in the tax and transfer system and about the effects of alternative constitutional rules on the behavior of governments. This paper summarizes the major contributions of public choice analysis to these types of questions and illustrates these contributions with some examples that are roughly representative of the our contemporary economic and political systems. All of these major contributions and some of the examples were developed by other scholars. My own role is limited to developing the implications of these contributions for the specific issue of the structure of the tax and transfer system and some examples to illustrate these issues.

A Positive Analysis of Taxes and Transfers

Contemporary economic and political systems use two types of currencies – money and votes. Since the distributions of money and votes among the population are quite different, one should expect a "market" to develop in which some groups use

D. Bös and B. Felderer (Eds.)
The Political Economy of Progressive Taxation
© Springer-Verlag Berlin Heidelberg 1989

their relative surplus of votes to acquire money and other groups use their relative surplus of money to influence votes.[1] The outcomes of this market, in turn, depend on whether the effective constitution permits such transactions, the decision rules in this market, and the relative distributions of money and votes. This paper addresses only one side of this market, the use of votes to acquire money. Some other paper will have to summarize the similarly complex process by which groups use money to influence votes. Actual tax and transfer systems, in turn, will reflect the net outcome of these two processes.

A Simple Example of Majority Rule

Consider the following example to illustrate the process of using votes to acquire money:

- A polity consists of five groups, designated as A, B, C, D, and E.

- Each group has an equal number of votes.

- The level of income before taxes and transfers of these groups is, respectively, 10, 20, 30, 40, 50. (This corresponds roughly to the level and distribution of income per worker before taxes and transfers in the United States.)[2]

- Each group votes to maximize its own income after taxes and transfers. (In other words, no group has any net benevolence or malevolence with respect to other groups.)

- Any group may propose a change in taxes and transfers, and any proposal must be approved by a minimum of three of the five groups.

- And, for this example, the level of income before taxes and transfers in each group is given – in other words, is independent of the characteristics of the tax and transfer system.

---

[1] Several related activities also affect this market. Groups with a relative surplus of votes will attempt to constrain the use of money to influence votes. And groups with a relative surplus of money will attempt to discredit the processes by which people use votes to acquire money. In the spirit of truth in advertising, may I acknowledge that the Cato Institute is financed by this second type of group.

[2] A careful reader will observe that the median income in this example is the same as the mean income. For all observed income distributions, in contrast, the median income is lower than the mean income. Since voting is a positive function of income, however, the median income of voters appears to be close to the mean income of the population.

Progressive Taxation and Democratic Government 3

Table 1 illustrates a representative set of outcomes for the conditions specific to this example.

Table 1: The Distributional Effects of Majority Rule

	Group					
	A	B	C	D	E	
Before Taxes and Transfers			Income			Transfer Share (%)
	10	20	30	40	50	0.0
After Taxes and Transfers						
Coalition						
1. ABC	16	26	36	36	36	12.0
2. ADE	20	20	30	40	40	6.7
3. ABC	24	24	34	34	34	14.7
4. CDE	10	20	40	40	40	6.7
5. ABE	13.3	23.3	30	40	43.3	4.0
6. ABC	17.3	27.3	34	34	37.3	13.1
etc.						

This set of outcomes reflects the standard results of this type of analysis. The more important lessons from this type of analysis are the following:

1. The effective coalition on each proposal will be the minimum necessary coalition for approval, and the net gains to each group in the effective coalition will be equal.

2. All transfers will be received by one or more of the lower-income groups, and all taxes will be paid by one or more of the higher-income groups.

3. There is no dominant coalition, however, on taxes and transfers. In other words, some new coalition can gain approval to replace any existing distribution of taxes and transfers.[3]

4. Moreover, the level and distribution of taxes and transfers differs substantially among the set of viable proposals. Among the limited set of proposals described in Table 1, for example, the tax and transfer share of total income varies from 4 percent to 14.7 percent, and the amount of transfers to the lowest income groups varies from 0 to 140 percent of their income before transfers. (For comparison, it is interesting to note that total transfer payments in the United States are

---

[3] The possibility that majority rule may lead to cycles was apparently first discovered by Condorcet in 1785. For an efficient summary of the conditions that lead to such cycles, see Mueller (1979), pp. 38–49.

about 13 percent of net national product, and the poor receive less than one-half of the total transfers.)

5. There is no consistent pattern of marginal tax rates. For this example, marginal tax rates range from zero to 100 percent but, in some cases, the marginal tax rates on some lower-income groups are higher than on higher-income groups.

Several obvious extensions of this analysis lead to some additional lessons.

6. An increase in the variance of income before taxes and transfers (or a broadening of the franchise to lower-income groups) increases the maximum level of taxes and transfers.

7. An increase in the share of votes required to approve a tax and transfer proposal reduces the maximum level of taxes and transfers. In the limit, the only transfers that would be approved by a rule of unanimity would be those that reflect the marginal benevolence of the groups subject to taxes toward some other group.

8. The tax rates on any group are not likely to be higher than that which maximizes revenue from that group. Specifically, $t_i \leq \frac{1}{1+S_i}$, where S_i is the elasticity of supply of taxable income with respect to the income after taxes for group i.[4] The level of both taxes and transfers, thus, declines as function of the magnitude of these supply responses to the tax and transfer system.

9. The extension of this type of analysis to transfers-in-kind is relatively straightforward. Transfer recipients would prefer a transfer of money to a transfer of food, housing, medical care, etc. of equal cost to the groups subject to tax. One or more of the groups subject to tax, however, may prefer a transfer of goods or services to a transfer of money, either because they may be suppliers of that good or service, there may be some marginal external benefit of the consumption of these goods or services by the transfer recipients, or the groups subject to tax may have some paternalistic concern about the mix of consumption spending by the transfer recipients. In this case, the level of taxes and transfer payments will be higher than if only money transfers are considered, and some part of total transfers will be in the form of goods and services.

10. Most important, the tax and transfer system is likely to be stable only if it reflects some marginal benevolence by the groups subject to tax or if some group has the authority to set the voting agenda. A clever agenda-setter, by structuring the sequence of votes and determining when the voting will end, can achieve any

---

[4] This formula for the revenue-maximizing tax rate applies strictly only when there is only one source of income or if income from all sources is taxed at the same rate. If income from only one source is subject to tax, the revenue-maximizing tax rate is $t_i = \frac{D+S_i}{D(1+S_i)}$, where D is the (absolute value of the) elasticity of demand for the factor of production subject to tax.

outcome within a wide range. The specific tax and transfer system of a democratic government, thus, may depend on the objective of the specific group that has the authority to set the voting agenda.

An Agenda for Future Research

This simple analysis, of course, is not sufficient to explain all of the characteristics of actual tax and transfer systems. We observe, for example, that low-income groups pay some taxes and high-income groups receive some transfers. In addition, many tax rates appear to be lower than the revenue-maximizing rates. Actual tax and transfer systems are much more stable than indicated by this analysis, suggesting that the outcomes of the political process may be shaped by some amount of benevolence or by those who establish the voting agenda. And finally, the level of taxes and transfers has increased substantially over time and differs substantially among nations without any obvious change or difference in the structure of the political system.

In conclusion, a rather simple public choice analysis explains many of the characteristics of tax and transfer systems. Moreover, this analysis contributes to an understanding of the effects of changes in the economy and political system on the level and distribution of taxes and transfers. Much more work, however, needs to be done. The following types of questions deserve more analysis:

- What is the income distribution of voters?

- What are the effects of the various ways by which money is used to influence votes?

- How much does the actual level and distribution of tax and transfers reflect some benevolence?

- Who are the agenda setters? What are their objectives? What are the effects of the specific rules used by legislatures affecting who is allowed to make a proposal, the sequence of votes, and the termination of voting on a specific issue?

- And what explains the rapid growth of taxes and transfers in most countries in this century and the substantial differences that remain?

The first major contributions to economics were made about 200 years ago. The major contributions to public choice were made in my adult life. There is reason to be pleased about how much public choice has accomplished. One should not be surprised about how much work remains to be done.

A Normative Analysis of Taxes and Transfers

The normative stream of public choice analysis builds on the same foundations as modern welfare economics. Every person is the only judge of his or her welfare. The welfare of individuals are not comparable by any common measure; in other words, the welfare of individuals may not be aggregated in any way to form a "social welfare function." And, most important, the consent of all individuals with the relevant rights is the only valid test of a "social optimum."

In fact, there are two normative streams of public choice analysis with quite different implications. One stream, which might best be described as "libertarian", is premised on the consent of all persons to each transaction, assuming that each person knows his or her own conditions. The other stream, which is best described as "constitutional" or "contractarian", is premised on the consent of each person to the rules that will determine future transactions, assuming that the persons choosing these rules act as if they do not know their own conditions.

A Libertarian Perspective

Let's first evaluate the implications of the libertarian perspective for three types of goods and services provided by government – private goods, public goods, and transfers. The distinctive assumption of the libertarian perspective is that each person has full rights to any property that he has acquired legally, including by inheritance, even if there may have been a buccaneer somewhere in the family background. The only basis for coercive transfers consistent with this perspective would be to redistribute property that the directly-affected individual has acquired by illegal means.

Private Goods

For various reasons, governments provide a range of "private" goods and services. The appropriate distinction between private goods and public goods is not whether average costs decline with respect to the number of people served but whether there is an efficient means to exclude nonpaying beneficiaries. Indeed, private markets provide many types of goods and services subject to declining average costs if there is some means to charge a sufficient number of beneficiaries to cover total costs.

The pricing rules for private goods supplied by the government are the same as for efficient markets. All people should pay the same price or "user fee" per unit of these goods provided, regardless of their income. For goods subject to declining average costs, some type of two-part pricing structure is preferable to a uniform price based on average costs. There is reason to question why the government should supply any of such goods, but there is no normative basis for using the tax structure to finance these goods. Although governments do not broadly follow these rules, this is a relatively straight-forward analytic issue and need not be further elaborated.

Public Goods

The level of public goods provided, by definition, is uniform across the affected population. The normative issue is to select a level of the public good and a distribution of tax shares that would be approved by unanimous consent. This issue, fortunately, was resolved some years ago.[5] The optimum level of public goods is that for which the sum of the marginal values across the population affected is equal to the unit price of the good. For individual demand functions of the form

$$Q = a_i y_i^b (s_i P)^{-c} \quad ,$$

where Q is the common level of the public good, P is the unit price, y_i is the income of group i, and s_i is the share of taxes paid by group i, the optimum income elasticity of the tax share is

$$E(s_i : y_i) = \frac{b}{c} \quad .$$

In other words, the income elasticity of tax shares that would be approved by every person is equal to the ratio of the income elasticity over the (absolute value of the) price elasticity of demand for the public good. The optimum tax structure is progressive if the income elasticity is higher than the price elasticity and is regressive in the opposite case. The optimum tax structure for the financing of public goods, thus, cannot be derived from first principles but must be derived from the revealed demand for these goods.

Table 2 provides an example of the optimum financing of public goods, for conditions that are roughly representative of those in the United States. The several available studies of the revealed demand for government services do not provide precise estimates of the relevant elasticities, but they each conclude that

---

[5] This implication of the "Lindahl" pricing rule for public goods was first brought to my attention by James Buchanan.

8 William A. Niskanen

the income elasticity appears to be higher than the price elasticity for most such services.[6] For this example, the income elasticity of tax shares is assumed to be equal to 1.5.

Table 2: The Distribution of Taxes for Public Goods

	Group					
	A	B	C	D	E	Sum
			Income			
	10	20	30	40	50	150
Tax Share	.035	.099	.183	.281	.393	1.000
Taxes	1.054	2.951	5.477	8.433	11.785	30.691
Average Tax Rate	.105	.149	.183	.211	.236	
Marginal Tax Rate	.105	.193	.250	.296	.335	

For this example (by design), the structure of average and marginal tax rates is quite similar to the combined structure of income and social security taxes in the United States following the federal Tax Reform Act of 1986. For several reasons, however, one should not conclude that the U.S. tax system is close to optimum. The available studies, for example, indicate that the "publicness" of most government services is very small. In this case the optimum tax structure would consist of equal payments for each person using these services plus a lower level or progressive taxation to finance the public component of these services. In addition, many government services are financed by other types of taxes or by borrowing, and the overall structure of taxes may not be appropriate to finance the combination of private goods, public goods, and transfers provided by the government. The primary lesson of this example is that a progressive income tax may be appropriate to finance the public component of the services supplied by government, depending on the revealed demand for these services.

---

[6] The technique for estimating the demand functions for public goods was independently developed and first applied by Borcherding and Deacon (1972) and Bergstrom and Goodman (1973). Both of these articles indicate that the income elasticity of the demand for public goods is higher than the (absolute value of the) price elasticity and that the degree of "publicness" for most of these services is very low.

Transfers

Given the libertarian perspective, what type and amount of transfers might be preferred by both the donors and recipients? Which of these transfers might best be provided by the government, specifically by the federal government?[7] The first implication of this approach is that the level and characteristics of transfers should be determined entirely by the preferences of the *donors*, as long as the recipients prefer some amount of some type of transfer to no transfer. Recipient preferences for higher income or that reflect malevolence or envy with respect to the donors are irrelevant, because they do not provide a basis for a unanimous consensus on transfers.

Donors may have one or more of three motives for transfers, and each of these motives implies a different type of transfer. Donors may have some amount of pure benevolence with respect to some other people, in which case the optimal type of transfer is a money transfer. Donors may be concerned about some condition specific to some other people – such as their income, health, education, or housing – in which case the optimal form of transfer is that which maximizes the specific post-transfer condition of concern, such as a voucher based on earnings or on some measure of the consumption status of the recipient. And third, donors may be uncertain about their own future status, in which case the optimal transfer is a money transfer based on the insured condition, such as unemployment or disability.

In each case, for each donor, the optimal amount of the transfer is that for which the marginal value of the transfer *to the donor* is equal to the marginal value of the other goods and services foregone. The amount of preferred transfers is likely to increase with the income of the donor but may differ among donors of the same income. Such transfers will generally reduce the post-transfer variance of income or some measure of the consumption status within the affected population but will not necessarily be restricted to the poorest individuals.

Some amount of some types of consensual transfers will take place without any government action, especially within families and other small cohesive social units, or where there is an established market for some forms of insurance. The necessary case for government transfers must be based on one or another of the following two conditions:

---

[7] This "libertarian" perspective on taxes and transfers is based on my development of the approach first developed by Hochman and Rodgers (1969).

- Numerous potential recipients may be concerned about the condition of the same set of potential recipients, *or*

- There is no potential market for some forms of desired insurance.

The sufficient case for government transfers must be based on both of the following two conditions:

- The benefits to the potential donors must be incremental to the conditions resulting from the combination of recipient behavior and any nongovernmental transfers including private insurance, *and*

- The incremental benefits to the potential donors must be higher than the transactions costs of an agreement among the donors through governmental processes, where these costs reflect the probability that the amount, nature, and recipients of governmental transfers may not be the same as preferred by each donor.

The case for transfers by the federal government must meet each of the above conditions plus one other:

- The benefits to potential federal donors must be incremental to the conditions resulting from the combination of recipient behavior, private transfers including insurance, and any transfers by state or local governments.

Federal transfers pose both advantages and disadvantages. Transfers by the federal government greatly reduce the "free-rider problem" among potential donors, because the costs of emigration from the nation are much higher than from an individual state or local government. At the same time, the transactions costs of federal decisions are likely to be much higher because such decisions require agreement of a larger number of voters with less homogeneous preferences. The greater potential for federal transfers is not a sufficient basis for assuming that any specific transfer or welfare service should be provided by the federal government.

The implications of this perspective for the structure of governmental processes are interesting. Conceptually, all transfer programs should be decided by referendum or by a separate legislature responsible only for each such program, in each case for which only donors are allowed to vote. The voting process should be structured to minimize the incentive for "strategic" voting. And the implicit decision rule, as in private charity organizations, is that all transfers should be approved by a unanimity of the donors (or their representatives) or, in the absence of unanimity, each donor must be allowed to withhold his contribution. One must shift to a constitutional perspective to understand the ethical basis for a decision rule on routine legislation that requires less than full unanimity.

It is instructive to compare the implications of this perspective with the current system of transfers and welfare services. This normative perspective is quite consistent with the current types of transfers and the distribution of recipients. We observe a combination of lump-sum money transfers, a substantial amount of conditional transfers of money or specific services, and several forms of social insurance. We also observe that the set of transfers leads to some reduction of the variance of post-transfer conditions, but that a substantial portion of transfers do not go to the pre-transfer poor. There is no clear case that the general character of the current transfer system is inconsistent with the preferences of most potential donors. For the most part, the case for change in the details of this system must be made on narrow technical grounds.

The major differences between the implications of this perspective and the current system concerns the amount of transfers. The current system is the result of a political process that is influenced by the preferences of both donors and recipients, as well as by the political agents that structure the alternatives considered. The major results of the actual decision process are that the amount of transfers are larger than are preferred by the current donors and that the nature of the transfers are biased somewhat toward money transfers that are not conditional on the behavior of the recipient.

The Constitutional Perspective

What are the characteristics of a "fair" system of taxes and transfers?[8] All too often, contemporary political discussion of taxes and transfers uses a concept of fairness that provides little basis for agreement. A proposed change in taxes or transfers is usually considered fair only when it benefits one's own group or some other group that one favors, whether or not the existing taxes and transfers are fair by any standard. In this context, agreement is possible only if those who would pay higher taxes have some marginal benevolence toward those who would receive higher transfers (or lower taxes), given the existing distribution of income taxes and transfers. Given the existing welfare state, this set of consensual redistributions may be empty. In this context, without such marginal benevolence, any increase in taxes and transfers is a negative-sum game, a form of legalized theft, reducing the total income of the community. The conventional focus on the distributional outcomes of this game, thus, is not a sufficient basis for determining whether these outcomes are the results of a fair game.

---

[8] This section is based on my own article, Niskanen (1986).

This section develops a "constitutional" or "contractarian" approach to taxes and transfers. This approach, thus, addresses the rules by which taxes and transfers are determined, rather than the results of a specific application of these rules. The distinctive assumption of this approach is that each person selects the rules affecting later taxes and transfers without knowledge of his specific position in the post-constitutional distribution of natural endowments. Given a consensus on these rules, unanimous post-constitutional agreement is neither a necessary nor sufficient basis for judging the fairness of the outcomes. In this sense, this approach is strictly individualistic but not strictly libertarian. The promise of this approach is based on the prospect of a much broader consensus on these rules than on any post-constitutional decisions on policies affecting the distribution of income.

For each application of this approach, each person is assumed to have a general understanding of human behavior, to know his own preferences, to know the post-constitutional distribution of natural endowments, but does not know his specific position in that distribution. In this sense, these examples are better characterized by uncertainty rather than ignorance. Two specific assumptions are common to both examples. For each individual, the utility of the outcomes is proportional to the square root of disposable income and leisure, but the general results are common to any utility function with a declining marginal utility of each condition.[9] The distribution of natural endowments is symmetric, with a mean of $30,000 (about equal to the current U.S. net national product per worker) in the first example, and a mean of $15 per hour (equal to $30,000 for a 2,000 hour work year) in the second example.

Redistribution of Unearned Income

The first example demonstrates the effects of different distributions of future income, given that all income is "manna," that is, independent of human effort.[10] Consider the following choice: an individual faces a lottery with a probability of .5 that he will receive an income of $12,000 or $48,000. A certain income of $30,000 would maximize utility. For the assumed utility function, however, he would prefer any certain income higher than $27,000 to this lottery and would be willing to pay the state up to $3,000 to provide the tax-transfer program. Table 3 summarizes the results of this type of choice for three distributions of natural income.

---

[9] Specifically, $U(y, z) = y^{.5} z^{.5}$, where y is the level of income after taxes and transfers, and z is the hours of leisure.

[10] This example was suggested, but not fully developed by Zeckhauser (1974).

Progressive Taxation and Democratic Government

Table 3: Redistribution of Unearned Income

	Natural Income		
Minimum $(p = .5)$	$ 20,000	$ 12,000	$ 6,667
Maximum $(p = .5)$	40,000	48,000	53,333
Equivalent Income	29,142	27,000	24,428
Minimum Transfer	9,142	15,000	17,761
Maximum Tax	10,858	21,000	28,905
Maximum Rent	858	3,000	5,572

The first implication of this example is that the level of taxes and transfers increases with the variance of natural income. The first column, for example, could represent the choice of someone selecting social insurance for his own generation, and the third column the choice of the same person for the social insurance available to his distant grandchildren. This comparison illustrates that the difference between a person's decision on a law or on a constitutional rule is a matter of the degree of uncertainty, not a different type of analysis. A second implication is that the constitutional rule would limit the range of taxes and transfers but may not specify the amount. For the conditions of the second column, for example, taxes may range from $ 18,000 to $ 21,000, and transfers may range from $ 15,000 to $ 18,000, depending on the distribution of the social rent. This rent, which increases with the variance of natural income, could be used to administer the tax and transfer system, finance the protective and productive services of the state, increase transfers or reduce taxes, or could be wasted by the state or in various forms of rent-seeking activities – an allocation that cannot be fully determined at the constitutional stage. In this case, since all income is "manna," disposable incomes would be equal.

For some, this example may suggest a constitutional basis for a substantial tax on estates. Such an interpretation, however, would be strictly correct only if the level and distribution of the estate is independent of the behavior of those who inherit the estate. In many cases, of course, people "earn" their inheritance by behavior that serves the interests of the person who leaves the estate. One should be cautious about weakening the ties that bind one generation to the next. Nevertheless, an inheritance is closer to "manna" than is most other forms of wealth, and there may be a constitutional consensus on a higher relative tax rate on income from this source.

Redistribution of Earned Income

A second example demonstrates the characteristics of the optimal tax and transfer system, given that taxes and transfers affect the hours worked, for a specific distribution of natural wage rates.[11] For this example, the observed wage rate is equal to the natural wage rate; that is, taxes and transfers are assumed to affect hours worked but not the choice of jobs or an individual's investment in his skills. An individual faces a lottery with a .25 probability of a natural wage rate of $6, $12, $18, or $24 per hour. The sum of taxes and transfers in this case is assumed to be equal. That is, no amount of taxes are necessary to administer the tax and transfer system or any other role of the state. The annual earnings are based on 50 weeks of work per year. Table 4 summarizes the characteristics of the tax and transfer system that maximizes expected utility for these conditions.[12]

Table 4: Redistribution of Earned Income

	Natural Wage Rate			
($p = .25$ for each rate)	$6	$12	$18	$24
Hours Worked Per Week	27.8	41.5	46.7	49.7
Annual Earnings	8,347	24,900	42,016	59,584
Annual Transfer or				
Taxes ($-$)	6,095	1,222	$-2,473$	$-4,844$
Average Tax Rate (%)	-73.0	-4.9	5.9	8.1
Marginal Tax Rate (%)	33.3	25.6	17.6	9.4
Annual Disposable Income	14,442	26,122	39,543	54,740

The most important implication of this example is that the marginal tax rates decline as a function of earnings. This induces those who are most skilled at generating earnings to work more than those who are less skilled and leads to a higher variance of earnings than of the natural wage rate. Average tax rates, of course, increase with earnings, reflecting the redistribution of income from higher

---

[11] This example was fully developed by Zeckhauser (above reference). The numbers presented in Table 4 are only a scalar change of the Zeckhauser calculations plus the correction of one error.

[12] For the symmetric distribution of natural wage rates in this example, the optimal level of taxes and transfers is approximated by the quadratic function

$$T = -a + bE - cE^2; \quad \frac{\partial T}{\partial E} \geq 0 \quad,$$

where T is the level of taxes ($+$) or transfers ($-$), and E is the observed level of earnings before taxes and transfers.

skilled workers. For this example, taxes and transfer payments are 5.4 percent of total earnings and the variance of disposable income is only slightly less than the variance of natural wage rates.

This example assumes that there is only one form of transfer payment, similar to a negative income tax. A superior solution may be to allow the poor to choose one of two forms of transfers, either a negative income tax or an earnings subsidy. Similar calculations for a tax and transfer system that includes an optional earnings subsidy, unfortunately, have not been developed.

Our current tax and transfer system differs from this example in two important ways. One, marginal tax rates are now much higher than the optimal rates for both the lowest and highest-skilled workers. This reduces the hours worked and earnings of both of these groups. Second, government transfer payments in the United States are now about 13 percent of net national product, an amount that would be appropriate only if the variance of natural wage rates is much higher than in this example.

Effects of Other Conditions

For the same distribution of natural wage rates and the same utility function, any change in other conditions would reduce the total amount of transfers relative to this example.[13] Any marginal tax rate on earnings leads people to choose more pleasurable jobs and to invest less in human skills. Any tax on the income from new investment would reduce the size of the complementary stock of physical capital. Any expenditure for the protective and productive services of the state would reduce the transfer share of total output. Any waste of resources by the state or in private rent-seeking activities would have a similar effect. Each of these probable conditions affecting the post-constitutional behavior of people and governments is realistic to expect at the constitutional stage and would lead to a lower preferred amount of transfers. And finally, the potential to emigrate or, with others, to secede from a state would limit the total amount of coercive transfers from any one individual to the difference between the value of residence in one state and that in the next best alternative, minus the personal costs of moving or of participating in an effective secession. Such rights of emigration and secession, moreover, are likely to be secured by a constitutional consensus, because they are consistent with the principle of maximum compatible liberty.

---

[13] The qualitative effects of changing these other conditions on the level of taxes and transfers were developed by Buchanan (1985).

Although some amount of social insurance may be preferred at the constitutional stage, a realistic consideration of these other conditions may lead to a set of constitutional rules that provides no authority for the redistribution of income. The U.S. Constitution, for example, provides no explicit authority for federal welfare programs. Article 1, Section 8 describes 18 specific powers of the federal government, without a hint that these powers authorize the redistribution of income or the provision of federal welfare services. The only constitutional authority for the modern welfare state rests on an obscure ruling by the Supreme Court in 1936, in United States v. Butler, that "the power of Congress to authorize appropriations of public money for public purposes is not limited by direct grants of legislative power found in the Constitution." Our contemporary national community may share a constitutional consensus for some amount of some types of federal transfers. Our contemporary problem, however, is that there are no effective constitutional limits on the amount or nature of these transfers.

Conclusion

Public choice analysis, in summary, provides both an explanation of why democratic governments choose a progressive tax structure and a normative basis for the system of taxes and transfers. The most intriguing conclusion of the positive analysis is that the relative stability of actual tax and transfer systems must reflect either some benevolence or the interests of some group that has the authority to set the voting agenda. The normative analysis of tax and transfer systems, in turn, leads to two intriguing conclusions. The optimal tax structure to finance public goods depends on the relative magnitude of the income and price elasticity of demand for these goods; given the crude available estimate of these two elasticities, some progression of both average and marginal tax rates to finance these goods appears to be appropriate. In addition, a constitutional perspective on tax and transfers concludes that some amount of transfers are desirable, average tax rates should increase with income, but that marginal tax rates to finance these transfers should decline over the whole income distribution.

Substantial additional development of these types of analyses would be desirable. Some development of positive public choice is necessary to explain some of the detailed characteristics of actual tax and transfer systems and, most important, why these systems have been relatively stable. Normative public choice should address the nature of the tax system that is appropriate to finance the combination of private goods, public goods, and transfers provided by governments.

For those of you who are concerned, as I am, about the absolute size of the state in contemporary societies, I would counsel you not to focus your concern on the progressive tax system. The primary problem of contemporary government is that it does too much, not that it finances its activities, in part, by progressive taxes. My own normative analysis leads me to conclude that the optimal size of government would be smaller than we now observe but would include some amount of transfers targeted to the poor. This government, in turn, should probably be financed by a tax system in which average tax rates increase but marginal tax rates decline with income. The challenge is to design a set of constitutional rules that would make such a tax and transfer system more consistent with the outcomes of democratic processes.

References

Bergstrom, T.C., and **Goodman, R.P.** (1973): "Private Demands for Public Goods." *American Economic Review* 63: 280–296.

Borcherding, T.E., and **Deacon, R.T.** (1972): "The Demand for the Services of Non-Federal Governments." *American Economic Review* 62: 891–901.

Buchanan, J. (1985): "Coercive Taxation in Constitutional Contract." Working Paper, Center for Study of Public Choice, George Mason University.

Hochman, H.M., and **Rodgers, J.D.** (1969): "Pareto Optimal Redistribution." *American Economic Review* 59, 542–557.

Mueller, D. (1979): *Public Choice.* Cambridge: Cambridge University Press.

Niskanen, W.A. (1986): "A Constitutional Approach to Taxes and Transfers." *Cato Journal.*

Zeckhauser, R. (1974): "Risk Spending and Distribution." In *Redistribution and Public Choice*, edited by Harold Hochman and George Peterson. New York: Columbia University Press.

Progressive Taxation: Models and Policies

Christian Kirchner, Hannover, West Germany

1. Methodological Issues

The normative part of Niskanen's paper attempts to achieve two goals:

(1) to illustrate the expected outcome of the libertarian and the constitutional (contractarian) perspectives insofar as transfers and progressive income taxes are concerned, and

(2) to compare these (anticipated) outcomes of various (ideal) political agenda with our actual tax and transfer systems and evaluate those systems in the light of the results of the normative analysis.

The author very cautiously introduces comparisons between such results from normative analyses and the actual world, arguing "that it might be instructive to compare the implications of the libertarian perspective with the current system of transfers and welfare perspectives" (p. 11). He determines that in actual transfer systems a substantial portion of transfers do not go to the pre-transfer poor (p. 11) and that the amount of transfers in actual tax and transfer systems is higher than that expected under the libertarian perspective (p. 11). Such a finding may induce a change from the actual tax and transfer system to the 'optimal' results under the libertarian perspective. But such a step – which undoubtedly would place more emphasis on individual liberties, as the present political systems of western democracies with majority rule and some degree of protection of individual liberties and minorities do – presupposes that we possess exact knowledge as to which factors in our political system should be modified. However, if individual preferences, for instance, are the source of 'excessive' transfers, there is no reason to decrease such transfers. A libertarian perspective would have to begin with such individual preferences. The difficulties arising from comparing results from normative analyses with actual facts stem from the problem that such discrepancies do not say much about the essential political process. Therefore, a more precise positive analysis is necessary. The Niskanen paper, therefore, appears somewhat unbalanced. It dismisses too many problems as "issues of future research" (p. 5). The well founded results of the normative analyses are very useful from a theoretical perspective, but they do not provide a sufficient fundament for designing constitutional rules which, according to the author, is an important step in the political process (p. 17).

One could counter this line of argument by pointing to the possibility of introducing new institutional devices for consensual transfers such as referenda or separate legislation in which only donors are allowed to vote and where the principle of unanimity is applicable (p. 10). But then one would have to solve the problem of how to introduce such new institutional devices under a majority rule. The first answer could be that one would have to find a majority which is willing to enact such new constitutional rules. But how could these new rules be protected against another change of the ruling majority coalition? The problem of unstable coalitions – as analysed in the paper (p. 3) – would arise here as well.

Niskanen is well aware of the methodological problems arising from mere comparisons between results from normative analyses and actual tax and transfer systems: after having stated the differences between the results of a normative analysis under the libertarian perspective and under the tax and transfer system of the United States, he returns to positive analyses and argues that the current system is the result of a political process that is influenced by the preferences of both the donors and the recipients, as well as by the political agents that structure the alternatives considered (p. 11). This clearly is an interesting hypothesis which deserves further examination. If we are able to demonstrate that there is not only a preference for benevolence on the part of representatives from high income groups but also a preference for malevolence (or envy) on the part of representatives from low income groups we would be in a better position to understand the actual stability of our tax and transfer systems and to evaluate the difficulties of changing the political system towards a libertarian perspective. A preference for malevolence (or envy) on the part of low income groups would work in the same direction as the incentive to improve one's own economic position (self-interest). Furthermore, if we analyse the activities of political agents – as mentioned in the paper (p. 11) – and if we take into account their self-interest, we could possibly find more arguments for the actual stability of the present tax and transfer systems. I shall, therefore, come back to these issues.

As far as the constitutional perspective is concerned, the Niskanen paper also compares the outcome of the normative analysis with the current tax and transfer system and argues that marginal tax rates are much higher in the present system than the 'optimal' rates would suggest (p. 15). Furthermore, this paper concludes that actual transfer payments are much higher than the ones to be expected under the constitutional arrangement, when the given variance of natural wage rates are taken into account (p. 15). The methodological problem here is identical to the one discussed in relation to the libertarian perspective. Any discrepancies found may be due to a higher risk aversion. The issue of how to lower marginal tax rates and the actual amount of transfers under a given majority rule cannot be answered. It is interesting to note that, in this context, the author discusses the issue of transfers under the given constitutional framework of the United States (p. 16).

If a given constitution outlawed transfers, the problem of realizing the 'optimal' transfer rate of the normative analysis would be very easy to solve. But despite the fact that the author characterizes the 1936 ruling of the Supreme Court (United States v. Butler) as "obscure", he has to acknowledge that this decision is binding so long as it is not overruled by a new decision of the Supreme Court. In a public choice framework, this means that predictions are necessary about possible changes in the jurisdiction of the Supreme Court under changing political factors. Then we are not confronted with the problem of just changing majorities within the legislature, but with the impact of such changes – and possibly with changes in the value structures of judges – on courts of law. The author is cautious enough to state that the present political system of the United States is characterized by a constitutional consensus for "some amount of some types of federal transfers" (p. 16). But this means that under given conditions, a change in the jurisdiction of the Supreme Court is unlikely. Here too – as in the case of the discussion of the libertarian perspective – a number of issues for further positive analysis are important.

2.   Agenda for Future Research

In his 'agenda for future research' (p. 5) the author mentions two issues which seem to be of utmost importance: the preference for benevolence on the side of donors, and the question, who are the 'agenda setters'. As mentioned in the preceding section, one should also take into account the issue of malevolence (or envy) on the side of recipients. In addition, agency theory should be included in the discussion of the problem of 'agenda setters' by analysing the role played by politicians and bureaucrats.

The introduction of progressive taxation in the last century was viewed by many as a kind of substitution for revolutionary changes in the social order. Instead of expropriating the rich members of society, redistribution was sought by means of progressive taxation. This line of argument certainly played a role in addition to the concept of "fairness" of taxation: if politicians seeking to maximize their voter support want to fulfil the desire either for revolutionary change or some kind of substitute, it is easy to them to promise to tax the rich and redistribute the wealth (or income) among the poor. If such a policy results in greater transfers from the rich to the state without really improving the lot of the poor, low income groups should then rethink their voting behavior and look for better alternatives. But if these actors have a certain preference for malevolence, it is not the improvement of one's own situation which counts, but the deterioration of the relative standing of the high income group. It is worthwhile, therefore, to research the direction of questioning as to whether preference for malevolence has actually played such a role in history and whether this factor is still relevant today. This could at least help to explain certain types of voting which otherwise would have to be viewed as irrational. If such a preference for malevolence can be proven, this would be relevant under majority rule, even in cases where constitutional rules are to be changed. For economists who favour results which are in accordance with the libertarian or constitutional perspective, this would mean that the problem of how such preferences may be changed would have to be tackled.

The case of malevolence has shown that this preference works best under a political system where political agents act on behalf of voters (representative democracy). If we now assume a majority rule democracy with such political agents, and if we further assume that in the principal-agent-relationship (between voters and politicians) political agents cannot be fully controlled by voters (which seems to be realistic), the politicians should be interested in any system of redistribution using the tax and transfer system which produces a social rent (p. 13). The hypothesis which seems worth testing then may be formulated as follows: politicians, as rational actors, have an interest in progressive taxation and transfers because their own position is improved by such a system. If there is a voter preference for malevolence (and benevolence on the side of others), it would be easy for politicians to install systems of progressive taxation and transfers. But even without such preferences the role played by politicians would work in the direction of consolidating majorities interested in redistribution. There are two more phenomena which let the hypothesis regarding the role of politicians appear more plausible:

- If politicians can improve their own position when the share of state activities increases, and if the financing of a growing share of state activities is more manageable by promising voters that this will done by taxing the rich, then politicians should employ the tax and transfer system to increase the share of state activities.

- If a substantial portion of transfers do not go to the pre-transfer poor

(p. 11), this portion can only be explained as follows: representatives from high income groups who must make these transfers to representatives of other groups are simultaneously donors and recipients under a progressive taxation system. That does not seem to make any sense, but if the one side of the transfer – the progressive taxation – is done openly and the other side – the subsidization – is managed covertly (as often is the case in actual tax and transfer systems), the incentive for politicians to behave in this way is a double one: they can count on a preference for malevolence among representatives of low income groups, and they can build up a clientel of subsidy recipients.

Both phenomena are consistent with the hypothesis regarding the role of politicians in a representative democracy. Hypotheses built on these phenomena, therefore, would have to be tested separately.

Finally, the role of bureaucrats should also be considered insofar as bureaucrats should be interested in any increase of their tasks. The line of argument and the formulation of hypotheses to be tested should be very similar to those discussed for politicians.

The Rise and Fall of the Laffer Curve

Alan Peacock, Edinburgh, U.K.*

1. Introduction

The history of fiscal doctrine is strewn with statements concerning the critical point at which taxes will become 'dangerous' to the economy, by which is meant that the economy has to endure efficiency losses and even social disturbances which could undermine good government.[1] The Laffer curve is therefore at the end of a long line of such statements, but it is one which, in the course of professional discussion, has been given much more precision than previous ones. The incentive for doing so has been provided not merely by mathematical economists in search of a model to refine which contains some semblance of reality, but also by the intense interest displayed by policymakers in search of an economic justification for lowering the average burden of taxes combined with reduction in tax progressivity.[2] The attraction is obvious when one considers the basic features of the curve itself. The demonstration of its existence, whether observable or not, is based on the mathematical truism that if tax rates levied on a given tax base, say income, are zero, then the revenue yield is zero and if they are 100 percent, the yield will also be zero, it being assumed that the tax base will disappear.[3] There is a presumption, therefore, that, as tax rates move from zero to 100 percent, the tax yield will rise, reach a maximum and then fall. It follows that there could be circumstances where a government could reduce tax rates, with associated improvements in the supply of effort, and yet still maintain the revenue yield.

The author believes that a study of the controversy surrounding the realism and relevance of the Laffer analysis is instructive for those of us whose value judgments lead one to conclude that the case for progressive and 'heavy' taxation is in the famous word of Blum and Kalven (1953), an 'uneasy' one. Even though he claims to demonstrate that the Laffer analysis does not offer the support for

---

* The help of Oliver Heavens and Ron Edwards in checking through the mathematics of alternative versions of the Laffer curve is gratefully acknowledged.

[1] For a useful survey and critique of the concept of an economic limit to taxation, see Shoup (1980).

[2] The history of the Laffer curve in US policy discussion is described in fascinating detail in Roberts (1984).

[3] The disappearance of the tax base is not a mathematical requirement. As Blinder (1981) points out, excise taxes have no such natural bound, and there are many examples of taxes on liquor, tobacco and petrol in which taxes have exceeded 100 percent of the producer's price.

D. Bös and B. Felderer (Eds.)
The Political Economy of Progressive Taxation
© Springer-Verlag Berlin Heidelberg 1989

tax reform for which it was intended, the investigation of its properties does draw attention to other ways in which a large and growing public sector may be detrimental to the aspirations of a free society.

The study begins with a simple exposition of the Laffer analysis (Section 2). It then presents and comments upon the critical literature which the analysis has spawned (Section 3 and 4). Most of that literature accepts the underlying thesis that taxpayers are passive reactors to stimuli offered by the fiscal authorities. The author then considers the implication for the analysis of adopting a 'public choice' approach to the Laffer 'paradox' and produces a rather different scenario describing the relation between the rise in tax rates and tax revenue (Section 5). A final section offers some conclusions (Section 6).

2. The Laffer Model

There are several mathematical versions of the Laffer model, which use different assumptions. The version used here is based on an amalgam of the Blinder (1981) and Fullerton (1982) models but these accord with the Laffer original as developed by Canto, Joines and Laffer (1981). For simplicity, following Fullerton, I assume that all income is labour income.

By definition:

$$Y = \bar{w}H \tag{1}$$

where $\bar{w}$ is some weighted average gross wage rate and H is the total hours worked in the economy.

The tax yield will depend firstly on the tax regime. A progressive income tax system is introduced in a very simple fashion by assuming a fixed exemption limit, E, and a linear tax system, so that

$$T = t(\bar{w}H) - \bar{E} \tag{2}$$

where t is the tax rate and T is the tax yield.

Now if $\bar{w}$ and H are positive constants, then

$$\frac{dT}{dt} > 0 \quad .$$

If this were so, then the yield of tax would go on growing even if $t > 1$, i.e. exceeds 100 percent. Workers would go on working even if their income after tax is negative! This implausible situation is recognized by introducing a functional relationship between H and t. Following Fullerton (1982) a constant elasticity of supply of labour with respect to the wage rate after tax, $\bar{w}(1-t)$, is used such that

$$H_s = B[\bar{w}(1-t)]^\epsilon \quad , \quad \epsilon > 0, \ B > 0 \quad . \tag{3}$$

Whereas the supply of labour is assumed to depend on the after-tax wage rate, the demand for labour is assumed to depend on the gross wage. Using a constant elasticity of demand function, we can write:

$$H_d = A \cdot \bar{w}^\eta \quad , \quad \eta < 0 \quad . \tag{4}$$

Assuming that the labour market clears so that $H_s = H_d = H$, when we can express $\bar{w}$ as a function of t.

Therefore equation (2) is re-written as

$$T = t(\bar{w}(t) \cdot H(t)) - \bar{E} \quad . \tag{5}$$

By total differentiation

$$\frac{dT}{dt} = \bar{w}H \left[1 + \frac{\partial H}{\partial t} \cdot \frac{t}{H} + \frac{\partial \bar{w}}{\partial t} \cdot \frac{t}{\bar{w}} \right] \quad . \tag{6}$$

Equation (6) tells us that whereas an increase in t will have a positive effect, ceteris paribus, the effect of such an increase in t could produce a fall in hours worked and thus in the tax base. We can no longer be sure that $dT/dt > 0$. Before we can determine whether the relationship between T and t traces out a Laffer curve, it must be remembered that the number of hours worked, and therefore the tax base, will depend on the demand for labour.

We are now able to solve for t and to determine, by setting (6) equal to zero, whether there is a maximum value for t. After some very tedious algebra, the interesting result is obtained that a maximum value for T is obtained when

$$t = \frac{\eta - \epsilon}{\eta(1 + \epsilon)} \quad . \tag{7}$$

Before exploring the properties of equation (7), let us proceed quickly to an illustration of the claimed policy significance of the Laffer curve.

Using the familiar technique of a four-quadrant diagram in which all axes are positive, a simple shorthand method may be used to demonstrate the curve's fiscal implications. Taking the origin of the four-quadrant diagram at 0, then the right-hand bottom quadrant displays the Laffer curve. It shows the relationship,

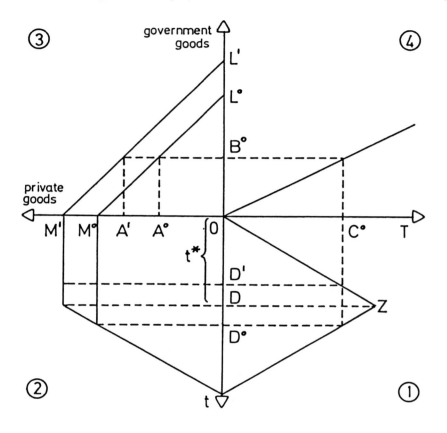

Diagram

therefore, between t and T. For simplicity, the curve is given as a triangle with the apex at Z. In the left hand bottom quadrant the relationship between GDP and t is shown. Again for simplicity it is assumed that GDP is independent of the tax rate, t, if $t < t^*$. When the tax rate rises above $0D$, hours of work fall in response to the further fall in the net wage, and when the tax rate is 100 percent, hours of work fall to zero. The distance $0A$ on the abcissa represented the GDP available for distribution between private and government goods. In the left-hand upper quadrant the opportunity slope is drawn depicting the exchange rate between private goods and government goods and, again, for simplicity's sake, the slope is assumed to be linear throughout its length. In the righthand upper quadrant the relationship between total tax revenue and the supply of government goods is shown. It is assumed that the government is constrained by total revenue

The Rise and Fall of the Laffer Curve   29

in the amount of goods it can purchase. Again for simplicity it is assumed that
the government goods 'sanctioned' by the available revenue rise in proportion to
total revenue available. In short, the prices of government goods are fixed.

Consider an economy which is 'over the Laffer Hill' where the tax rate is $0D^o$.
The associated level of Y is $0M^o$, and the tax revenue T is $0C^o$. Given the price of
government goods, this enables the government to 'buy' $0B^o$ level of such goods,
leaving $0A^o$ of private goods.

The government can be just as 'well-off', in the crude sense of being able to
buy the same level of government goods, if the tax rate were reduced to $0D'$, where
the lower tax rate produces the same total tax revenue. However, this is because
H increases in response to the fall in t, and, with given $\bar{w}, Y$ increases to $0M'$.
The private sector is 'better off', as a result. All is for the better in the best of
Lafferian worlds. Taxes are lower, output is higher and so the opportunity slope
showing the trade off between private and government goods shifts upwards from
M^0L^0 to $M'L'$.[4]

3.   A Confusion of Curves

I have cheated in presenting the model in a form which dramatises its policy content, for a number of important assumptions have been omitted, some of which are
recognized by its author. These assumptions do not question the basic character
of the relationship between the government and the taxpayer but they relate to
any idea that there is a Laffer curve which is unique and immutable. These are
now considered seriatim:

(i)   The Tax Base

We have to be clear whether broad-based or narrow-based taxes are being considered. Imagine a government which places a tax on tartan rugs. It is obvious that
the cross elasticity of demand for tartan compared with other rug material is so
high that raising the tax rate on the area of tartan used would produce negative

---

[4] This illustration draws attention to the naivety of textbook presentation of alternative
choices open to society between public and private goods. These presentations normally assume
that the opportunity slope determining the limitations on choice is independent of the process
of transfer of resources from the private to the public sector. For an important exception see the
recent textbook of Stiglitz (1986).

marginal revenue even in Scotland. Broader-based commodity taxes might also display Laffer-like properties. As David Hume (1752) remarked: "a duty upon commodities checks itself; and a prince will soon find that an encrease of the impost is no encrease of his revenue". He adds, characteristically, that "(i)t is not easy, therefore, for a people to be altogether ruined by such taxes". These cases are obvious enough, but more graphic examples may be found in countries where local governments have taxing powers but know that they are constrained in raising rates by the possibility that their marginal revenue receipts will diminish if their inhabitants buy goods in neighbouring jurisdictions.

These homely examples indicate that the Laffer effect very much depends on high elasticities of demand in the case of commodities and, where the tax base is some form of factor income, on high elasticities of supply. However, presumably if we are concerned primarily with macroeconomic effects, the analysis is meant to apply to tax regimes where the taxes are broad-based. The question that this gives rise to is whether such taxes will be associated with high elasticities. I shall return to this question at a later stage.

(ii) The Tax Regime

Consider a government which wishes to raise a large proportion of its revenue (say 30 percent) from a tax on persons and has a fixed revenue yield in mind. The observed elasticity of supply of labour will depend on whether the tax varies and how much it varies with personal income. In theory at least, the use of a poll tax would avoid a tax on margins and would have less disincentive effects than a progressive personal income tax. A change in the tax regime from the former to the latter would presumably mean that although the revenue yield would be the same, the Laffer curve would have shifted. This is, of course, an extreme example but it serves to underline the point made by Hemming and Kay (1980) that a Laffer curve can only be defined by reference to one particular point in time and must refer to a particular tax regime and a particular distribution of skills.

(iii) The Pattern of Expenditure

Unless we are looking at some set of mini-Laffer curves associated with narrow-based taxes, which is surely not the case to which the Laffer analysis has been meant to apply, then one is faced with the further question of what to assume about the use of the proceeds of the taxes raised using different tax rates. This is the familiar problem of 'balanced-budget incidence' as it was christened by Richard Musgrave (1959).

An obvious ploy to remove this awkward problem is to try to assume an expenditure pattern which eliminates any effects on labour supply caused by government expenditure. Thus in the Canto, Joines and Laffer (1981) model, it is assumed 'for simplicity' that (a) government expenditure takes the form of transfers payments to individuals, receipt of which is unrelated to factor supply; (b) there is no waste or inefficiency on the part of the government; and (c) taxes and transfers are costless to collect and distribute, respectively. These conditions, as they claim, would eliminate any net income effects, leaving it possible to confine the analysis to the change in the relative prices of work and leisure resulting from the tax regime(s). Clearly, this can be no more than a subterfuge, and underlines once again the problem of how to devise a suitable empirical test when now the pattern of government expenditure as well as the pattern of taxes and the distribution of skills are changing through time.

There is a further problem which offers a pre-echo of our later analysis when taxpayers' perceptions of budgetary impacts are considered in more detail. Taxes are frequently earmarked to finance specific items of government expenditure, a state social security system being a prime example. In this case, the effects on incentives to work can be very complicated because the taxes and benefits received occur in different periods. Neo-classical models of individual behaviour might throw some light on how to formulate some suitable behavioural hypothesis. Lindbeck (1982), for example, in another context, considers a two-period model of household behaviour for a social security scheme in which it is assumed that social security taxes are paid in period 1, and benefits received in period 2. If the individual can borrow freely in a perfect capital market, and if the discounted capital value of expected benefits for working an extra hour is smaller (greater) than the capital value of the taxes on that extra hour, there is a negative (positive) substitution effect against work in general, and in both periods! Even more complicated effects can be imagined, for the individual might also reassign his work effort through time. Thus even the simplest example, which takes no account of the complicated rules in actual social security schemes, produces a hornet's nest of problems, remembering also that the fastest growing taxes on income in OECD countries over the last two decades have been social security taxes.

The study of expenditure effects and of earmarked taxes reinforces the earlier point that a Laffer curve cannot be identified by reference to plots of tax revenue against tax rates (quadrant 2) and tax rates against GDP (quadrant 3) derived from time series, unless the tax and expenditure regimes and the distribution of skills remain unaltered during the period under scrutiny. It follows that tests of the shape and height of the Laffer curve have to eschew the familiar time series analysis.[5] The crucial question as to whether economies are likely to ever be on the 'downside' of the Laffer curve has to be tackled by some other method. A last-ditch argument which might be employed is to argue that, despite the conscious efforts of governments to redistribute income by fiscal means, the empirical results suggest that little redistribution has taken place. That being so, could it not be the case that at least net income effects of fiscal action are negligible? This is implausible because, if we concede the point, the fact still remains that even small changes in the distribution impact can mask major changes in the composition of taxes and expenditures, changes which are bound to have different impacts on the supply of effort.

4. Can We Be Over the Hill?

Returning to the original question raised by the Laffer curve analysis entails a demonstration as to whether or not it is likely that there will be circumstances in which a major economy would find itself in the position where a cut in the average (direct) tax burden would raise the total tax yield. Given the insuperable difficulties presented by time series analysis, recourse is had to the identification of a given Laffer curve and the derivation from it of the value of 'the' tax-rate (t) which would maximize total tax revenue (T). This particular value of t, call it t^*, is then compared with existing average tax rates in whichever country we have in mind.

The first stage in the investigation is to identify the characteristics of the economy which determine the shape and location of the Laffer curve itself. This means assuming

(i) a given tax regime. A simple way of introducing a progressive tax system would be, as in Section 2, by introducing an exemption limit;

(ii) no change in the income distribution so that the distribution of skills remains unaltered with any change in t, and no change takes place in relative net incomes so that everyone's income after tax is reduced in the same proportion. This means that if there is to be no change in the progressivity of the tax, then, when the marginal tax rate is increased, the exemption limit must be raised;

---

[5] For an interesting, but far from convincing, attempt to establish the shape and the position of a Laffer curve for the UK, see Beenstock (1979). For criticism of Beenstock's conclusions, see Hemmings and Kay (1980).

The Rise and Fall of the Laffer Curve
33

(iii) some functional relationship between levels of remuncration after tax and the supply of work effort which identifies both substitution elasticity and income elasticity effects, as in equation (5).

The next stage is to examine the relationship between the values of the elasticities and the tax rate t^*. Table 1 shows that the value of t^* falls as we move towards the right hand bottom corner of the matrix.

Table 1: Matrix of Values of t^* for Given Values of ϵ and η

η ϵ	−0.5	−1	−2	−3	−4	−5	−∞
0.5	1.33	1.00	0.83	0.77	0.75	0.73	0.67
1	1.50	1.00	0.75	0.67	0.63	0.60	0.50
2	1.67	1.00	0.67	0.55	0.50	0.47	0.33
3	1.75	1.00	0.63	0.50	0.44	0.40	0.25
4	1.80	1.00	0.60	0.47	0.40	0.36	0.20
5	1.83	1.00	0.58	0.42	0.38	0.33	0.16
∞	2.00	1.00	0.50	0.33	0.25	0.20	0.00

The third stage considers the question – how do we choose particular values of ϵ and η which accord with what is known about these elasticities? It is at this stage that anti-Lafferites have deployed what appears to be a successful pincer movement against the existence of the curve. In order for the value of t^* to come within a plausible range, say circa 0.5, then the elasticities of supply of and demand for labour have to be fairly high, or, in Blinder's words, "quite sizeable". However, such evidence as has been produced to quantify the elasticity of supply of labour alone, supports the opposite conclusion. Consequently, any value of η of −1 or more, whatever the value of ϵ, produces a value of t^* of 100 percent or more (see Table 1)! Within the strict confines of the Laffer analysis, as depicted by a whole string of academic journals, one is bound to conclude that the Laffer curve is a highly suspect construction. If we are looking for arguments and evidence to support the reduction of tax progressivity and the lowering of tax rates generally, then we must look elsewhere.

5. The State-Taxpayer Relationship Reconsidered

The Laffer analysis may have had an immediate appeal to those of us who have been concerned about the consequences of the growth of 'Leviathan', who also number amongst them many who have based their arguments in support of 'collective failure' on analysis of public choice. It is therefore somewhat paradoxical to find that the Laffer curve is based on a policy-making model, very similar to that used to explain how Keynesian fiscal policy is meant to operate, in which the taxpayer is subject to various stimuli and reacts rather like a Pavlovian dog. The only counteraction open to taxpayers faced with an increase in marginal tax rates is to fold their tents and to creep uncomplainingly into the pastures of leisure – already a strong assumption for it presupposes that the substitution effect dominates the income effect. As I have argued elsewhere (Peacock, 1979) firms and households are not passive adjusters to a change in their opportunity sets forced on them by government, except perhaps in the short run. It is worth parenthetic mention that Buchanan and Lee (1982) emphasise, rightly, that the distinction between the short and long perspective of taxpayers makes a great deal of difference to how we view the Laffer approach. They argue that those supply-side economists who argued in terms of Laffer curve effects were implicitly adopting a long-run perspective. While, therefore, it may be an open question whether taxpayers will form firm expectations about the permanency of any changes in tax rates introduced by government, labour supply elasticities might be very different in the longer run when taxpayers have time to consider any compensatory effects produced by tax changes, e.g. their effect on government services (already mentioned in Section 3 below). But what is interesting in this context is that in the longer run this kind of 'command model' used by Buchanan and Lee is suspect for the very reasons which Buchanan-type public choice theory has emphasised. Taxpayers adjust their behaviour not only through 'investment' in ways of minimising the effects of tax measures where it is assumed that such measures are imperatives. They can try to remove the coercive element in government action by exercising their power as voters and by their bargaining skills in dealing with the tax authorities who require their cooperation.

It would be entirely legitimate to start from a position in which, instead of assuming that government has complete control over the rates if not the yields of taxes, an antithetic, voluntaristic position is taken. This would require us to believe that in Western democracies, the electorates' preference systems have required a relative increase in the resources transferred to government use as inputs for the production of publicly-provided services and that redistribution through the transfer system reflects the importance in individual utility functions of concern for the welfare of others.[6] This view has excited sufficient interest to stimulate empirical investigation, and it has been claimed that there is no reason to suppose that a growing average tax burden will be associated with growing voter alienation. The corollary of this position is that if voter preferences change and fewer public goods are demanded then the tax burden will be adjusted downwards. Consequently, it is unnecessary to rely on Lafferian legerdemain to move taxpayers to preferred positions. Of course, those holding such a view will admit that the political system only approximates to a competitive market. Governments are not simply passive adjusters to electoral demands any more than taxpayers passively react to government-imposed tax regimes. However, there is one clear piece of evidence that a voluntaristic position, even as a first approximation to a model government, is untenable. If it were broadly true, then how is it possible to explain the observed growth in tax avoidance and evasion which have accompanied if they have not been caused by the growth in the average tax burden?[7]

It so happens that the phenomenon of tax evasion and the associated growth in the black economy offer a further dimension to taxpayers' reactions to changes in tax rates and their effects on t^* and T. The tax base now becomes a function not only of changes in H, hours of work, but also in the extent to which income is under-reported. Not surprisingly, therefore, the effect of the 'propensity to evade' on the original Laffer model has excited some interest and has been deployed to rescue its policy conclusions (see, for example, Feige and McGee, 1983, and Waud, 1986; but criticism by Peacock, 1983).

The mathematical complications of embodying an evasion component, and even an avoidance component into equation (5) are best left to the imagination, but fortunately the results obtained are intuitively obvious if we stick to the formulation of the Laffer curve used in this paper. Assuming that the elasticity of evasion with respect to t is positive, then at the very least we can establish that an evasion-adjusted Laffer curve will have a value of t^* which is lower than for the evasion-unadjusted curve, and that the value of T will also be lower. In a model which embodies both tax evasion and avoidance, Waud is able to show that a value of t^* as low as 0.33 can be obtained, even when the elasticity of demand for labour is < -1.

The problem with the extension of the model to cover evasion is that it has been done on the implicit assumption that the probabilities of achieving avoidance

---

[6] For an authoritative review of these propositions, see Musgrave (1986).

[7] I cannot embark on an analysis of the tricky question of how the extent of evasion and avoidance may be calculated. The David Hume Institute commissioned a study of the determinants and the magnitude of evasion which may be found useful. The study also includes a 60-item bibliography. See Pyle (1987).

and/or evasion objectives by taxpayers are fixed. Tax authorities are not simply passive adjusters to taxpayers' actions and they are normally dedicated to the business of rigging the odds against the taxpayer so that any bargaining advantages achieved by tax avoiders and the cheating of evaders can be circumscribed. It is clearly very difficult to embody changes in 'tax collection technology' into a formal model and no attempt is made to do so. However, there is one obvious weapon which the tax authorities may use if evasion grows with the rise in the average rate of direct taxes, recalling that all the models we have examined concentrate on taxes on factor incomes. They may decide that the marginal revenue return from devoting resources to improving the yield of taxes on expenditure is higher than the marginal revenue return from reducing avoidance/evasion of direct taxes. As I shall demonstrate, it is not even necessary to assume that the tax rates on goods and services need be adjusted in order to show that losses of revenue from Laffer effects may be compensated, if not fully, so, by changes in the yield of other taxes.

Let us retrace our steps a short distance and consider the evasion-adjusted Laffer model somewhat more closely. The first point to be made about it is that it implicitly assumes that the possibility of evasion either has no effect on the demand for labour or that it reduces that demand. This is certainly not intuitively obvious. As Peacock and Shaw (1982) argue: "There is a strong presumption that if evasion is possible then the GDP will be higher than in the non-evasion case. (Of course, it has to be accepted that those who work in an employed or self-employed capacity in the shadow economy may add a risk premium to their offer price, so that the gross wage would not be a function solely of the income tax rate.) Nevertheless, in the absence of evasion possibilities, GDP is likely to be lower because at the margin the demand for labour services will fall if higher wages have to paid to cover tax obligations. Provided that the demand for labour reveals positive price elasticity, and this does not seem an unreasonable assumption, it is clearly incorrect to estimate the revenue due to evasion by applying some tax coefficient to productive activities that would not otherwise exist". This argument has been considered a substantial one by the UK Board of Inland Revenue (1981) who have described tax evasion as a "random tax-subsidy towards price reduction", though they strongly condemn evasion for other reasons. The second point concerns the question of the interdependency of tax yields, taking on board but without being dogmatic about the direction of change in H as a result of changes in the degree of tax evasion. For simplicity, assume initially Y divided between two groups of earners, evaders and non-evaders. The proportion of income earned in each sector is determined by an evasion coefficient, a, such that aY represents the income of evaders and $(1-a)Y$ the income of non-evaders. Y is initially independent of t and a.

As evaders pay no direct tax, then

$$T = tY(1 - a) \quad . \tag{2a}$$

However, if they buy goods and services, evaders of direct taxes will pay taxes on expenditure embodied in the price of goods and services. Assuming a uniform consumption tax T_i with rate t_i

$$T_i = t_i C = t_i[b_1 Y(1 - a)(1 - t) + b_2 a Y] \tag{8}$$

where b_1 is the proportion of income spent on goods and services by non-evaders and b_2 the proportion by evaders.

From (2a)

$$dT/dt = Y[(1 - a) - t \cdot da/dt] \quad . \tag{5a}$$

We shall not attempt to find a general solution, but consider what would happen, using alternative assumptions if both the tax rate, t, and the evasion coefficient, increase. If Y is constant (denied by Laffer of course) then the sign of dT/dt is indeterminate. The increase in evasion will reduce the tax base, but the rise in the rate will increase the yield per unit of income. What is interesting is that whatever the sign of dT/dt, the yield of the tax on non-evaders' expenditure will fall because of the combined effect of t and a on the size of disposable income. On the other hand, the disposable income of evaders rises, and so will the yield of the tax on goods and services which evaders buy (cf. equation (8)). If we remove the assumption that Y is constant and adopt the Laffer assumption that a rise in t reduces hours of work of non-evaders, and a rise in the evasion coefficient, a, increases the hours of work in the evading sector, then it is possible to envisage a situation on the downside of the Laffer curve (defined in terms of the relation between direct rates and yields, as is normal), where a fall in the yield of direct taxes might be fully compensated by a rise in the yield of taxes on expenditure (5).

The extension of the Laffer curve analysis in order to reflect a bargaining situation between taxpayers and the fisc, i.e. a minimum concession to realism, does nothing much to restore our confidence in its policy conclusions. The 'rescue operation' simply lands one in a minefield of further complications.

6. Concluding Remarks

The purpose of this contribution was to examine how far the Laffer curve increased our understanding of the 'dangers' of high and progressive taxation. What conclusions do we reach?

i) As an attempt to establish a generalisation about the relation between the marginal rate of tax and the yield of tax garnished with empirical backing, the analysis does not seek to establish any particular set of tax principles. Such principles concerning the desirability or otherwise of progression, the degree of progression and the size as well as the distribution of the tax burden are matters for debate, even amongst those who share the same general economic philosophy. However, it is frequently the case that strong, attractive economic propositions are used to buttress widely different philosophical positions, and the Laffer curve is no exception. Nothing could be more attractive to those who prefer the public sector to remain large than a proposition that this can be done by cutting income taxes so that the budget can still remain balanced. Simultaneously, the curve demonstrates, as the Diagram shows, that the fruits of tax reduction can be reaped in the form of a higher rate of growth of private real expenditure with the growth of the public sector kept in check. *A fortiori*, reducing the average direct tax burden by lowering marginal rates will be even more in keeping with this position. Laffer cannot be blamed if it is convenient to believe that he is correct. As Jonathan Swift put it:

All philosophers who find
Some favourite system to their mind
In every point to make it fit
Will force all nature to submit.

(For philosopher, perhaps one should rather substitute 'politician'. After all, philosopher means 'lover of wisdom'.)

ii) It is comparatively easy to show that the Laffer analysis is based on a model which, in order to prove his basic proposition, adopts assumptions about elasticities of supply and demand for labour which seem implausible. Furthermore, it neglects important features of the working of government and the economy which insofar as they can be embodied in the model itself, do nothing to enhance its credibility.

iii) An examination of the growth in the average tax burden in Western industrial countries brings out an important 'design fault' in the model, for it presupposes that throughout the period of growth, taxpayers have only one weapon against growing tax obligations – reducing their hours of work – or perceive that the marginal costs of tax avoidance or evasion exceed the benefits. Attempts to rescue the Laffer position by taking account of the phenomenon of 'tax bargaining' may improve our understanding of the implications of alternative assumptions of taxpayer behaviour, but that is not enough to restore one's faith in the presumed shape and location of the curve itself.

iv) Nothing in what I have said is meant to suggest that the time and energy spent by economists crawling over the Laffer analysis and its assumptions represents some major malinvestment of intellectual resources. The question as to whether there are limits to the amount of taxation that can be raised is an important one for both the supporters and opponents of progressive taxation. Those who, following Rawls (1971), argue that society should choose that tax rate which maximises the welfare of the worst-off individual are concerned about the determination of the point at which raising the tax rate further would mean lowering the standard of living of the least well-off if redistribution of income through budgetary action were to proceed further.[8] Those like the author who are of a more libertarian disposition and who are therefore suspicious of large government, are anxious to know at what point the marginal benefit from extra public expenditure exceeds the marginal cost, but as perceived by the voter/taxpayer, and whether or not the implied average tax burden is above that rate. The fact that an answer is more difficult to find than Lafferian analysis has suggested is something which it has been worth finding out.

References

Beenstock, M. (1979): "Taxation and Incentives." *Lloyds Bank Review* 134: 1–15.

Blinder, A. (1981): "Thoughts on the Laffer Curve." In *The Supply Side Effects of Economic Policy*, edited by Laurence Meyer. Boston: Kluwer Nijhoff Publishing.

Blum, W.J., and **Kalven, H. Jr.** (1953): *The Uneasy Case for Progressive Taxation.* Chicago: The University of Chicago Press.

Buchanan, J.M., and **Lee, D.R.** (1982): "Tax Rates and Tax Revenues in Political Equilibrium : Some Simple Analytics." *Economic Inquiry* 20: 344–354.

Canto, V.A., Joines, D.H., and **Laffer, A.B.** (1981): "Tax Rates, Factor Employment, and Market Production." In *The Supply Side Effects of Economic Policy*, edited by Laurence Meyer. Boston: Kluwer Nijhoff Publishing.

Feige, E.L., and **McGee, R.L.** (1983): "Sweden's Laffer Curve: Taxation and the Unobserved Economy." *Scandinavian Journal of Economics* 85: 499–519.

Fullerton, D. (1982): "On the Possibility of an Inverse Relationship between Tax Rates and Government Revenues." *Journal of Public Economics* 19: 3–22.

---

[8] For a formal demonstration of the proposition that, assuming that the Laffer curve is not devoid of realism, the sacrifice of private consumption in order to reduce inequality can result in taxes which are 'too high', see the intriguing article by Lambert (1986).

Hemming, R., and **Kay, J.** (1980): "The Laffer Curve." *Fiscal Studies* 1: 83–90.

Hume, D. (1752): "Of Taxes." In his *Political Discourses*. Reprinted in David Hume, *Essays, Moral, Political and Literary*, edited by Eugene F. Miller. Indianapolis: Liberty Classics 1985.

Lambert, P.J. (1986): "Getting on the Wrong Side of the Laffer Curve." *European Journal of Political Economy* 2: 193–202.

Lindbeck, A. (1982): "Tax Effects Versus Budget Effects on Labor Supply." *Economic Inquiry* 20: 473–489.

Musgrave, R.A. (1959): *The Theory of Public Finance.* London: McGraw Hill.

Musgrave, R.A. (1986): "Leviathan Cometh – Or Does He?" Chapter 13 of the author's *Public Finance in a Democratic Society, Volume II.* Brighton: Wheatsheaf Books Ltd.

Peacock, A.T. (1979): *The Economic Analysis of Government,* Chapter 1. Oxford: Martin Robertson.

Peacock, A.T. (1983): "The Disaffection of the Taxpayer." *Atlantic Economic Journal* 11: 7–15.

Peacock, A.T., and **Shaw, G.K.** (1982): "Tax Evasion and Tax Revenue Loss." *Public Finance* 37: 269–278.

Pyle, D.J. (1987): *The Political Economy of Tax Evasion.* Hume Paper No. 6, The David Hume Institute, Edinburgh.

Rawls, J. (1971): *A Theory of Justice.* Cambridge, Mass.: Harvard University Press.

Roberts, P.C. (1984): *The Supply Side Revolution.* Cambridge, Mass.: Harvard University Press.

Shoup, C. (1981): "Economic Limits to Taxation." *Atlantic Economic Journal* 9: 9–23.

Stiglitz, J.E. (1986): *Economics of the Public Sector.* New York and London: W. W. Norton and Co.

Waud, R.N. (1986): "The Tax Aversion and the Laffer Curve." *Scottish Journal of Political Economy* 33: 212–227.

On the Irrelevance of the Laffer Curve

Clemens-August Andreae and Christian Keuschnigg, Innsbruck, Austria

When discussing the magnitude of marginal tax rates, we do not consider the Laffer curve to be particularly helpful. The change in tax revenues due to a change in marginal tax rates is a misleading measure of the benefits or losses to society. In designing a tax system one cannot avoid the fact that a dollar of tax revenues costs the taxpayer a dollar. This is the income effect of taxation. If taxes alter relative prices by discriminating between different activities, they introduce incentives to shift private activities from heavily taxed to less heavily taxed activities. This is the substitution effect. The substitution effect leads the taxpayers to persue a combination of activities with lower social returns. Although this reaction is privately advantageous at the new after-tax prices, society suffers a welfare loss. In designing a suitable tax system, one must be concerned with minimizing welfare costs or excess burden of taxation.

"Excess burden" measures the efficiency costs of the tax system. There is considerable evidence in recent empirical research in public finance that high tax rates may burden society with large welfare losses. Depending on elasticity assumptions, the marginal welfare costs of current tax rates vary between 17 and 56 percent of additional revenues, or, an average of 33 percent. These numbers were recently calculated for the United States by Ballard–Shoven–Whalley (1985). If the government were to increase tax revenues from current levels, it would inflict a welfare cost of approximately 33 cents per dollar of additional revenues.

In Europe, where tax systems mostly operate with higher marginal tax rates, marginal welfare costs are expected to be even higher. We are inclined to think that the benefits from additional government expenditures can no longer justify the costs of additional revenues accrued through rate increases. Since marginal welfare costs increase progressively with the increasing marginal tax rates, even small decreases in marginal tax rates can be expected to yield large gains to society. Peacock's empirical reasoning with the Laffer curve reveals that no informed economist should expect the rate reductions of broadly based taxes to be self-financing. Tax rate reductions can be financed by elimination of a myriad of tax exemptions which are often found to serve the special interest of small groups at the cost of a silent majority. In eliminating these tax exemptions and special tax treatments there may be an unsatisfied demand for courageous Schumpeterian politicians who, for the sake of long run gains to society, can withstand the pressure and protest from a myriad of lobbies and pressure groups.

Whether tax rate reductions are partly or wholly self-financing, as implied by the Laffer curve, is not particularly relevant for discussing the magnitude of marginal tax rates or tax progressivity. Because of the large efficiency gains at the margin, it is fundamentally a good policy to lower marginal tax rates even if these rate reductions are not wholly self-financing. In a free society there is an additional political reason for low marginal tax rates. The government may find tax exemptions an attractive instrument to elicit a certain pattern of investment, saving and working behavior on the part of the taxpayer. In combination with high marginal tax rates the control of taxpayer behavior becomes very effective through the use of tax exemptions. The taxpayer may have good economic reasons for *not* behaving according to the priorities of government, but he will suffer a heavy economic penalty if he does not take advantage of the tax exemptions and acquiesce to the priorities of the government. In a free society the state has no business to control individual economic decisons. Since we, like Alan Peacock, are of a more libertarian disposition and are suspicious of a large and omnipotent government, for economic *and* political reasons we prefer a broadly based tax system with very few exemptions and low marginal tax rates.

Reference

Ballard, Ch., Shoven, J. and **Whalley, J.** (1985): "General Equilibrium Computations of the Marginal Welfare Costs of Taxes in the United States." *American Economic Review* 75: 128–138.

The International Consequences of Less Progressive Taxation

Erich Streissler, Vienna, Austria

1. Setting the Problem

1.1 The last three decades have seen a resurgence of international economic integration on a hitherto unprecedented scale. Advances in transport and particularly in communication technology have knit markets together more closely and have formed a nearly instantaneously working network of interactions. At the same time in all advanced economies the public sector has become huge. To a large extent, it is thus no longer only (or even predominantly) the interaction of private economic decision taking and of the production and consumption of private goods that we face in international trade. It is the size of the public revenue and the way in which it is raised that determine which countries prosper and which are retarded in the great game of economic competition: the decisive factor is no longer comparative advantage now but comparative taxation. But it is not only the balance of international commodity flows that is shaped by the international differences in taxation and the more or less concerted international changes in predominant types of taxation, right now e.g. the manifest world wide movement towards less progressive income taxation. Even more clearly the development of exchange rates and the long-run preconditions for international financial stability depend upon changes in the structure of taxation.

Taxation would be of little international interest if it occured just in the form of lump-sum deductions from otherwise determined factor incomes. But we know that lump-sum taxes are nowhere even remotely the order of the day. Particularly if taxation is progressive it distorts commodity supply and demand and the domestic supply of given factors as well as their international movement and finally their additional creation. The international consequences of these distortions are the topic of this paper. For centuries the theory of public finance has inquired into these consequences on an national level; the international consequences have, however, not yet found the general attention they merit.

1.2 The time is now ripe to face squarely the issue of the international consequences of more or less progressive taxation. Practical experience of progressive income – or wealth – taxation has accumulated by now, and theoretical developments in economics have posed the problem afresh.

D. Bös and B. Felderer (Eds.)
The Political Economy of Progressive Taxation
© Springer-Verlag Berlin Heidelberg 1989

For at least a century before the 1970s economists had regarded progressive taxation mainly from the angle of interpersonal equity and consequently mainly as a question of the redistribution of given incomes. It had been deduced in one of the first applications of marginal utility theory that with a declining marginal utility of income equal sacrifice (in some sense) implied progressive taxation. What was not made sufficiently clear was the basic assumption of this line of argument: that the "income" analysed had to be pure rent. Under rapidly shifting economic conditions pure rents, however, practically do not exist, only temporary quasi-rents. In other words, all income is "earned" income and none is "unearned". But then, as Sadka (1976) points out, we have to qualify our judgements about progressive taxation already on equity grounds. Sadka approvingly quotes J. S. Mill (1948/1970, V/ii § 3, p. 808): "To tax the larger incomes at a higher percentage than the smaller ... is ... to impose a penalty on people for having worked harder". As has been recognized more and more since the 1960s and the 1970s, we have to face the work-leisure choice lying behind the process of income generation, a choice highlighted by modern mainstream economics only relatively recently (for reasons of the typical theoretical structure of economic reasoning; Streissler and Neudeck, 1986, p. 229). If, in addition, earning potential is itself acquired by learning (Brunner, 1986), the equity argument for progressive taxation of labour income is even further weakened.

Furthermore, since the 1970s more and more theoretical authors have questioned the concentration on tax equity as altogether one-sided: we certainly have to balance equity considerations against efficiency arguments, even if we wish to favour on balance only the poor. This has been brought out in the literature on optimum income taxation. Among many others perhaps the most influential author on this topic was Mirrlees (1971). Assuming a given distribution of innate (not of acquired) abilities in the population and examining only a tax on wage income he found neither the arguments for progressive nor even for high income tax rates persuasive. Mirrlees concludes: "I must confess that I had expected the rigorous analysis of income-taxation in the utilitarian manner to provide arguments for high tax rates. It has not done so" (ibid., p. 207). In his illustrative calculations "the maximum marginal tax rate occurs at a rather low income level, and falls steadily thereafter" (ibid., p. 207). And finally: "Perhaps the most striking feature is the closeness to linearity of the tax schedules" (ibid., p. 206; one of the latest contributions in this vein is Hellwig, 1986). All this is very evocative of the measures taken in the most recent (1986) United States tax reform. In this case, at least, it cannot be said that abstract economic theorizing has not led political practice.

The case for less progressive taxation of wage income is relatively new in rigorously argued theoretical economics, but has been taken up vigorously from different angles by a number of authors. The theoretical case for less progressive taxation of capital formation on the one hand and of economic risk taking on the other is already quite traditional. But it has gained renewed practical importance with the decline in the growth performance of the industrial world during the last fifteen to twenty years. For though there is some disagreement among economists about the exact composition of causes behind economic growth, everyone seems to agree that some mixture of capital formation, costly technical progress and risk taking is certainly crucial to it.

1.3 If we wish to determine the international consequences of less progressive taxation we must first ask four questions for each country: (1) What will happen to the labour supply if taxation becomes less progressive? (2) What will happen to saving and thus to capital formation if taxation becomes less progressive? (3) What will be the effect on risk taking if taxation becomes less progressive? And finally: (4) What is going to happen to the inefficiencies of economic control between principals and agents (the moral hazard problem) if taxation becomes less progressive?

Once these four questions have been answered, we can derive the effects of the expected changes on capital intensity, commodity composition and economic growth; we can then proceed to conclusions about the likely effects of these changes on international competitiveness and on international financial conditions. Unfortunately, the theoretical answers to the first three questions are highly ambiguous, as will be sketched in some detail in the next chapter. Therefore, in order to reach even tentative conclusions, we shall be forced to make a large number of assumptions. Hard and fast answers will be impossible. Our whole analysis unfortunately will have to remain wide open to criticism. Once we leave the preliminary one-country stage of analysis a fifth question comes up: (5) What factor movements will be elicited between countries with less and with more progressive taxation, taking into account the effects of questions (1) to (4)? In this context, we shall assume that the country introducing less progressive taxation is a "small" open economy. Such an assumption is no longer absurd even for the United States, as certain consequences of factor movements on the rest of the world will have to be faced explicitly in the case of US.

1.4 There is a final preliminary question: What is a progressive tax; and, in consequence, what is less progressive taxation? This seemingly elementary question is not so easy to answer as one would think in a disquisition on political economy intended to lead to practicable conclusions.

As is all too well known, progressive taxation is defined as taxation where the average tax rate rises with an increase in the tax base; or, alternatively, as taxation where the marginal tax rate always lies above the average, the size of this gap measuring the degree of progression.

In using the results of the prevailing theoretical models the first problem to be faced is that most models adress themselves only to studying the effects of higher or lower – and in most cases proportional – taxation as such and not of progression proper. We shall therefore, in fact, sometimes just speak of the consequences of lower and not of less progressive taxation. This is quite legitimate when the taxed activity studied is itself positively dependent on the tax base, e.g. on income or wealth. We shall assume that both income from non-human wealth and saving rise with income or total wealth; and assume this in contrast to the simple life-cycle theory without bequest motive. Less controversial will be the assumption that risk taking rises with income or wealth. Merely lower taxes on capital income or risky income can then stand for less progressive taxation. In general, however, we shall have to distinguish between lower average taxation and less progression keeping average taxation constant. In analyzing actual reforms the distinction often is not at all easy to make.

Secondly, and even more importantly, actual tax schemes never merely impose the same tax rate upon the same increment of income, regardless of how it is derived. Usually in effect distinct sources of income (or distinct sources in the change of wealth) are taxed quite differently; and these differences seem to be correlated with the degree of progression of the tax schedules.

For instance, the Austrian income tax is highly progressive in its tax schedule. This progression is, however, practically reversed by the treatment of capital income: depreciation allowances are highly accelerated, verging nearly upon free depreciation, so that investment activity is favoured to an unlimited extent. In many different specified ways saving, too, entails many different kinds of tax deductions which are nearly unlimited in extent (full use of the copious saving allowances, which, for families with several children rise up to some 50,000 $ a year, can at best be made with incomes in substantial excess of 100,000 $ a year). Furthermore, interest income is – already legally and even more so illicitly – also virtually untaxed, so that the Austrian tax-scheme has jokingly been called "a consumption tax raised to the second power". Finally even realized capital gains are completely untaxed if the wealth instrument in question has been held for more than one year (or five in the case of real estate). It will therefore not come as a surprise that the Austrian income tax has been found to be on average practically proportional as between different levels of income classes. But such a proportionality *in effect*

– after all economic adaption to an income tax schedule has taken place – must be distinguished from proportionality *ex ante*, the proportionality of the schedule. When we speak of less progressive taxation we can only mean changes of the tax schedules, i.e. lower progression ex ante.

The Austrian tax system is certainly an extreme case but does not seem to be untypical in its general tendency. The most dramatic and – on a world scale – also the most important recent fundamental change in the income tax system, that of the United States, seems to show similar features: a still relatively progressive tax system with top rates of 50 percent has been converted into a system with a final average tax rate of 28 percent, which is, for higher incomes, also the marginal rate. But at the same time many business investment allowances have been cancelled and realized capital gains are now taxed as income. The US-tax system has thus changed from a progressive tax system favouring capital formation to a much less progressive system treating capital formation neutrally. In effect, this change discourages capital formation; or, at least, home investment in contrast to saving (Sinn, 1987). This would not be the normal effect we should expect from less progressive taxation without a concurrent shift in the relative treatment of different sources of income.

This analysis leads us to distinguish two cases: we shall speak of *less progressive income taxation of the first type* in cases where *all* the sources of a high income level are treated more favourable in the *same* proportionate degree. For instance, the German or the Swiss tax system does not much favour capital formation, so that lower average tax rates in the top brackets in Germany or Switzerland would approximate this first type of case. On the other hand, we shall speak of *less progressive income taxation of the second type* in cases where a progressive income tax *highly favouring capital formation is changed* into one treating all sources of income *roughly equally*, but at lower average rates in the top brackets. The recent US tax reform entails such a second type lower progression; and so would an Austrian reform as presently envisaged. Needless to say, other tax shifting types of cases of lowered progression would also be possible. But we shall explicitly distinguish only these two cases.

1.5 A recent OECD study (McKee et al., 1986) presents highly interesting estimates of comparative tax rates on (1) the use of labour and (2) of capital and (3) of marginal income tax rates at average production worker income levels for 1983. (No attempt is made to estimate the incidence of taxes in this study.)

For a single worker taxes were both much lower and much less progressive (as measured by the gap between marginal and average rates) in OECD non-Europe (Australia, Canada, Japan, New-Zealand and the United States) than in OECD

Europe. In Europe, only Switzerland was comparable to the non-European OECD nations. Marginal and average tax rates of single workers for non-Europe were on average 43.5 percent and 33.5 percent, respectively, for Europe 62.5 percent and 46.3 percent, respectively. The difference was not quite as marked for the single earner of a married couple with two children, where average progression was about equal for the non-European and the European OECD, but tax rates were about 15 percentage points lower in non-Europe: 59.3 percent vs. 42.5 percent for the former, but only 44.6 percent vs. 27.9 percent for the latter. Successful economies, like Switzerland and Japan, have low marginal tax rates on labour. (My own country, Austria, has the third highest progression so that its economic success in the Seventies has to be explained by its very low capital taxation.) By now, of course, the United States have the lowest marginal tax rates of any OECD country; or, at least, the lowest degree of progression. In general, marginal total taxes on labour use are closely paralleled by marginal income taxes for the average production labourer: the rank correlation between the two is 0.82 for single workers. More astonishingly, there is also a relatively close correlation between high marginal total tax rates on labour and the progression of taxes on wage incomes, as measured by the gap between marginal total and average total taxes: here the rank correlation for single workers is a highly significant 0.71. Exceptions are Switzerland and above all Japan (and to a much lesser extent Germany), which have low but progressive taxes, and Sweden and to a lesser extent Denmark, which have very high but only mildly progressive taxes. For married workers with two children, who are sole family supporters, this correlation is at $R = 0.49$ much weaker, though still significant. Thus it is astonishing to what an extent the concept of low taxation and of less progressive taxation can be used interchangeably, at least for single workers.

Taxes on the use of capital differ markedly more or less in all OECD countries as between various types of financing of capital formation and as between inventories, equipment and structures. Furthermore, taxes on labour and capital, as the authors of this study remark, in general "are not the same; they are rarely close". Because of the diversity of tax clauses it is difficult to draw firm conclusions. But the general impression seems to be that countries with high marginal tax rates and high progressive income taxes tend, on the other hand, strongly to favour capital formation by their tax system. This statement can be weakly proved by various barely significant rank correlations between measures of relatively favourable tax treatment of capital formation and measures of highly or progressive taxation. Our conclusion thus gives occasion for the distinction made between less progressive income taxation of the first type and of the second, the latter being distinguished

The International Consequences of Less Progressive Taxation   49

by an abolition of favourable treatment of capital formation at the same time as marginal rates for upper income groups are lowered.

2. Short Run Partial Consequences of Less Progressive Taxation on Factor Supply

2.1 In what follows we shall examine one by one the consequences for the different factor supplies named in chapter 1.3 of a less progressive tax raised solely on the factor in question.

2.2 Let us first look at the work-leisure choice. Income taxes, progressive or otherwise, normally tax only income from market activities and thus normally do not tax leisure activity; at least not directly, though consumption taxes might tax activities complementary to leisure particularly heavily, for instance motor car driving. We shall assume this is not the case. Thus labour income is thought to be taxed and leisure consumption untaxed. As is well-known even in this case it is, unfortunately, not possible to determine unambiguously whether lower taxation will lead to higher or lower labour supply: the substitution effect of raising the after-tax price of labour through lower taxation would raise the amount supplied of the now better priced labour at the cost of leisure; but the income effect would work in the opposite direction: being now better paid per hour worked the individual could afford to take more leisure and work less. These statements, of course, already assume what is not self-evident, i.e. that wage income taxes are in the main actually borne by workers; but on balance this seems to be likely.

Empirical studies on which effect (the substitution or the income effect) is likely to predominate are summarized in the modern public finance literature (Break, 1974, pp. 180 ff.; Atkinson and Stiglitz, 1980, pp. 48 ff.; Stiglitz, 1986, p. 372) to the effect that these opposing effects seem roughly to cancel out so that changes in tax have no appreciable effect, at least not on basic male labour. This is all the more true if workers are frequently rationed in the labour market (they wish to work longer, but cannot find the opportunity to do so). Furthermore, a zero effect on labour supply is the theoretically expected result for the widely used logarithmic utility function for work and leisure (Atkinson and Stiglitz, 1980, p. 36). It seems to be agreed, on the other hand, that there is likely to be some small increase in female labour participation (of wives of the main earners) at lower tax rates. In addition, with lower tax rates labour would certainly flow from the shadow into the official economy; though it is hard to say whether, on balance, this would change the supply of the economically relevant amount of labour at all. Basically, these labour increasing effects of lower taxation (women and workers drawn from the shadow economy) are most likely in service trades, where wages are relatively low. But this also means that a merely *less progressive* tax schedule (with the same average tax) as applied to the lower wage spectrum would actually mean higher taxation there, so that we should expect slightly *lower* labour supply in services. In addition service trades are of little international importance apart from those countries (like Austria) that heavily depend on tourism.

Some substitution of an interemporal nature is also possible. Ippolito (1985, p. 347) remarks: "Tax progressivity stimulates workers to take less leisure in the form of retirement in exchange for more leisure during work life"; and the opposite would, of course, be true for less progressive taxation.

Another labour effect may be more important: there is some evidence that highly qualified "workers", e.g. managers and professionals, might work slightly more at higher wage rates. And it is also not unlikely that the willingness to work on overtime depends positively on the wage rate. Less progressive taxation would mean higher effective wage rates for the most highly qualified in the labour force and possibly also for many types of overtime work, which are frequently supplied by highly paid workers.

We can therefore conclude: production of services may be slightly favoured by lower, but not by merely less progressive taxes. Less progressive taxes, on the other hand, may slightly increase the supply of the most highly qualified types of work and may make the response of the economy slightly more flexible in the sense that it would be easier for firms to get the most highly qualified workers (who are difficult to substitute by capital) to supply additional overtime in case of high demand pressure. On the whole the effect on labour supply is likely, however, to be not the most important effect of less progressive taxation.

2.3 Turning now to the consumption-saving decision we note first that a tax on wealth or a tax on capital gains is basically the same as a tax on interest so that we can stick to an analysis of the latter.

First the question has to be settled whether interest income actually bears the tax. With free exchange of commodities but inelastic investment the conclusion at least for the short run in growing open economies seems to be: "Capital bears roughly the entire burden on capital income" (Bovenberg, 1986, p. 348). A lower tax on interest income thus raises the effective rate of interest for the saver; and assuming savings to increase with income, and probably more than proportionately so, a less progressive tax works in the same direction as a lower tax.

If we take the simple life cycle explanation (without bequests) as the explanation of saving the effect of lower taxation of interest income on saving is for positive wealth holders once more ambiguous: by the substitution effect saving is raised because of its higher return; but the income effect of an increased return lowers the need to save in order to achieve a given desired level of wealth in the future; or, in other words, higher interest income increases consumption.

On the other hand, for borrowers, who can tax-deduct interest payments, this explanation leads to unambiguous conclusions: now the income effect works in the same direction as the substitution effect. If interest on debt (especially on mortgages) is deductible, a lower tax level on interest income increases the effective interest to be paid, thus increasing saving by the substitution effect; and it also lowers the remaining income, thus once more lowering consumption and raising savings. One of the most important questions in judging the effect of less progressive taxation on saving is, therefore, whether borrowers are to be found more in the lower or in the upper eschelons of the income distribution; and whether interest on debt is tax deductible, which it generally is for firms, though for households only in the US and Britain, but not in many other European countries (e.g. neither in Germany nor Austria).

Conclusions become more clear-cut, if we assume – contrary to the simple life cycle model without bequests – a saving propensity rising with income (or wealth) and examine progressive taxation. In this case less progressive taxation means that high savers are taxed less and saving will thus increase. This is all the more true if saving follows more or less the classical saving assumption that the saving propensity out of capital income is much higher than out of wage income. This assumption seems to be favoured more in Europe than in the United States, possibly because credit markets are much less perfect in Europe and it is thus much more difficult to borrow. In this case saving rises unambiguously already with lower taxation of interest income and all the more so with a less progressive taxation if we assume that capital income is bunched at higher income levels.

The way to introduce into the life cycle theory by the back door a saving propensity rising with income or a higher saving propensity out of capital income is to assume a bequest motive. And, in fact, as Tobin (1967) remarked long ago, a bequest motive more or less has to be assumed in life cycle models in order to get a positive macroeconomic stock of capital in a child rearing society. If we analyse the effect of lower taxation on savings for bequests we once more get the type of ambiguity so beloved by theoreticians: everything depends crucially upon parameters we know nothing about. But at least we can be sure that "the level of bequests is always reduced by a wealth tax" (Atkinson, 1971, p. 218). And this effect seems likely to dominate saving behaviour for bequest purposes during the first decades after a change in the tax system, that is to say before the wealth increasing effects of higher bequests due to the division of the bequests among their recipients becomes strong. We may thus conclude: lower and, even more so, less progressive taxation of capital income is likely to increase saving for bequest purposes at least during the (rather long) middle run.

The empirical results of numerous studies also seem to favour the conclusion that less progressive taxation will somewhat increase saving; and the evidence is more reliable than with the labour supply though the increase in saving is possibly not very strong (Atkinson and Stiglitz, 1980, pp. 90 ff.).

A final aspect in the field of saving is the effect of less progressive taxation on the accumulation of human wealth, which is, after all, an investment decision. Here the result seems to me more clear cut. Human capital is accumulated particularly by the children of parents in the upper income groups and in turn leads to upper income group earnings. In human capital formation the cost has to justify (at least) the expected returns. The burden of effective cost is lowered by less progressive taxation: for instance a given sum is more easily saved with lower taxes on interest. And the effective after tax return on human capital is increased. Thus on both counts less progressive taxation encourages the accumulation of human capital.

2.4 Let us next turn to the effects of less progressive taxation on risk taking, which we shall consider as a quasi-factor of production and which is perhaps the most crucial aspect as far as economic growth is concerned. Again the problem is highly complicated (Kihlstrom and Laffont, 1983). We shall, however, only study so-called *private* risk taking and not the effect of the tax in shifting risks towards or away from government via the uncertainty of the government's tax returns (so-called social risk taking). Our reasoning for concerning ourselves only with private risk taking is the following: it is appropriate to consider private individuals as risk averse, living, as they are, under the threat of bankruptcy or even starvation. The government, on the other hand, should be considered as risk neutral: perhaps unfortunately it cannot go bankrupt nowadays and, moreover it is under no threat whatsoever to do so because of uncertain returns taken from private individuals, as long as these are uncorrelated (the government is the largest possible insurer in an economy). If private returns are not uncorrelated, the government should bear these risks all the more; because then they are mostly either of its own making, or, at least, partly its own responsibility.

If assets are valued for tax purposes in a conventional way independent of short run fluctuations in their market value (e.g. if they are valued at their long-run average value) then the question of the tax effect on risk taking is reduced merely to the effect of the taxation of the cash returns derived from them.

Now it has long been known that with a full loss set-off of negative income a higher proportional rate of taxation of the returns on a venture will lead to *more* (private) risk taking: the government serves as a silent partner (or insurer) to both gains *and* losses, which, for a risk averse individual, increases the certainty equivalent of the project. This is probably the case for additional ventures of larger corporations which on the one hand tend to be subject to more or less proportional (corporate) taxation in most countries and on the other have several ventures running at the same time, so that they can easily set off losses against other incomes. Thus in this case lower taxation will reduce risk taking.

The situation is quite different for the individual small entrepreneur venturing into business: with only one venture he will, in general, have no income against which heavy losses can be set off (lower occasional, i.e. uncorrelated, losses over time might be set off against future income). Such an entrepreneur is then basically in the situation where the government eats into his gains but leaves him all of the losses. In this case higher taxes will reduce risk taking (at least for sufficiently high tax rates; see Atkinson and Stiglitz, 1980, p. 112); and lower taxation will increase it.

A similar situation is also treated in the literature (Atkinson and Stiglitz, 1980, p. 44 ff.): safe, cushy jobs frequently have attractive fringe benefits that go untaxed; risky jobs, on the other hand, are more typically remunerated by money income alone (and possibly even money income varying with profits). Higher taxation will then cause a shift away from such socially useful risky jobs and towards the frequently much less useful cushy ones.

Even in the first case considered, the case with the full tax set-off of losses, things change when we switch to considering progressive instead of proportional taxation: then gains are taxed more heavily than taxes are rebated due to losses. Thus a highly progressive taxation will reverse the stimulating tendency towards more risk taking of a high level of proportionate taxation. This will be particularly important for larger unincorporated businesses, though not so much for corporations where the tax tends to be proportional.

We finally turn to an income tax on risky returns which takes account of the short term market valuation of the asset financing a risky venture in the sense of treating increases in the value of this asset as positive and decreases as negative income. In this case it can be shown unambiguously that a lower rate of taxation will increase private risk taking if, as is commonly assumed, absolute risk aversion is a declining function of wealth (Atkinson and Stiglitz, 1980, pp. 106 and 111). As risk taking income is likely to be on average high income the results for a lower rate of taxation carry over to less progressive taxation.

We can thus conclude: as perhaps its most important effect less progressive taxation is likely to increase private risk taking of individuals and small firms, though possibly not that of large corporations. As the risks taken by large corporations are frequently treated in a preferential way by governments anyhow, the latter caveat may not be of great importance.

2.5 The effect of lower taxation on the control problems of principals relative to their agents, or on the problem of moral hazard as a cause of economic inefficiency, is straightforward.

The case of shareholders as principals controlling corporate managers as agents is quite obvious. If managers are able to maximize to a certain extent their own utility, that is their ease and convenience, because they are not fully controlled by shareholders or by competition in the managerial labour market, shareholders have to offer them an additional incentive reward. This is especially necessary in order to get managers to take up sufficiently risky ventures (as seen from the viewpoint of shareholders), for managers tend frequently to opt for the safer course. If the incentive income of managers (for instance their profit share) is taxed instead of untaxed the incentive becomes insufficient. Its pre tax level has to be raised to such a degree that its after tax level remains the same. But this means that risky projects which also need control of managers via incentive pay become less profitable for shareholders and some are therefore no longer undertaken. More will be undertaken at low tax rates. As managers are likely to have relatively high incomes, this argument about low tax rates carries over to less progressive taxation. We can conclude: less progressive taxation makes it cheaper for shareholders to guide corporate managers towards riskier projects. This aspect thus counteracts the risk reducing effect of lower corporate taxation found in the last subsection.

The same argument carries over to most of the efficiency wage reasoning (Yellen, 1984). If a certain optimum wage has to be paid to insure a certain work effort or to insure other productivity increasing effects, it is evidently the effect of the after tax wage that counts. Thus with lower tax rates lower pre tax wage rates can assure the same degree of economic efficiency. In so far as efficiency wages are paid to above median income earners, less progressive taxation thus assures the same degree of economic efficiency of labour productivity at lower real wage rates.

In similar ways other types of efficiency can be more cheaply reached at lower tax rates; and as most not directly controllable agents tend to have above median incomes it will also be reached by less progressive taxation. If, for instance, the public imposes a payment on polluters of the environment, a given tax deductable payment geared to the amount of pollution is more painful at low tax rates than at high, for it then reduces after tax returns by more. Thus pollution control via tax deductable pollution taxes becomes cheaper. If there are only indirect means of public control of moral hazards the optimal tax problem becomes, however, more complicated (Arnott and Stiglitz, 1986).

We can conclude: in most cases less progressive taxation will increase economic efficiency or, rather, reduce the cost of assuring it. Thus the productivity of given factors will be increased. And less progressive taxation may also increase corporate risk taking when this is insufficient without incentive pay of managers.

2.6 In the main part of this section we have examined the consequences of less progressive taxation without a lower yield of revenue on factor supplies and factor efficiency. But many actual reductions of progressivity will also entail a reduction in tax yield: it may be politically impossible to increase the taxation of the poor so that lower taxation of the upper income groups also entails a reduction of average taxation. And as it appears implausible that lower taxation will stimulate total factor supply to such an extent already in the short run that total tax yield will increase in spite of lower tax rates – in other words as the Laffer curve may easily be upward sloping at the relevant tax rates, if not even up to the 100 percent marginal tax rate (Malcolmson, 1986) – we must then face the question of lower total yield. Let us therefore finally turn to an examination of the effect of a reduction in total tax revenue and therefore also lower government expenditure on factor supplies.

Government expenditure will fall into two categories: the spending for goods and services proper and transfer expenditure. In view of the bureaucracy models prevalent in the literature on the economics of politics it is reasonable to assume that a moderate lowering of government expenditure on goods and services will in the present bloated state of most OECD governments have no appreciable effect on the provision of government services at all: it will just force the government to reduce somewhat its high degree of inefficiency in the provision of services; or, to put it in another way, it will just lead to some reduction in the large number of superfluous civil servants and to the reduction of civil service pay. This can be surmised from the near ubiquitous desire of present electorates to reduce their tax burden. Evidently they assume that lower taxes will not appreciably reduce valuable government services but will just reduce government inefficiency. If this is indeed the case, no effect on private factor supply is to be expected apart perhaps from an increased labour supply for private production because of reduced public employment opportunities.

In the case of transfer expenditure administrative costs, though usually excessive, are in general relatively not very large, so that a cut in transfer expenditure will cause a nearly equal cut in transfers actually reaching private citizens. In this case individuals will have to provide more for themselves against the emergencies up to then insured by social security; and they will also have to provide more against old age. This means that both life-cycle saving for retirement and precautionary saving for emergencies (or saving for the provision of education of children) will have to increase. A lower total tax yield which leads to smaller government transfer will therefore certainly increase the supply of private capital.

3. Long Run Total Effects of Less Progressive Taxation

3.1 Once we turn to the interaction of all the various effects of less progressive taxation on factor supply, once we turn to the long run adjustments to these supply changes, their interaction with aggregate demand and finally their impact on the rate of growth of an economy, the number of possible counteracting effects mount geometrically and our conclusions therefore have to become even more tentative.

In this chapter we shall not yet turn to the international consequences of the various changes analysed but only look basically at a closed economy. Or, alternatively, in an international setting we examine an economy that is so large (for instance the whole EEC or even the United States) that changes in its tax system affect the whole world, for instance raising the world rate of growth on average or lowering the world rate of interest.

We shall have the international setting at the back of our mind only in so far as we are going to neglect in this chapter the effects of tax changes on factor use because of changes in aggregate demand. There appears to be a prima vista case that aggregate demand might change because of tax changes. Less progressive taxation is likely to imply higher private saving. Lower taxation, on the other hand, is a redistribution from governments, which seem at present to have saving propensities not only of zero but even negative ones (they constantly run deficits), to private individuals that have positive saving propensities. Thus less progressive and even more so lower taxation has demand reducing effects as long as we leave aside its effects on investment. We shall, however, assume here that there is no effect on aggregate demand, because investment will rise pari passu with saving. And we can do this all the more easily because additional saving is not likely to have effects on aggregate demand in an open economy: for what will not be invested here will either increase exports or reduce imports or both, in other words will (by the absorption approach reasoning) only change the balance of trade, so that in the home country no possible capacity or employment reducing effects of higher saving have to be faced.

3.2 Let us first examine once more the effects of lower taxation of upper income earners on labour supply and consequently on investment.

The desire to save more at lower tax rates, which we have found likely, will by itself also have repercussions on the work-leisure choice about which it is difficult to generalize. Even more important, in a closed economy a higher rate of saving will ceteris paribus lower the rate of interest, and this will lead to higher wages, if labour is a substitute for capital (Feldstein, 1974). Thus lower taxation for upper income groups will have a double effect in raising effective wages: once because wages are taxed less and once because they rise due to the increase in the supply of capital. For lower wage earners, on the other hand, these effects tend to cancel out with less progressive taxation: they receive higher wages because of the stimulus to saving; but these higher wages are more heavily taxed.

If, as we have argued, the substitution and the income effects of wage changes on labour supply more or less cancel out, these changes do not matter one way or the other as to their effect on the labour supply. Possibly, we have found, there will be some increase in high quality, managerial and entrepreneurial labour; and this is now seen to become more likely because of the wage (or profit) stimulating effect of lower interest rates. But this partial increase in the labour supply of managers and entrepreneurs is of a kind that is probably much rather complementary to capital and not a substitute to it.

For business investment we thus reach the conclusion: as the amount of basic labour is likely to remain the same and as managerial and entrepreneurial labour, which is likely to be complementary to it, is possibly going to increase, business investment, stimulated by lower interest, will move in the same direction as saving. Less progressive taxation will therefore lead to a more capital intensive mode of production.

3.3 We can reinforce this argument by assuming that total taxation is an optimal taxation and that taxation is lowered (as we have argued less progressive taxation may in actual practice often go hand in hand with lower average taxation). In the long run we can consider all factor supplies to be perfectly elastic (at least if they are not exhaustible resources). Then, as is well known, optimal taxation should not change the proportions of commodities consumed from what they would be without taxes. That is to say a lower optimal tax would differ from a higher optimal tax by increasing the consumption of all commodities proportionately. Let us assume that the standard consumer values the following three commodities in his utility function: private consumption, saving (seen here only as a bequest type saving which creates provision for others; or as capital accumulation valued, for instance by business men, for its own sake), and finally leisure. A tax cut from one optimal level to another would then increase private consumption, saving and leisure equiproportionately. But that would unambiguously mean a lower supply of labour at lower tax rates. Thus investment would be doubly stimulated in this case: firstly because labour would become scarcer and secondly because saving would increase. The conclusion that the capital intensity of production would increase – in this case by lower, but optimal taxes – would become even stronger.

3.4 We have seen that less progressive taxation of the first type is likely to increase saving and thus increase the capital intensity of the economy and reduce the rate of interest. Furthermore it is likely to increase the formation of human capital, shift superior labour into business management and increase the labour supply of existing managers. It is likely to increase risk taking by small enterprises and individual inventors. Finally it is likely to decrease managerial slack and other inefficiencies of the economy.

All this will mean that it will raise the level of productivity as well as the rate of growth of the economy. Increases in economic efficiency are once-and-for-all-effects; but as they may well be spread over several years to become fully effective, they have short term "growth" effects in a statistical sense. According to some growth theories higher capital formation again only pushes national income up to a higher level but does not affect the final growth rate. The transition may, however, be long, so that again "growth" will be higher in a statistical sense for the medium term. Capital formation may, however, also cause a higher rate of technical progress, for instance via various learning by doing effects (Streissler, 1980). Furthermore it has been found that more capital intensive industries tend to have a higher rate of technical progress (Ferguson, 1965). Such rises in technical progress will raise the rate of growth even in long run equilibrium. The same arguments can be made about an increase in human capital which, after all, is in effect just an increase of "capital intensity" of another kind: more human capital will certainly push up the ecomomy to a higher level income, thus creating medium run "growth" effects; but it may also raise the rate of creation of technical progress, thus increasing the long run equilibrium rate of growth.

Possibly the most important effect of less progressive taxation on the rate of economic growth will be due to the likely increase in risk taking by small firms and individual inventors. A large percentage of the most important technical advances are due to small firms and individual inventors (Jewkes et al. 1969); and Schumpeter (1912) thus rightly centered the creation of technical progress in the newly formed small firm, the one, as we argued, most likely to be stimulated to higher risk taking by less progressive taxation. Though this may not be true for large oligopolistic markets (Weizsäcker, 1980), in competitive markets there is likely to

The International Consequences of Less Progressive Taxation 59

be too little risk taking from the standpoint of society, so that less progressive taxation would here partly remedy an economic inefficiency. The stimulus to more entrepreneurial activity and to higher risk taking of less progressive taxation will thus unambiguously increase economic growth in the short as well as in the long run.

To summarize: less progressive taxation of the first type will increase economic growth particularly during a lengthy medium term transitional period, but also in long run equilibrium. This would raise investment demand, thus mitigating the fall in the rate of interest due to higher saving. Production would tend to become more capital intensive, particularly transitionally till the higher capital demand of more rapid growth pushes interest rates up again. Production is also likely to shift towards more human capital intensive products and especially towards more innovative ones.

3.5 Turning now to less progressive taxation of the second type, that is to say to lower progression with a simultaneous reduction of tax advantages for capital formation, these conclusions may well be reversed.

Favourable tax treatment of real capital formation, particularly accelerated depreciation schemes, may have extremely strong effects on the rate of investment (Jorgenson and Hall, 1967) and on the total capital stock (Sinn, 1984). Rescinding them at the same time as less progressive taxation of private and of corporate income is introduced may thus have a strong and protracted growth reducing effect. At the same time the likely stimulus of less progressive taxation towards higher saving remains, a type of saving that is now no longer synonymous with investment. In an international context a country that introduces less progressive taxation of the second type is thus likely to become a strong international lender: its increased saving will be invested abroad. If it is an important country, as the United States are at present, it is, on the other hand, likely to carry other countries with it in its growth decline.

It is difficult to say what is likely to prevail in the long run: the growth decreasing effects of lower capital formation or the growth increasing effects of more managerial and entrepreneurial activity and of more risk taking by small firms. If we take the Schumpeterian view of the pre-eminence of innovative entrepreneurial activity over all capital accumulation the latter will be the case. Eventually, after a probably protracted period, which may well outlast a decade, the growth increasing effects of less progressive taxation even of the second type are likely to take over.

The product mix in such a country will, on the other hand, be markedly different from one with less progressive taxation of the first type: because of the dampening effects on capital accumulation production will become on average less intensive in physical capital though more intensive in human capital. For the formation of human capital is not impeded by smaller tax favours for real capital formation. Production is also likely to be more innovative due to the higher risk taking by small firms. We are thus likely to get a mixture of production veering particularly to those types of so-called "intelligent" products which use capital only sparingly.

4. Real International Consequences

4.1 Less progressive taxation of any kind is above all likely to create more human capital intensive and more innovative products. These products are typically non-homogeneous "quality" products. Normally their price elasticity of demand is likely to be low; or, in other words, these products are highly competitive but themselves little subject to competitive pressures. The most important effect of less progressive taxation may therefore be that it makes international trade more profitable for the country which has resorted to it. In the long run less progressive taxation may thus favour international economic integration by increasing the gains from trade which can be achieved. Selling human capital intensive and innovative products at relatively good profit margins abroad is therefore also likely to increase the rewards to risk taking once again and thus to cause a further virtuous spiral of innovation.

A side aspect of changing international trade towards products with low price elasticity must also be remarked upon: such products are more immune to exchange rate fluctuations which are largely shifted to their consumers. Less progressive taxation may thus change the trade mix towards products which are more immune towards international financial disturbances.

4.2 By Rybczynski's theorem capital intensive productions will rise more than proportionately in countries with less progressive taxation of typ one; and the production of commodities which use basic labour will decline absolutely. Thus the exchange of capital intensive for labour intensive commodities through world trade will be intensified. This has the added advantage for world trade that if the advanced countries decrease the progression of their income tax schedules it becomes easier for less advanced countries with their generally more labour intensive domestic productions to gain a foothold in world markets.

If trade is unimpeded and international commodity markets are near perfect, one of our conclusions for the closed economy will, however, no longer hold: be-

The International Consequences of Less Progressive Taxation   61

cause of factor price equalisation higher rates of saving will no longer necessarily entail lower interest rates and no longer higher wages. The whole substitution process necessary in order to take up a larger amount of capital per worker will come about by the shift in the commodities produced, not by a substitution of factors of production against each other in the production of one and the same commodity.

If the country that introduces less progressive taxation is very large or if many important countries introduce less progressive taxation of the first type more or less simultaneously, world capital will increase relatively. In this case we are more or less back in the closed economy world: rates of interest will decline and more capital intensive production of each commodity receives an additional stimulus.

As countries with less progressive taxation of the first type will grow more rapidly they will capture a larger share of world trade. If many important countries turn to less progressive taxation, world growth on average will rise. Other countries are going to benefit as well: the demand for their products will rise too.

In the 1960s one tended to assume that a more rapidly growing economy was likely to suffer a worsening in its terms of trade and/or its balance of trade (see, e.g., Johnson, 1958). This is, of course, certainly the case with higher growth due to higher aggregate demand. But the models in question found that also true for the case of a pure supply side growth, one due merely to a higher increase in productivity, which would be the effect of less progressive taxation of the first type. These models have, however, not been borne out by experience: the balance of trade and the terms of trade, if anything, rather seem to have turned in favour of the more rapidly growing economies. This may be due to two effects: technical progress, as far as production processes are improved by it, frequently also entails relative savings in inputs, so that growing countries tend to become less dependent on imports per unit of production at the same time that they become more dependent on imports as their volume of production increases; and these two effects may nearly cancel out. On the other hand technical progress, as far as it improves finished products, also constantly creates new monopolistic quasi-rents. It therefore pushes up the terms of trade in the not fully competitive markets for its new products. A worsening of the terms of trade and/or of the trade balance due to less progressive taxation of the first type is therefore unlikely. To put this point in a nut-shell: less progressive taxation of the first type increases both the rate of growth and international competitiveness of a country (competitiveness being appropriately measured by the profitability of trade).

4.3 International capital markets tend to become more perfect all the time and capital is by now highly mobile internationally in the middle or longer run. With perfect capital markets and mobile real capital, proportional capital taxation is fully shifted away in the very long run in contrast to various forms of favourable tax treatment of capital, like accelerated depreciation allowances (Sinn, 1984), which remain. (Mobility merely of financial capital is, however, not enough for this result, as Bovenberg, 1986, points out.) In other words: apart from such advantages after tax marginal returns on capital are equalized. Thus in internationally integrated economies the whole tax burden tends to fall on labour.

This has a highly important consequence: less progressive taxation becomes a powerful weapon in the international competitive race for highly qualified entrepreneurial and managerial labour. Labour is not fully mobile, as is well known. But managers and other business leaders tend to be particularly internationally minded and therefore comparatively mobile. Low tax rates in the upper range of income – in other words less progressive taxation – will be one of the most important ways to attract them to a country.

As international firms are not oblivious to the preferences of their staff, a less progressive taxation even of labour will be of great importance in attracting direct investment to a country as well: subsidiary companies of international firms, particularly those using much high powered staff, will tend to be located in countries with low marginal tax rates for high incomes.

Thus less progressive taxation will tend to attract additional high quality factors: managerial staff and also some capital complementary to it. This attraction for factors and the consequent international factor movements will further increase the level of income and even the long run growth rate of a country with less progressive taxation. The attraction for additional factors may even justify a lower rate of taxation, and not only a less progressive one: the argument for Laffer-curve effects, somewhat ludicrous on a closed economy level and as regards mere changes in work effort, becomes much more persuasive in the case of international competition for markets and factors.

4.4 In fact, it may not be inappropriate to transfer some of the arguments of tax competition on the national level to the international sphere. As Turnbull and Niho (1986) point out, a lower demand for public services and consequently a lower level of taxation may attract capital – and, I may add, also qualified labour. A reduction in social security expenditure with a consequent reduction in social security payments may be particularly attractive to factors, certainly to qualified labour and, if the social security load is borne in non-perfect capital markets also partly by capital, to capital as well. Top level managers are usually not very much interested in social security benefits, which they frequently do not, or even cannot, use, for instance because of time constraints. To them social security payments are therefore mostly redistributive taxation only. Thus a reduction even in proportional social security contributions may have similar effects as less progressive taxation proper in attracting factors internationally. Furthermore, as noted, a "privatisation" of social care may have the effect that individuals will wish to save more in order to provide for themselves; or that they will take out private insurance. These effects will further increase the effects less progressive taxation already has on saving and all the consequences noted which higher saving will entail.

4.5 For less progressive taxation of type two (lower marginal tax rates in upper income brackets with simultaneous reduction of favourable treatment of capital formation) the international consequences will be quite different. As pointed out the medium term effect is likely to be a reduction in the rate of growth; furthermore capital intensity of production will be decreased. Thus the export of capital intensive products will be reduced.

In the case of the United States we have witnessed from 1981 to 1986 the effects of less progressive taxation of – so to speak – a "reverse type two", that is to say a (slightly) less progressive tax, which also entailed on average lower taxation, coupled with the introduction of very marked tax favours for capital formation. From 1988 onwards (with preliminary steps already in 1987) we are now going to witness one of the most drastic cases ever known of less progressive taxation of the second type: a reduction of the top marginal income tax to 28 percent (effectively 35 percent for medium high incomes between roughly 50,000 and 150,000 $) and of the marginal corporation tax rate of 34 percent (again effectively 39 percent in a medium range). This less progressive taxation will not lead to lower taxation on average; and the tax advantages of capital formation in the form of accelerated depreciation will mostly disappear. The present shift thus basically works like the introduction of an additional tax on capital which is a substitute for a reduced pay-roll tax. Such a tax, as Feldstein (1974) showed, is not shifted away much from capital but is mainly borne by it.

The consequences of the first named experiment ("Reverse" second type less progressive taxation together with lower taxation) were as to be expected: a marked surge in economic growth, and, as Sinn (1984) has pointed out, capital imports of gigantic proportions. (The resulting budget deficit of lower taxation, with its increase in demand, will also have tended towards this result.) The present experiment is likely to have the opposite effect (Sinn, 1987): the tax change favours saving but discourages investment. The United States will therefore tend to become once more an exporter of capital, at least if the present budget deficit, that gobbles up private saving, is reduced. American firms will once more seek invest-

64   Erich Streissler

ment abroad. The growth rate of the United States, on the other hand, is likely
to be damped down for a considerable period.

4.6 The upshot of this discussion on the real consequences of less progressive
taxation on international trade is the following: the tax system has nowadays
become one of the most decisive influences in shaping the exchange of factors
and of commodities between nations. Less progressive taxation is likely to give
decisive competitive advantages. The United States have taken the lead in shaping
a revolutionary new tax system of few exemptions but of a breath-taking low degree
of progression, not known anywhere in industrial countries (apart perhaps from
Switzerland) for the last fifty or even sixty years. The other industrial nations
will have to follow suit, and soon at that, if they do not wish to be hopelessly
outperformed in international markets. In following the lead of the United States
they need not emulate its example, however, of eliminating favourable treatment
of capital formation. In fact, they will be well advised not to do so.

5.   Financial International Consequences

5.1   Let us now turn to the likely effects of less progressive taxation on the exchange rate in a world of flexible rates. As we have noted, less progressive taxation
is likely to lead to higher economic growth and higher saving as well as investment;
and finally to a more capital intensive production on average.

According to the now usual monetarist models of exchange rate determination,
a higher rate of economic growth will by itself lead to an appreciation of the
exchange rate: ceteris paribus domestic money will become scarce relative to goods
so that its value in foreign markets (e.g., the exchange rate of the country) will
appreciate. As we have argued the full effect of an increase in the rate of growth due
to less progressive taxation will take some time till human capital is accumulated
and qualified occupations are shifted towards a higher share of managerial and
entrepreneurial activities and till technical advances reach their full swing. The
effect of outperforming other economies is thus likely to mount and a tendency
(given the exchange rate) towards a more favourable balance of trade for the future
has to be assumed. This leads once again to an appreciation of the currency
(Mussa, 1984, p. 36). A third effect will be the attraction of foreign factors. As
has been argued, even if only highly qualified owners of human capital move to
a country with less progressive taxation, some capital, being complementary to
them, will move at the same time. Thus the demand for the currency of the coun-

try with less progressive taxation will rise. Once more the exchange rate is pushed up.

We next turn to the increase in the degree of capital intensity of production. If we use a portfolio model for the demand for money, the additional investment entailed in creating this relatively higher capital stock will also push up the demand for money. Thus we have found a fourth reason why the exchange rate will appreciate, even without a change in the rate of interest (Obstfeld and Stockman, 1985, p. 954). If capital markets are not perfect and the rate of interest falls because of higher saving the demand for money will increase, as it is negatively interest elastic. A domestic increase in the demand for money provides a fifth reason why the domestic currency will appreciate.

Thus we have found no less than five reasons why the exchange rate is likely to appreciate in a country with less progressive taxation relative to others. All the arguments apply, of course, to a real appreciation of exchange rates, not a nominal one. These tendencies may feed upon themselves for a considerable period. Appreciation over some time tends to reduce the rate of inflation. Such a country will therefore appear financially "sound" to international investors. Furthermore, a more rapidly growing country may also appear "sound" in a real sense: even though in non-perfect capital markets the rate of interest would rather decline, foreign investors might hope to share in the higher and more numerous innovation rents likely to accrue, as argued, in a country with less progressive taxation. They will therefore also tend to speculate on balance more in favour of this currency than otherwise. Continuous appreciation of a currency increases the return for the foreign investor. Thus the more rapidly growing and more capital intensive country will tend to attract additional capital just because it has an appreciating currency for a considerable period.

As the appreciation of the exchange rate will be one in real terms, the terms of trade of the country with less progressive taxation will also tend to increase. Clearly, imports with prices denominated in the currency of their origin will become cheaper. Less progressive taxation is likely to lead to more innovative products which normally will show a relatively low price elasticity of their foreign demand. Thus the price of these export goods will not have to be lowered much because of exchange rate appreciation. On balance, more import goods will be received for every unit of commodities exported. Thus a further favourable effect on real incomes will be exerted in the country with less progressive taxation.

Some worsening in the balance of trade might be the effect of these changes. In fact the "purpose" (so to speak) of the appreciation of the exchange rate is to make a real inflow of capital possible; and that is to say a worsening of the balance of trade. In the experience of more rapidly growing countries, however, this worsening of the balance of trade via appreciation has not been substantial.

5.2 With less progressive taxation of the second type the effect on exchange rates is likely to be the reverse rather. If a country saves more due to less progressive taxation but wishes to reduce investment because its capital stock after the cancellation of investment allowances is already too high, it will have an outflow of capital. Furthermore, readjustment will lead to a temporary depression in economic growth. Both lower growth and the capital outflow will depress the exchange rate.

In fact, we have just witnessed this type of change in the case of the US dollar. From 1981 to 1986 the USA had a system of less progressive taxation of a "reverse" second type with increased investment allowances. During this period an accumulation of capital in the USA was therefore desired. In the process of capital accumulation the exchange rate has to stand above its equilibrium level (Mussa, 1984, p. 35). When it was realized during the spring of 1985 that this tax system was not likely to last, the dollar started to drop. The fall accelerated, when the new system was introduced. By the same argument, during a period of relative domestic capital decumulation and of a build up of foreign capital holdings the exchange rate must stand below its equilibrium level for a considerable period. The dollar therefore switched rapidly from overvaluation to undervaluation. Other changes may also have worked in the same direction: notions for instance that the persistent budget deficits might lead to higher inflation in the USA (Sargent and Wallace, 1981/1985) or the realisation that the US balance of trade tended to be deeper and longer in deficit than expected. But the changes in the US tax system were certainly important and yield the most consistent explanations of exchange rate movements.

During the whole period from 1981 up to now the sucking off of capital from other nations by the United States has exerted a depressing effect on growth in other countries: real interest rates have been pushed up because of favourable conditions of investment in the United States. On the other hand the balance of trade deficit of the US has created favourable growth conditions for other nations. It is difficult to say which effect has dominated; on balance in industrial nations probably the depressing effects of higher real interest rates. It is good that the situation is likely to change soon.

5.3 It is also good for the stability of the international financial system that the change to a less progressive system of taxation of the second type is likely to turn the United States once more into a net capital exporter. The United States turned a net debtor in 1986 or – according to other calculations – is going to turn into one in the near future. Never before in history has the leading financial nation, the nation providing the key currency in the world, been a debtor.

It has been sagely remarked that one of the reasons why the international gold standard worked so well under the leadership of Great Britain before the First World War was that Great Britain was a huge creditor nation. If Great Britain in this period ran an increased balance of trade deficit, its exchange rate depreciated mildly within the gold points, thus slightly stimulating its exports and discouraging its imports. But the real burden of adjustment fell on the rate of interest. In such a situation the rate of interest was pushed up. As Great Britain was a huge creditor, this automatically tended to balance its current account: its interest inflow increased. Thus it was easy for Great Britain to balance out its real shocks with small changes in its exchange rate and small changes in its rate of interest. Its currency was "sound": only small price fluctuations were needed. The gold standard thus imposed little real burdens; at least not on the leading financial nations: the debtor nations had to pay for its advantages with interest movements against them. And the other nations were forced to stick to the gold standard all the same, because opting out of the gold standard, once it had been introduced, would have imposed heavy losses in terms of transaction costs.

If the United States, however, were a debtor nation, its periodic balance of trade problems would be aggravated by interest payments: interest rates would still go up if it had a trade deficit. But then interest payments would reinforce instead of dampen its trade deficit. (Fortunately the United States is not yet a debtor on interest terms: it still receives more interest than it pays out, but only just so.) Thus fluctuations in the exchange rate of the US dollar would have to become very large in order to balance out real shocks. In fact, we are just now already experiencing the first pangs of these difficulties. Huge fluctuations in the exchange rate of the leading currency of the world might' by and by create unbearable international tensions. The present change in the US tax system may thus be seen as a timely move in the direction of greater stability of international exchange markets.

References

Arnott, R., and **Stiglitz, J.E.** (1986): "Moral Hazard and Optimal Commodity Taxation." *Journal of Public Economics* 29: 1–24.

Atkinson, A.B. (1971): "Capital Taxes, the Redistribution of Wealth and Individual Savings." *Review of Economic Studies* 38: 209–227.

Atkinson, A.B., and **Stiglitz, J.E.** (1980): *Lectures on Public Economics.* Maidenhead: McGraw Hill.

Bovenberg, A.L. (1986): "Capital Income Taxation in Growing Open Economies." *Journal of Public Economics* 31: 347–376.

Break, G.F. (1974): "The Incidence and Economic Effects of Taxation." In *The Economics of Public Finance.* Washington, D.C.: The Brookings Institution.

Brunner, J.K. (1986): "A Two-Period Model on Optimal Taxation with Learning Incentives." *Journal of Economics/Zeitschrift für Nationalökonomie* 46: 31–47.

Feldstein, M.S. (1974): "Incidence of a Capital Income Tax in a Growing Economy With Variable Savings Rates." *Review of Economic Studies* 44: 505–513.

Ferguson, C.E. (1965): "Time-Series Production Functions and Technological Progress in American Manufacturing Industry." *Journal of Political Economy* 73: 135–147.

Hellwig, M.F. (1986): "The Optimal Linear Income Tax Revisited." *Journal of Public Economics* 31: 163–179.

Kihlstrom, R.E., and **Laffont, J.J.** (1983): "Taxation and Risk Taking in General Equilibrium Models With Free Entry." *Journal of Public Economics* 21: 159–181.

Ippolito, R.A. (1985): "Income Tax Policy and Lifetime Labor Supply." *Journal of Public Economics* 26: 327–347.

Jewkes, J.; Sawers, D., and **Stillerman, R.** (1969): *The Sources of Invention.* (Second Edition.) London: Macmillan.

Johnson, H.G. (1958): *International Trade and Economic Growth.* London: Allen & Unwin. (Ch. III and IV.)

Jorgenson, D.W., and **Hall, R.E.** (1967): "Tax Policy and Investment Behavior." *American Economic Review* 57: 391–414.

Malcolmson, J.M. (1986): "Some Analytics of the Laffer Curve." *Journal of Public Economics* 29: 263–279.

McKee, M.J.; Visser, J.J.C., and **Saunders, P.G.** (1986): "Marginal Tax Rates on the Use of Labour and Capital in OECD Countries." *OECD Economic Studies* 7: 46–101.

Mill, J.S. (1970): *Principles of Political Economy.* London: Parker.

Mirrlees, J.A. (1971): "An Exploration in the Theory of Optimum Income Taxation." *Review of Economic Studies* 38: 175–208.

Mussa, M. (1984): "The Theory of Exchange Rate Determination." In *Exchange Rate Theory and Practice*, edited by J. F. O. Bilson and R. C. Marston. Chicago: University of Chicago Press.

Obstfeld, M., and **Stockman, A.C.** (1985): "Exchange-Rate Dynamics." In *Handbook of International Economics, Vol. II.*, edited by R. W. Jones and P. B. Kenen. Amsterdam: North-Holland.

Sadka, E. (1976): "On Progressive Income Taxation." *American Economic Review* 66: 931–935.

Sargent, T.J., and **Wallace, N.** (1981/1985): "Some Unpleasant Monetarist Arithmetic." *Quarterly Review, Federal Reserve Bank of Minneapolis* 1981, Reprint Winter 1985, pp. 38–44.

Schumpeter, J.A. (1912): *Theorie der wirtschaftlichen Entwicklung.* Leipzig: Duncker & Humblot.

Sinn, H.W. (1984): "Die Bedeutung des Accelerated Cost Recovery System für den internationalen Kapitalverkehr." *Kyklos* 37: 542–576.

Sinn, H.W. (1987): "Der Dollar, die Weltwirtschaft und die amerikanische Steuerreform von 1986." Münchner Wirtschaftswissenschaftliche Beiträge No. 87–01. University of Munich.

Stiglitz, J.E. (1986): *Economics of the Public Sector.* New York: Norton & Company.

Streissler, E.W. (1980): "Models of Investment-Dependent Economic Growth Revisited" In *Economic Growth and Resources, Vol. 2*, edited by R. C. O. Matthews. London: Macmillan.

Streissler, E.W., and **Neudeck, W.** (1986): "Are there Intellectual Precursors to the Idea of Second Best Optimization?" *Journal of Economics/Zeitschrift für Nationalökonomie* Supplementum 5: 227–242.

Tobin, J. (1967): "Life Cycle Saving and Balanced Growth." In *Ten Economic Studies in the Tradition of Irving Fisher.* New York.

Turnbull, G.K., and **Niho, Y.** (1986): "The Optimal Property Tax with Mobile Non Residential Capital." *Journal of Public Economics* 29: 223–239.

Weizsäcker, C.C. von (1980): *Barriers to Entry. A Theoretical Treatment.* Berlin: Springer-Verlag.

Yellen, J.L. (1984): "Efficiency Wage Models of Unemployment." *American Economic Review, Papers and Proceedings* 74: 200–205.

Tax Reforms and International Mobility

Leland B. Yeager, Auburn, Alabama, USA

At first glance, the assignment given to Professor Streissler might suggest a knee-jerk reaction in organizing a symposium on almost any topic, whatever it might be: "Now let's include a paper on its international aspects." Nevertheless, Streissler has responded well to what could have been a stultifying assignment. He introduces necessary distinctions between types of reform, considers the possible consequences of each, recognizes ambiguities and necessary qualifications (for example, the tension between income and substitution effects of taxes on both effort and saving), reaches tentative conclusions about effects within a country, and draws implications about likely effects on balances of payments, exchange rates, and the international financial system.

Summarizing its real international consequences, Streissler finds less progressive taxation likely to give a country decisive competitive advantages. The United States, he thinks, has taken the lead in cutting back progression; and other countries will have to follow suit if they do not wish to be hopelessly outperformed in international markets. However, he advises them not to emulate the United States in eliminating tax breaks for capital formation.

Turning to financial variables, Streissler finds that higher economic growth and the attraction of productive factors from abroad are likely to make a country's currency appreciate – and in real terms, that is, relative to purchasing-power parity.

These tendencies may be reversed – the currency may depreciate instead – if a reform removes tax breaks for investment. The U.S. dollar, previously buoyant on capital inflows, started to fall on the exchange markets in 1985, Streissler says, when people realized that those tax breaks were not likely to endure. Also possibly depressing the dollar has been the growing idea that persistent budget deficits might rekindle inflation. However, Streissler finds it good for the stability of the international financial system that a type-2 move to less tax progression is likely to make the United States once more a net capital exporter. If the United States remained a net debtor, interest payments would aggravate its periodic trade-balance problems. The dollar rate would have to fluctuate widely "to balance out real shocks", whose first pangs, Streissler says (p. 67) we are already experiencing. So tax changes tending to promote U.S. capital exports may prove "a timely move in the direction of greater stability of international exchange markets".

72
Leland B. Yeager

I wonder if this is right – to applaud dollar-weakening developments at a time when the dollar is already weak. I might also quibble over Streissler's apparent confidence (p. 64) in his conclusions about how reduced tax progression affects a country's exchange rate. Many other influences are at work besides those he is able to take account of. Even Streissler's more momentous conclusions about the effects of tax reduction are iffy, as he himself recognizes. This is not the fault of his method of analysis. Firm generalizations are hard to come by. Even in the mathematical models deployed in a couple of the other conference papers, the effects of specified changes depend on particular functional forms and parameter sizes.

Another possible quibble concerns Streissler's evident assumption that tax breaks for investment are generally a good thing, presumably because he thinks that resources allocated to real capital formation would be too few in some sense in the absence of corrective measures. Such a judgment should be explicitly stated, defended, and examined.

Since Streissler is discussing the international aspects of what is, after all, a redistributionary measure – progressive taxation – I wish he had gotten into the issue of redistribution between rich and poor countries. What are the economic consequences of such redistribution? Is it ethically permissible or ethically required?

In his remarks about how taxation affects international movements of capital, skilled and managerial labor, and business enterprise, Streissler is alluding to a situation on the world scene reminiscent of Charles Tiebout's (1956) analysis of different levels of government within a single country. Federalism, together with people's mobility among jurisdictions, promotes competition among local governments and so makes the activities of governments and the desires of their citizens match better than they would under a unified national tax and expenditure system. Citizens can discipline local governments by "voting with their feet".

Streissler in effect makes one point that Tiebout neglected: with regard to redistributionary measures, including progressive taxation, geographical mobility gives particular weight to the wishes of their potential victims, the people best endowed with productive abilities and wealth. These people can restrain predatory governments by moving away (or showing readiness to move). Competition among countries to attract brains, entrepreneurial ability, capital, and other sources of wealth gives each government some incentive to restrain the progressivity of its taxes.

This may be a practical argument against redistributive taxation, but it is no moral argument. If redistribution is a moral imperative, one implication of

Streissler's analysis may be that the governments of the world should form a cartel to keep the victims of redistribution from escaping.

For those of us who see no compelling moral basis for progressive taxation, however, Streissler offers hope. (I must make a qualification. I do not confidently condemn all redistribution. There is a difference between redistribution to relieve actual poverty and redistribution for more questionable purposes, such as achieving a closer approach to equality of income and wealth as a supposed goal in its own right.) Streissler offers hope that increased international economic integration will have liberalizing effects: it will further restrain governments from reaching into our pockets and dominating our lives.

Reference

Tiebout, C. (1956): "A Pure Theory of Local Expenditure." *Journal of Political Economy* 64: 416–424.

Equitability and Income Taxation [*]

Dieter Bös and Georg Tillmann, Bonn, West Germany

1. Introduction

There are many different concepts of equitability. The two most important for our purposes will be defined and explained in the next section. However, before doing so, we need an introductory description of the economy we are dealing with.

We distinguish various economies with different goods. In the first instance we have a pure exchange economy with n consumption goods. Any consumer $h, h = 1, \ldots, H$, is characterized by his consumption bundle $\xi_h = (\xi_{1h}, \ldots, \xi_{nh})$. This commodity vector can have no negative components. In another economy income y_h is the only good considered. Finally, in the usual Mirrlees tradition consumption c_h and labor supply ℓ_h are taken into account. The explicit inclusion of labor supply means a transition to a "production economy" where the consumers are treated not only as purchasers of output. The output is measured in monetary units, expressed by the income y_h. If the government levies an income tax, the consumer is left with his net income, $c_h \geq 0$, which he uses for consumption. He does not save, but spends all his money for consumption goods.

In pure exchange economies and in economies with income as the only good the consumers are characterized by their utility functions $u_h(x_h)$ where $x_h = \xi_h$ or $x_h = y_h$, respectively. The utility functions have the usual neoclassical properties.

In a Mirrlees economy consumers are characterized by neoclassical utility functions $u_h(x_h)$,[1] where $x_h = (c_h, \ell_h)$. Moreover, consumers differ in their individual skills. "Skill" means productive ability.[2] We measure individual skills by $w_h > 0$ and without restriction of generality order the individuals according to their skills $w_1 < w_2 < \ldots < w_H$. Each individual contributes to production

---

[*] We gratefully acknowledge comments by William Baumol, Udo Ebert, Peter Hammond and Lorenz Nett on an earlier draft of this paper.

[1] Details of the properties of these utility functions will be given in explicit definitions in subsequent sections.

[2] From the original meaning of the words one could distinguish between innate "abilities" which are the basis of acquired "skills" which determine the "productivity" of an individual. However, as we do not explicitly deal with this causal chain, in this paper the terms "ability", "skill", and "productivity" are used synonymously.

D. Bös and B. Felderer (Eds.)
The Political Economy of Progressive Taxation
© Springer-Verlag Berlin Heidelberg 1989

according to his ability. Therefore his "effective labor supply"[3] equals $w_h \ell_h$, measured in standardized units of "efficiency man-hours". ℓ_h is worktime measured in natural units, normalized to $0 \leq \ell_h \leq 1$. It is adequate, moreover, to normalize the wage rate to unity. Then the individual gross income equals $y_h = w_h \ell_h$. It may be noted that in many papers the above explanation has been abridged to saying wage rates are equal to individual skills.

For the various economies we define allocations in the following way: in a pure exchange economy let an initial endowment vector Ω be given. A vector ξ is called an allocation if $\Sigma_h \xi_h \leq \Omega$. In an economy with income as the only good a total amount of money Ω is given and a vector y is called an allocation if $\Sigma_h y_h \leq \Omega$. In the Mirrlees economy an allocation is a vector (c, ℓ) such that $\Sigma_h w_h \ell_h \geq \Sigma_h c_h$.

2. Equitability and Fairness

In this paper we consider two different concepts of equitability. We have considered the properties of many other concepts, too (Tillmann, 1984). However, the gist of all problems which arise from equitability, can already be found in an analysis which confronts Foley equitability and contribution equitability.

2.1 Foley Equitability

The best known concept of equitability is due to Foley (1967) and Varian (1974).[4]

Definition 1 (Foley equitability):
An allocation x is Foley equitable if $u_h(x_h) \geq u_h(x_j)$ for all $h, j; 1 \leq h, j \leq H$.

According to this definition an allocation is Foley equitable if no consumer prefers another's consumption, income, or consumption-labor bundle. Every consumer, comparing his bundle of goods with all others, is content with his bundle.[5]

---

[3] Ordover–Phelps (1975).

[4] For a short "Dogmengeschichte" see Baumol (1986), pp. 71–74.

[5] According to Varian's terminology, a consumer h *envies* consumer j if $u_h(x_h) < u_h(x_j)$. It can be doubted whether this terminology actually describes what is called "envy" in everyday-life. In Varian's definition consumer h does not care about j's bundle x_j. He only would prefer to have x_j instead of x_h. · The typical every-day-life definition of "envy" would rather mean $u_h(x_h, x_j)$ where j's higher income, or higher consumption or lower labor supply reduces h's utility. However, this semantic problem of "envy" does not influence the importance of the concept of "equitability".

Equitability and Income Taxation

This is a sort of stable allocation as nobody has an incentive to change the distribution.

The economic consequences of Foley equitability depend on the specification of the goods.

(i) Assume $x_h = \xi_h$. Utility depends on bundles of consumption goods, it is strictly increasing in the consumption of each good. (There is no satiation.) In that case we deal with Foley equitability in an exchange economy with n goods. The production of the commodities is not modelled, there is no labor or capital supply included in the model, so the analysis is restricted to the division of a fixed bundle of commodities. Hence Baumol (1986) starts his explanation of equitability by referring to the problem of the "just division" of a given cake and extensively applies the Edgeworth box diagram to explain equitability.

(ii) Assume $x_h = y_h$. Utility depends on income only, it is strictly increasing in income. So disutility from labor supply is not taken into account. Such an analysis is only meaningful if there is a fixed amount of income K which has to be divided among the consumers, $\sum_h y_h = K$. Equitability is reduced to a pure distribution problem.

If $x_h = y_h$, only the equal distribution of incomes is Foley equitable. The proof is simple. We require $u_h(y_h) \geq u_h(y_j)$ and $u_j(y_j) \geq u_j(y_h)$. If both utility functions are strictly increasing in income, the above inequalities require $y_h \geq y_j$ and $y_j \geq y_h$. y_h must be equal to y_j for any pair $h, j \leq H$.

However, in this paper one of our main intentions is the modelling of income taxation and all recent literature on the topic stresses the disincentive effects of taxation. So the cake may shrink depending on the process of division. This leads us to the third specification.

(iii) Assume $x_h = (c_h, \ell_h)$. Utility is strictly increasing in consumption and strictly decreasing in labor supply. The inclusion of labor supply means a transition from a pure exchange economy to a production economy.

As both consumption and labor are taken into account, reward is given for higher labor supply. An agent with a high labor supply needs high consumption, otherwise he would be discontent if he compares his utility with others. On the other hand, higher consumption, if coupled with higher labor supply, will be accepted by the others.

Unfortunately, Foley's definition of the reward for labor supply is deficient. Only the consumption-labor bundles are compared, regardless of the individual abilities. Consumer h compares $u_h(c_h, \ell_h)$ and $u_h(c_j, \ell_j)$ using his own utility function only. Hence he computes the utility he would obtain if he himself (with his own ability w_h!) worked ℓ_j hours and received c_j consumption as reward for the labor supply.

Before concluding this subsection it should be mentioned that Foley equitability requires equal utility for everybody if the individual utility functions are identical. The proof is simple. We have $u(x_h) \geq u(x_j)$ and $u(x_j) \geq u(x_h)$ for any pair h and j. The two inequalities can only hold if $u(x_h) = u(x_j)$.

2.2 Contribution Equitability

Foley's concept takes account of the individual needs only. It ignores the individuals' abilities. However, there exist theoretical concepts which consider both. So it seems natural to develop a concept of equitability which weights the labor time of a skilled person higher than the labor time of someone less skilled. This is exactly what Varian's (1974) "contribution equitability"[6] does.

Definition 2 (contribution equitability):
An allocation is contribution equitable if $u_h(c_h, \ell_h) \geq u_h(c_j, w_j\ell_j/w_h)$ where $w_j\ell_j \leq w_h$; $\forall h, j; \ h, j \leq H$.

Consider the output produced by agent h. If he works ℓ_h units, he produces $z_h = w_h\ell_h$. It makes sense to ask how much h would have to work to produce what j produces, that is $z_j = w_j\ell_j$. Denote this time by $Q_h(z_j)$. In our case $Q_h(z_j) = w_j\ell_j/w_h$. We define an allocation as contribution equitable iff $u_h(c_h, \ell_h) \geq u_h(c_j, Q_h(z_j)) \Leftrightarrow u_h(c_h, (w_h\ell_h/w_h)) \geq u_h(c_j, (w_j\ell_j/w_h))$. If it is impossible for agent h to produce what j produces, $Q_h(z_j)$ will be undefined and we will regard the contribution equitability as being vacuously satisfied for these two agents. Pazner (1977) has illustrated how this definition is not entirely ethically satisfactory: it favors the able and penalizes the less able by implicit sanctification of productivity.

The explicit treatment of the individual skills in the definition of contribution equitability has two properties:

(i) when comparing the own bundle (c_h, ℓ_h) with somebody else's bundle, the labor supply ℓ_j is weighted by w_j/w_h. Assume consumer h is less able than consumer

---

[6] The content of the idea is reflected best by accentuating the "contribution" of the different individuals, see Baumol (1986), pp. 42–47. Varian (1974) himself refers to it as "equitability*", Pazner (1977) as "wealth equitability".

Equitability and Income Taxation

j. For the two persons the Foley concept requires

$$u_h(c_h, \ell_h) \geq u_h(c_j, \ell_j).$$

Varian's contribution equitability, on the other hand, requires

$$u_h(c_h, \ell_h) \geq u_h(c_j, \frac{w_j \ell_j}{w_h}).$$

Here we have assumed $w_j/w_h > 1$, so agent h would have to work more than ℓ_j if he wanted to produce the output of agent j. Since $u_2 < 0$, consumer h suffers more disutility from his labor supply if producing the output of agent j. Hence it is easily possible that h is discontent if this is judged according to the Foley concept, but is content according to the contribution equitability concept.

(ii) when $w_j \ell_j > w_h$, the comparison breaks down because Mr h is not able enough to produce Mr j's output even if Mr h worked the maximum labor time $\ell_h = 1$. This is a meaningful mathematical restriction upon the comparison. Moreover, it is of great importance if the concept of contribution equitability is used as an instrument to evaluate equity in an economy. The discontinuation of comparison means you are not allowed to compare your own position with the position of somebody who is so skilled that you cannot produce his output even if you work as hard as possible.

Contribution equitability explicitly considers both differences in individual skills and in individual utility. Foley equitability considers skills only implicitly, as far as they influence utility. This problem is particularly evident if the utility functions are assumed identical. Then Foley equitability implies that individuals are treated as identical although they are different with respect to their skills. Thus it is not surprising that with identical utility functions Foley equitability leaves all individuals equally well off. Contribution equitability distinguishes people according to their skill, even if their utility functions are identical. Different people are treated as different. Hence, even for identical utility functions, in contribution equitable allocations utility levels vary across individuals.

We have a "normal ranking": the higher the skill, the higher the utility. Consider the definition of contribution equitability for two individuals h and j, where h is less able than j. Then

$$u(c_j, \ell_j) \geq u(c_h, \frac{w_h \ell_h}{w_j}) > u(c_h, \ell_h).$$

The second (strict) inequality results from $w_h/w_j < 1$ and $u_2 < 0$: lower labor supply means higher utility.

As higher skill implies higher utility, for identical utility functions contribution equitable allocations never are Foley equitable.

2.3 Fairness

2.3.1 Equity and Efficiency

Economists often consider the trade-off between equity and efficiency, between distribution and allocation. In the preceding section equitability has been presented as a pure equity concept. Fairness is a concept which combines equity and efficiency.

We characterize efficiency by means of Pareto optimality and define

Definition 3 (fairness):
An equitable allocation which is Pareto-optimal, is called "fair".

Here we use either Foley fairness or contribution fairness, corresponding to the two concepts of equitability.

If somebody ranks Pareto optimality supreme, he will start from Pareto optimal states in the first instance. However, most observers will consider some Pareto optima to be "unjust". Take for instance the endpoints of the contract curve in an Edgeworth box. Many attempts have been made to choose a subset of all Pareto optima as being "better" or "preferable from some higher point of view". The equitability of an allocation can be taken as a criterion that can be used to select some preferable Pareto optimal allocations from the entire set of Pareto optima.

If somebody ranks equity supreme, he will start from equitable states in the first instance. However, if one equitable state is Pareto better than other equitable states, he will be willing to choose this better state. Hence he will be willing to apply the efficiency criterion in addition to the criterion of economic justice. Once again, we obtain fair states.

In standard exchange economies fair states typically will exist. However, in production economies this is not necessarily the case. In the following we shall see that the existence of fair allocations depends on whether preferences alone, or preferences and productivities are taken into account. If we are in a pure exchange economy, no problems will arise. If productivities are taken into account, that is, if we are in a production economy, it matters essentially whether preferences are identical or different.

2.3.2 Fairness in the Case of Different Preferences

The treatment of fairness, in particular in large (continuum) economies, is rather difficult and requires the use of measure theory to an extent which is beyond the scope of this paper. Hence, in this subsection we will restrict ourselves to the main features of the problem. Details and proofs of the statements can be found in Tillmann (1986).

2.3.2.1 Pure Exchange Economy

Let us begin with fair allocations in pure exchange economies. As differences in productivity are irrelevant in exchange economies, Foley and contribution fairness coincide. Hence it suffices to deal with Foley fairness.[7]

It is well-known that in exchange economies Foley fair allocations always exist under standard assumptions, for instance for continuous, convex and monotonic preferences (Varian, 1974, pp. 68–70). Typically, there is not only one fair allocation, but a continuum of fair allocations. This raises the question of how to select further from among those fair allocations. Varian (1976) argued that equal income allocations are "especially fair", in particular in "large" economies with a continuum of preferences so that "very similar agents" have "very similar tastes". His argument is as simple as it is convincing: "it is clear that if an agent has tastes very similar to mine and a higher income, then I will envy his chosen consumption bundle. Now if there were a continuum of agents, each similar to his neighbors, then certainly each agent could have no larger income than his neighbors – or else envy would result." (Varian, 1976, p. 252). This argument meanwhile has been made precise (Kleinberg, 1980; Champsaur–Laroque, 1981). So we know that in large economies only equal income allocations are fair. Generically, therefore, we have a finite number of fair states, maybe even a unique fair allocation.

2.3.2.2 Production Economy

Matters are much more complicated if we explicitly consider that the individual contributions to gross national product vary across individuals. Let us first deal with *Foley fairness*.[8] The starting point of the discussion was an interesting counterexample presented by Pazner and Schmeidler (1974). This example assumes constant returns to scale and homogeneous utility functions in a two consumer

---

[7] This means $u_h(\xi_h) \geq u_h(\xi_j) \ \forall h, j$.

[8] This means $u_h(c_h, \ell_h) \geq u_h(c_j, \ell_j) \ \forall h, j$.

economy[9] and shows that fair allocations may not exist. They assume

$$u_1(c_1, \ell_1) = (11/10)c_1 + (1 - \ell_1)$$
$$u_2(c_2, \ell_2) = 2c_2 + (1 - \ell_2)$$
$$c_1 + c_2 = (1/10)\ell_2 + \ell_1$$
$$0 \le \ell_1 \le 1 \ , \ 0 \le \ell_2 \le 1.$$

The feasibility constraint shows the superior productivity of the first agent. Moreover, the marginal productivity of the second agent's labor is so low that efficiency requires him not to work. Consequently, in any efficient state, the first agent should do all the work. However, "in such a situation agent 2 will envy agent 1 because he consumes more of the goods and agent 1 will envy agent 2 because he consumes more leisure." (Varian, 1974, p. 72). So in this economy, *no* Pareto efficient state is equitable.

Existence and properties of Foley fair allocations in production economies have meanwhile been scrutinized in Tillmann (1986). He shows it is possible in finite economies that fair allocations do not exist if both preferences and productivities differ only "marginally" across individuals. If only preferences *or* productivities differ, fair allocations always exist.

To show that non-existence of Foley-fair states is not an exception, it is sufficient to consider economies with two agents. The following results hold:[10]

(i) for any two different productivities two different utility functions can be found such that no Foley fair state exists;

(ii) for any class of preferences where the individuals' indifference curves intersect at most once, we can show the reverse of (i): for any two different utility functions two different productivities can be found such that no Foley fair state exists;

(iii) in large economies where preferences and productivities, vary continuously, no Foley fair state exists at all.

Cases (i) and (ii) say that it is always *possible* that preferences and productivities are related to each other in such a way that no fair state exists. Case (iii) is far more general. It fully excludes the possibility of fair allocations in large production economies which are defined as above.

What is the reason for the fundamental impossibility (iii)? We will not give a proof, because it is too complicated. However, the basic reason can easily be demonstrated. As we have continua of both preferences and productivities, we

---

[9] This presentation of Pazner–Schmeidler's example follows Varian (1974), p. 72.
[10] Tillmann (1986), propositions 2–5.

can *always* have people with very similar (= nearly identical) preferences and very similar (= nearly identical) productivities. Others may have very different preferences and productivities. Now consider two different preferences, u_a and u_b, and two different productivities w_h and w_j, where $h < j$.

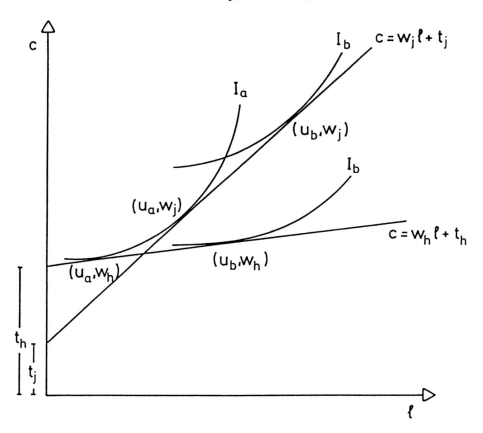

Figure 1

Figure 1 exhibits indifference curves $I_a(c,\ell), I_b(c,\ell)$ in the consumption-labor space. "a" and "b" are types of consumers with different preferences u_a, u_b. The preferences do not take account of the individual productivities. Figure 1 also exhibits the budget equations $c = w_h\ell + t_h$ and $c = w_j\ell + t_j$ where t_h, t_j are lump sum taxes or subsidies. Here productivities matter. In a Foley-fair state individuals with identical preferences must attain the same utility level, independent of their productivity. On the other hand it can be shown that individuals with the same productivity must optimize with respect to the same budget equation. The assumption of a continuous variation of preferences and of skills implies that for any preference ordering there are individuals with different skill and vice versa. Now consider Figure 1. Everything is fine in the case of the u_a-preference. There are two individual optima (u_a, w_h) and (u_a, w_j) which attain the same utility. However, in the case of the u_b-preference (u_b, w_h) yields a lower utility than (u_b, w_j) and so Mr h is discontent when comparing his utility with that of Miss j (and others). The assumption of a continuous variation of preferences and of skills implies that situations as illustrated in the figure do always occur. So there is no Foley fair allocation.

The negative results on Foley fairness suggest we should look at other definitions of fairness. Hence, let us consider *contribution fairness*. The non-existence of Foley fair allocations in large economies is due to the neglect of individual productivities in Foley's definition of equitability. As the utility functions do not depend on productivity, we have to equate utilities of individuals facing different budget lines which cannot be equitable. If utility functions are redefined so as to depend on productivity , the above problem vanishes. Therefore, *contribution fair* allocations always exist. Uniqueness, alas, cannot be guaranteed if a fixed distribution of skills is given.

In large economies, however, there is one and only one contribution fair allocation. However, this unique allocation is the laissez-faire state. There is no redistribution which would compensate for different productivities. Once again we face the implicit sanctification of productivity which characterizes contribution equitability. The implied laissez-faire fairness will be considered unjust by most policy makers.

2.3.3 Fairness in the Case of Identical Preferences

In pure exchange economies fair allocations always exist, even if the preferences vary across consumers. The same holds, of course, if preferences are identical. In production economies, on the other hand, we faced serious problems with the existence of Foley fair allocations. A natural way out of the dilemma would be a combination of equitability and second best Pareto optima, or a consideration of other definitions of economic justice. However, for the time being, let us stay in the first best framework and restrict the class of utilities to identical preferences. Needless to say we dislike the assumption of identical preferences. However, the literature on optimal income taxation has had to live with that assumption from the days of the sacrifice principles to the days of the Mirrlees model.

This subsection therefore deals with fair allocations in production economies with individuals who have identical preferences $u(c, \ell)$, but different productivities

Equitability and Income Taxation 85

$w_1 < \ldots < w_H,$[11] which implies different budget constraints $c_h = w_h \ell_h$. The result is as follows:

Proposition 1:
(i) Foley fairness: in any case exactly one fair allocation exists;

(ii) contribution fairness: those allocations always exist, but are non-unique.[12]

Proof:
See Tillmann (1984).

Until now we have considered only whether fair allocations do exist. In the following we want to scrutinize whether those states can be decentralized: does there exist a tax such that the optimal bundles of utility-maximizing agents are an equitable or fair allocation? A trivial answer to that question is as follows.

Proposition 2:
Given lump sum taxation all Pareto-optima can be obtained by decentralization.

The proof of Proposition 2 is well known and can be omitted. However, in economic practice lump-sum taxation is not available. Hence we turn to the investigation of how fair allocations can be decentralized by means of an income tax.

3. The Mirrlees Approach to Income Taxation

Let us now deal with income taxation as an instrument to achieve equitable, and possibly fair, allocations. For this purpose we must carefully distinguish between two concepts of *individual skills*:

(i) A *fixed distribution of skills* is given if there is one and only one numerical representation of the skills for which our theories are formulated. We deal with the given skills at some given moment, say $w_1 = 2$; $w_2 = 4$; $\ldots$, $w_H = 20000$. The government has statistical information about the distribution of the skills. It does not know who is who. As all different values of skills are given, a tailor-made income-tax tariff can be built, which exactly considers the individual situations.

---

[11] In terms of the following Section 3, this is a fixed skill distribution with finitely many individuals.

[12] As already mentioned in the preceding subsection, uniqueness results if a continuum of consumers is assumed.

Unfortunately, skills change over time, and a tailor-made income tax which was equitable when introduced may cease to be equitable in the course of time. Hence, income tax schedules better should be formulated in such a way that they are equitable not only for one fixed distribution of skills, but for all possible distributions of skills. This leads us to the second concept.

(ii)   A *variable distribution of skills* is given if we do not only consider one given realization of the individual skills, but allow for all possible changes in the individual skills.

A variable distribution of skills is not only the appropriate concept to encompass all configurations of skills which change over time. It can also be seen as the natural consequence of dealing with large economies. Let us assume a continuum of consumers whose skill distribution is denoted by a function $f(w)$. This distribution is an approximation to the actual discontinuous distribution of the many consumers in the economy. Now take samples from the continuum economy. Every sample typically will be different. So by taking samples we can generate different distributions of skills, which is exactly what the concept of a variable distribution of skills implies. The informational setting is the same as in the case of a fixed distribution of skills. The government knows the distribution, but does not know who is who.

Whereas the skills vary across individuals, the *utility functions are identical* in our model. They have the following neoclassical properties:

Assumption 1:
$u : \ \mathbb{R}_+ \times [0,1] \to \mathbb{R}$ is twice continuously differentiable, monotone, strictly quasiconcave, $u_1 > 0$, $u_2 < 0$, $lim_{c \to 0} - \frac{u_2}{u_1}(c,0) = 0$, $lim_{\ell \to 1} - \frac{u_2}{u_1}(c, \ell) = \infty$. Consumption and leisure are normal goods. We normalize $u(0,1) = 0$.

If individual h works ℓ_h units, he or she obtains a gross income $w_h \ell_h$ and a net income $c_h = w_h \ell_h - t(w_h \ell_h)$ where t, $t : \ \mathbb{R}_+ \to \mathbb{R}$ denotes the tax function. We apply the following weak assumption on the tax function.

Assumption 2:
$t : \ \mathbb{R}_+ \to \mathbb{R}$ is continuously differentiable. The income tax is a pure redistribution tax, $\sum_h t(w_h \ell_h) = 0$.

The optimization problem of consumer h is as follows:

$$\max_{\ell \in [0,1]} \ u(w_h \ell - t(w_h \ell), \ell).$$

Equitability and Income Taxation

The skills w_h and the income tax function are exogenously given for the consumer. Hence his utility depends on his labor supply only. As u and t are continuous, u has maxima on the closed interval $[0,1]$.

The following Kuhn-Tucker conditions must be fulfilled in a maximum. The maximum is not necessarily unique.

$\ell_h = 0$:
$$w_h \cdot (1 - t'(0)) \cdot u_1(-t(0),0) + u_2(-t(0),0) \leq 0,$$
$1 > \ell_h > 0$:
$$w_h(1 - t'(w_h\ell_h))u_1(w_h\ell_h - t(w_h\ell_h), \ell_h) + u_2(w_h\ell_h - t(w_h\ell_h), \ell_h) = 0.$$

The Kuhn-Tucker conditions show when individuals work[13] and when they do not work. Consider the very plausible case of $t'(0) < 1$, consumers with "minimal income" must not be taxed totally.[14] From the first Kuhn-Tucker condition we then learn that all individuals $h = 1, \ldots, H$ work if

$$w_h > \frac{-u_2(-t(0),0)}{(1 - t'(0))u_1(-t(0),0)}.$$

Therefore the term at the right-hand side of the inequality separates the working and the non working population. If this term increases, less individuals will work, until even the most skilled stops working if

$$w_H \leq \frac{-u_2(-t(0),0)}{(1 - t'(0))u_1(-t(0),0)}.$$

Needless to say, an income tax does not make sense if it compels all individuals to stop working. Hence, if equitability happens to hold only for the $((0,0))$ allocation, this is tantamount to saying equitability cannot hold at all.

There is an interesting reformulation of the individual optimization approach which we will need for the understanding of contribution equitability. The concept we have presented on the preceding pages deals with identical utility functions u, but different budget constraints $c = w_h\ell - t(w_h\ell)$. The basis of the differences in the budget are the differences in the individual skills.

Let us now put the problem the other way round. We redefine utility in the (c,y) space

$$v_h(c,y) := u(c, \frac{y}{w_h}), \quad y \leq w_h; \quad v_{h1} > 0, \quad v_{h2} < 0.$$

---

[13] $\ell_h = 1$ is excluded by Assumption 1.

[14] Sometimes tax laws may lead to a poverty trap of $t'(y) > 1$ for small y. However, for $y = 0$ this phenomenon never occurs as it would lead to a negative net income.

Utility v_h depends on net income c and on gross income y. The dependence on net income measures the utility from spending income. The dependence on gross income measures the disutility from labor. Even if net incomes are equal, equal gross incomes do not lead to the same utility because the time one has to work for a given gross income depends on the individual's skill.

Hence, although v_h has been derived from u, it represents a different conception of utility. v_h is different across individuals although u is not. This means that the difference in the individual skills has been transformed into a difference in the individual utilities.

On the other hand, by switching to the (c, y) space, we can reformulate the budget constraint into

$$c = y - t(y).$$

The budget constraint is identical for all consumers.

After substituting the individual budget constraints into the utility functions, we have two equivalent concepts to describe the individual optimization:

(i) $\quad \max_{\ell \in [0,1]} \ u(w_h \ell - t(w_h \ell), \ell)$

(ii) $\quad \max_{y \in [0, w_h]} \ v_h(y - t(y), y).$

4. Income Taxation to Achieve Fairness

4.1 The Impossibility of a Foley Equitable Income Tax

Proposition 3:
Consider Foley equitability. Assume a variable skill distribution. Then there does not exist any income tax such that the resulting allocation is equitable if we exclude the trivial allocation $((0,0))$. As there is no equitable allocation, there is no fair allocation, either.

Proof:
As the $((0,0))$ allocation is excluded, at least one person works, $\ell_h > 0$. The individual maximum may be non-unique. In that case we choose any of the various maxima. As we have a variable skill distribution, there is some $\hat{w} > w_h$. Then there exists an $\tilde{\ell}$, $0 < \tilde{\ell} < \ell_h$ such that $\hat{w}\tilde{\ell} = w_h \ell_h$. Therefore $\max_\ell u(\hat{w}\ell - t(\hat{w}\ell), \ell) \geq u(\hat{w}\tilde{\ell} - t(\hat{w}\tilde{\ell}), \tilde{\ell}) > u(w_h \ell_h - t(w_h \ell_h), \ell_h)$, as $u_2 < 0$.

Proposition 3 is a very general result. It applies for progressive, proportional and regressive taxes in the same way. The deeper reason for this negative result

Equitability and Income Taxation

is as follows. We have identical utility functions, but exogenously given different abilities. Each individual optimally adjusts his labor supply to his individual skill, taking account of the income taxation. Therefore the individual's optimum depends only on his ability and no tax function that leaves some incentive for work, can enforce an equitable allocation. Hence we had explicitly to exclude the trivial $((0,0))$ allocation and we see that this exclusion was crucial for the proof.[15] So the impossibility of an equitable income tax is deeply rooted in the whole philosophy of the taxation model.

The assumption of a variable skill distribution also turned out to be decisive for the proof. A simple example may illustrate the importance of variability in the skill distribution. Assume we have a fixed skill distribution. Now consider the case

$$w_H > \frac{-u_2(-t(0),0)}{(1-t'(0))u_1(-t(0),0)} \geq w_{H-1}, \qquad t'(0) < 1.$$

In this allocation only the person with the highest ability supplies a positive amount of labor. Now it is possible that

$$u(-t(0),0) = u(w_H \ell_H - t(w_H \ell_H), \ell_H).$$

Then we have a Foley equitable income tax which does not lead to the $((0,0))$ allocation, because $\ell_H > 0$. Admittedly, this example is of no economic interest, but only a sort of logical puzzle to exemplify the importance of assuming a variable skill distribution.

It is adequate at this point of the paper to ponder how Foley equitable allocations can be brought about if income taxation fails to do so. We would have to apply other instruments, for example

(i) suitably chosen lump sum taxes or a tax on individual abilities (instead of incomes);

(ii) an egalitarian education policy: if all individuals are equally able, in our model an equitable allocation results.

The reader should not misunderstand the preceding remark on education policy. We do not really believe it is possible to achieve equally able individuals by education. We only want to accentuate the importance of the different skills in our model. Moreover, we want to make clear the basic value judgments inherent in it. If some socialist policy maker strives for an equitable allocation, he may actually

---

[15] For another concept of equitability, which requires equal consumption, this total disincentive effect has been stressed by Baumol (1986), pp. 184–188.

see a progressive income tax and an egalitarian education policy as two instruments which complement each other. The model we are dealing with encourages such a way of thinking.

4.2 Contribution Fairness and Income Taxation

Let us now scrutinize whether the concept of contribution equitability leads to more positive conclusions on fairness and income taxation. We obtain the following proposition which holds for both fixed and variable distribution of skills.

Proposition 4:
Let *any* continuous tax function t be given. The resulting allocation is contribution equitable.

Proof:
Incomes $y_j > w_h$ are not feasible for consumer h and contribution equitability is vacuously fulfilled by definition. Incomes $y_j \leq w_h$ are never preferred to the own utility maximizing income y_h because $v_h(y_j - t(y_j), y_j) \leq max_{y \in [0, w_h]} v_h(y - t(y), y) = v_h(y_h - t(y_h), y_h)$.

Proposition 4 provides the very opposite of Proposition 3. There it was impossible to achieve a Foley equitable allocation by means of an income tax. In the case of contribution equitability, however, every income tax yields an equitable allocation.

The reason for the result is the following. Consider the consumer's choice of an optimal gross income in the (c, y)-space. If somebody's ability is higher than mine, it may be that I cannot possibly reach his income; which leaves undefined a utility function which postulates that I achieve this income. So any such comparison is excluded from the analysis because it is undefined. On the other hand, as long as I can reach somebody else's income, I will be content with my own utility maximizing position. Hence, if utility is defined on the income space, it is possible to levy an income tax in such a way that everybody is defined to be content.

We do not find contribution equitability satisfactory from an ethical point of view. There are two main arguments. First we follow Pazner (1977). We do not regard it "just" that equity is based on individual abilities which may be distributed across individuals according to some random process.

Moreover, if there is enough variance between the less able and the more able, one can oppose contribution equitability on the following grounds. In that case contribution equitability divides the possibilities into two cases:[16]

- either it is possible to achieve another's income. Then no envy occurs because one always (weakly) prefers the own utility maximizing income.

- or it is impossible to achieve another's income. This is a statement of physical impossibility. However, the statement is taken as the basis of a value judgement on equity. The income of the less able simply is not compared with the income of the more able in such a case.

To scrutinize the point, this dichotomization excludes by definition all possible envy of the better-off and then just asserts as a result that nobody envies the worse-off.

Even if one were to reject the caveats mentioned above, there is one more problem which arises when taking contribution equitability as a measure of economic justice in the case of income taxation. If we require Pareto optimality, i.e., if we deal with contribution fairness, we obtain the following unsatisfactory result.

Proposition 5:
Assume a variable skill distribution. There is exactly one contribution fair allocation which can be obtained by decentralization. The corresponding tax is $t(y) \equiv 0$.

Proof:
For the general proof see Tillmann (1986). As this proof needs measure theory, we give a simpler proof, based on the assumption of a differentiable tax function. Proposition 1 (ii) states that for $t \equiv 0$ a Pareto optimum, i.e., a contribution fair allocation, is given. Other optima cannot be reached. We have $-u_2(c_h, \ell_h)/w_h u_1(c_h, \ell_h) = 1 - t'(w_h \ell_h)$ from the Kuhn-Tucker condition. Moreover, at a Pareto optimum marginal rate of substitution times wage rate must be equal to unity, and therefore $-u_2(c_h, \ell_h)/w_h u_1(c_h, \ell_h) = 1$. Hence $1 = 1 - t'(w_h \ell_h)$ which implies $t(y) = $ constant. As we have assumed a purely redistributive tax, $t(y) = 0$.

---

[16] Compare the proof of Proposition 4 where the following dichotomization can clearly be seen.

Once again, the assumption of a variable skill distribution is crucial for the proposition. For a fixed skill distribution we could decentralize every contribution fair allocation by a tailor-made income tax as illustrated in Figure 2.

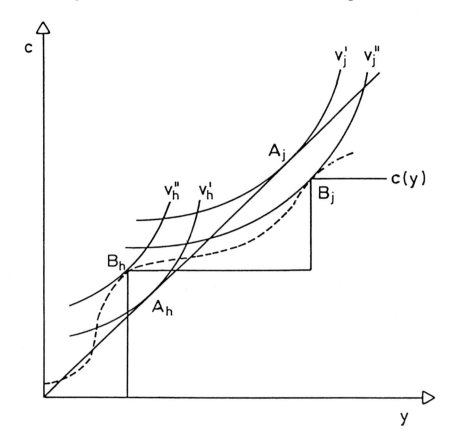

Figure 2

The laissez-faire state is illustrated by the points A_h and A_j. We introduce an income tax which favors the less able individual h. The resulting allocation B_h and B_j is contribution fair and can be decentralized by a step function $c(y) = y - t(y)$. Alternatively a differentiable function $c(y)$ could be chosen which also leads to the allocation B_h, B_j, as illustrated by the dotted curve.

5. Equity and Efficiency Reconsidered: Fairness and Incentive Compatibility

The recent literature on optimal income taxation accentuates the problems which result from the government's incomplete information. This does not mean the government is taken to be totally uninformed. Quite the contrary: the government is assumed to have statistical knowledge of all individual characteristics.[17] So it knows the distribution of the individual productivities, and it knows the individual utility functions (!). However, the government does not know who is who. When facing individual tax payers it cannot distinguish who is the man with the ability w_{115}, say, although it knows there is somebody with this ability.

The government can only observe some variables like individual incomes or individual labor supply.[18] These variables are correlated with the underlying individual characteristics. However, they are not perfectly correlated, so it is impossible to gain exact information about the characteristics from the knowledge of income or labor supply.

The government's incomplete information makes it impossible to levy a system of lump sum taxes that achieve the first best optimum. Income taxation normally is a second best device only, because it restricts the range of instruments to changes of the observable variable "income".

Incomplete information leads to the problem of incentive compatibility. When the government plans the income tax, it assumes that the man with ability w_{115} earns an income y_{115} which results from his individual utility maximizing labor supply, adjusted to the income tax. The tax must be designed in such a way that the government can be sure that the one who earns the income y_{115} is the man with ability w_{115}. The tax must be designed in such a way that individual abilities could be "screened" on the basis of incomes. This solves the problem of the government's not knowing who is who.

---

[17] If the government lacks statistical information of characteristics, incentive-compatible allocations require mechanisms where the bundle every agent obtains, depends on the distribution of characteristics. See for example Hammond (1979). These approaches are beyond the scope of this paper.

[18] In models of tax evasion the government cannot even observe the incomes which are actually earned. This problem is excluded in this paper.

If an income tax is not incentive compatible, it is possible that income y_{115} is earned by the man with ability w_{320} who decided to "hide" his ability by earning a lower income than anticipated by the government. It is clear that the entire planning process of the government breaks down in such a case. The government had anticipated that the man with the ability w_{320} will earn income y_{320} and had planned its redistribution policy on the basis of this assumption. However, this man has manipulated the government policy. A consistent tax policy under incomplete information is only possible if the policy maker anticipates exactly how the taxpayers will adjust and incorporates this adjustment in his tax policy. Then the taxpayers actually behave as anticipated (revelation principle) and the plan of the policy maker is realized in practise.

How can the government make sure that nobody deviates from the behavior which was anticipated when the tax was set up? This can be guaranteed if each utility maximizing individual attains his best result by honestly "declaring" his ability or labor supply than by signalling false characteristics. To make sure the skilled participate in the economic system in a way which actually earns high incomes, the policy maker considers the "self-selection" constraints of the taxpayers. If the government is informed about incomes only, the following constraints must be fulfilled:

$$v_h(c_h, y_h) \geq v_h(c_j, y_j); \quad y_j \leq w_h; \ \forall h, j \leq H.$$

For $y_j > w_h$ this inequality is vacuously fulfilled because $v_h(c_j, y_j)$ is not even defined. The government has statistical knowledge of all incomes y_h. So the government also has knowledge of consumption $c_h = y_h - t(y_h)$ because it sets $t(y_h)$ and consumption is only the difference between income and tax payment. Moreover the government knows all utility functions without being able to impute a particular function to a particular person. Each individual chooses its income y_h which optimally adjusts to the income tax $t(y_h)$. If each individual attains maximum utility by choosing the income y_h which corresponds to its ability w_h, then the taxpayers can be distinguished by their incomes. Everybody acts as anticipated by the government. The tax is incentive compatible.

Stiglitz (1982) explicitly[19] posed the problem of Pareto efficient income taxation with self selection. The policy maker solves the following optimization approach:

$$\max_{c,y} v_1(c_1, y_1)$$

subject to

$$v_h(c_h, y_h) = v_h^o \qquad h = 2, \ldots, H$$
$$v_h(c_h, y_h) \geq v_h(c_j, y_j) \qquad y_j \leq w_h \; \forall h, j \leq H$$
$$\Sigma c_h \leq \Sigma y_h$$

where c, y are vectors of the instrument variables, $c = y - t(y)$, and v_h^o are exogenously given utility levels.

The self-selection constraints, in this optimization approach, are identical with the conditions of a contribution equitable allocation. Moreover, the above maximization leads to a Pareto optimal allocation. Does that mean Stiglitz' Pareto efficient taxation with self selection is identical with the approach of contribution fairness? This is not exactly true. Contribution fairness means contribution equitability plus first best Pareto optimality. Stiglitz' approach yields first best and second best Pareto optima.

A first best Pareto optimum results from the following optimization approach:

$$\max_{c,y} v_1(c_1, y_1)$$

subject to

$$v_h(c_h, y_h) = v_h^o \qquad h = 2, \ldots, H$$
$$\Sigma c_h \leq \Sigma y_h.$$

It can easily be seen that for each consumer the marginal rate of substitution between consumption and income is equal to unity. When defining contribution fairness we intersected the set of contribution equitable allocations and of first best Pareto optima. Therefore, contribution fairness requires that the marginal rates of substitution between consumption and income are equal to unity.

In Stiglitz' approach there may be distortions by the self selection constraints. As soon as one of them is binding, the corresponding marginal rate of substitution is not necessarily equal to unity. So Stiglitz' analysis includes first best Pareto optima if all marginal rates of substitution are equal to unity. However, his approach also allows for second best Pareto optima where the marginal rates of substitution

---

[19] Implicitly Mirrlees (1971) has also dealt with this problem.

deviate from unity. The latter cases are not contribution equitable according to Definition 2. Hence, there is a noteworthy difference between the concept of Pareto optimal taxation with self selection and the concept of contribution fairness.[20]

However, in spite of this difference, we face a striking similarity of the two concepts. Apparently fairness can be approached from a different angle than we did in the preceding sections. We treated equitability as a pure concept of distribution. When moving to fairness, the basic distributional value judgment of equitability was enriched by additionally postulating an allocational value judgment, namely Pareto optimality. In the Stiglitz approach self selection is an allocational concept without any particular touch of a distributional concern of the policy maker. So, implicitly, Stiglitz treats equitability as a pure concept of allocation.

Hence equitability is a hybrid concept. Seen from one angle it is a distributional value judgment. Seen from another angle it is a self selection constraint which is based on allocational reasoning only. The reader should not be surprised too much about this hybrid nature of the concepts. Ever since the discussion about Musgrave's tripartition it has been well-known that distribution and allocation cannot be separated. In any case equitability starts from an allocational background. Let us assume, for instance, that we have fifty bundles of goods and fifty people, and we let them choose from the bundles. Equitability is given if everybody chooses one bundle and is content with it. He prefers his bundle to all others. This is both an allocational and a distributional problem. First, commodities are allocated to individuals according to their individual choice, their individual self selection. Second, economic justice is achieved if everybody is content with his bundle.

Therefore we do not share the opinion of those information economists who have twisted an equity criterion into an allocational concept only, disguising an egalitarian doctrine by relabelling it as a "self selection" concept. In fact we have one concept only which can be examined from either a distributional or an allocational angle.

*

Before concluding this section, let us deal briefly with the relation of self selection to Foley equitability. Until now we concentrated on a policy maker who is informed about incomes and decentralizes the economy by means of an income tax. If we compare self selection and Foley equitability, we have to deal with utility functions $u(c, \ell)$. We know from Proposition 3 that in the case of income

---

[20] It may be noted that one could think of defining contribution fairness in such a way that it is exactly identical with Stiglitz' concept. However, this is not done in this paper.

Equitability and Income Taxation

taxation consumers with higher skill always obtain higher utility. Hence a Foley fair allocation can never be implemented by an income tax. Let us now switch to a policy maker who observes labor supplies instead of incomes and imposes a labor tax $t(\ell)$. Foley fairness requires

$$u(w_h\ell_h - t(\ell_h), \ell_h) \geq u(w_j\ell_j - t(\ell_j), \ell_j) \quad \forall\, h, j.$$

What about the self selection constraints in the (c, ℓ)-space? Let the consumer h adjust to the tax and choose his optimal labor supply $\ell_h(w_h)$. He will choose $\ell_h(w_h)$ if this yields a higher utility than any other $\ell(w)$, for example ℓ_j. However, his productivity still is w_h, and so his "effective" labor supply is $w_h\ell_j$, and not $w_j\ell_j$.[21] Therefore, the self selection constraints are

$$u(w_h\ell_h - t(\ell_h), \ell_h) \geq u(w_h\ell_j - t(\ell_j), \ell_j) \quad \forall\, h, j.$$

The self selection constraints differ from the conditions of Foley equitability. Whereas the distributional concept of Foley equitability ignores the individual productivities, this is impossible for the allocational concept of self selection in the (c, ℓ)-space.

The difference between self selection and Foley equitability implies that it is impossible to decentralize a Foley fair allocation by a labor tax $t(\ell)$. At least in the Mirrlees framework it can be shown that a Foley fair allocation can be decentralized by a wage tax $t(w)$. It is clear that this tax is lump sum in character, but the information requirements are lower than in the case of "real" lump sum taxation where the policy maker must know exactly who is who. The wage tax $t(w)$ in the Mirrlees framework only requires knowledge of incomes and of the corresponding labor supply to compute $w = y/\ell$.

---

[21] Recall Ordover-Phelps (1975) as mentioned in the introduction. The wage rate, according to that explanation, is equated to unity.

6. References

Baumol, W. (1986): *Superfairness.* Cambridge, Mass.: MIT Press.

Bös, D., and **Tillmann, G.** (1983): "Neid und progressive Besteuerung." In *Staatsfinanzierung im Wandel,* edited by K.-H. Hansmeyer (Schriften des Vereins für Socialpolitik, New Series) 134, 637–660.

Bös, D., and **Tillmann, G.** (1985): "An 'Envy Tax': Theoretical Principles and Application to the German Surcharge on the Rich." *Public Finance/Finances Publiques* 40, 35–63.

Champsaur, P., and **Laroque, G.** (1981): "Fair Allocations in Large Economies." *Journal of Economic Theory* 25, 269–282.

Champsaur, P., and **Laroque, G.** (1982): "A Note on Incentives in Large Economies." *Review of Economic Studies* 49, 627–635.

Foley, D. (1967): *Resource Allocation and the Public Sector.* Yale Economic Essays 7.

Hammond, P.J. (1979): "Straightforward Individual Incentive Compatibility in Large Economies." *Review of Economic Studies* 46, 263–282.

Kleinberg, N.L. (1980): "Fair Allocations and Equal Income." *Journal of Economic Theory* 23, 189–200.

Mirrlees, J.A. (1971): "An Exploration in the Theory of Optimum Income Taxation." *Review of Economic Studies* 38, 175–208.

Ordover, J.A., and **Phelps, E.S.** (1975): "Linear Taxation of Wealth and Wages for Intragenerational Lifetime Justice: Some Steady-state Cases." *American Economic Review* 65, 660–673.

Pazner, E. (1977): "Pitfalls in the Theory of Fairness." *Journal of Economic Theory* 14, 458–466.

Pazner, E., and **Schmeidler, D.** (1974): "A Difficulty in the Concept of Fairness." *Review of Economic Studies* 41, 441–443.

Stiglitz, J. (1982): "Self-selection and Pareto Efficient Taxation." *Journal of Public Economics* 17, 213–240.

Tillmann, G. (1984): *Equity and Taxation.* In *Beiträge zur neueren Steuertheorie,* edited by D.Bös, M.Rose and Ch.Seidl. Berlin–Heidelberg: Springer-Verlag, 75–94.

Tillmann, G. (1986): "Equity and Production." Discussion Paper A-80, mimeo, University of Bonn.

Varian, H.R. (1974): "Equity, Envy and Efficiency." *Journal of Economic Theory* 9, 63–91.

Varian, H.R. (1976): "Two Problems in the Theory of Fairness." *Journal of Public Economics* 5, 249–260.

A Political Philosopher's View of Equitable Taxation

John Gray, Oxford, U. K.

I comment on this paper as a political philosopher and not as a political economist. My principal goal is not to criticise the paper's theoretical results – which, insofar as I possess any competence of judgement, seem to me unexceptionable – but instead to clarify, and thus to expose to criticism, its methodological and evaluative presuppositions. At the methodological level, I will argue, it is hardly surprising that most of the conceptions of equitability discussed in the paper are unrealisable in any actually existing economy. For the formal model which the authors deploy in a neoclassical intellectual tradition encompasses drastic abstractions from realistic contexts in which utilities and productivities are not only widely divergent, but typically also only partially knowable. At the level of substantive value-judgement, I will maintain that the quest for equity or fairness in income distribution is the search for a mirage. Fundamental questions of equity, fairness and justice arise most saliently in respect of market processes, not with regard to income flows, but instead with reference to the underlying structure of entitlements from which these flows are generated. If the notion of equity or fairness in income distribution is a mirage, akin to the mediaeval idea of the just price or wage, it follows that progressive taxation policies which aim to approximate such equity in income distribution are radically flawed. It does not follow from this, however, that considerations of justice are altogether irrelevant to policy for income taxation, since (I shall contend) important injustices may well be incurred under any regime of progressive income taxation. My argument here will be a variant of the Hayekian argument that proportional taxation of incomes is least offensive to justice (although in no sense uniquely equitable), but I will qualify this Hayekian position with the argument, inspired by Buchanan's work, that redistribution may be demanded by justice in the assignment of initial endowments and in the spending activities of government.

Bös and Tillmann show convincingly that Foley fairness cannot exist in large economies in which preferences and productivities vary continuously, and they argue from this that a Foley equitable income tax is likewise impossible. The reasoning in both arguments seems demonstrative, and the inference from the one to the other inexorable. Several methodological comments may be in order, however. The first is that Foley equitability – in which no agent prefers another's consumption-income or consumption-labour bundle to his own – is manifestly unrealisable in any plausibly imagined real-world context. Any world in which the sentiment of envy exists is a world in which Foley equitability is unachievable. Moreover, Foley equitability (like many another conception in the neoclassical tradition) postulates a complete knowledge on the part of agents of others' circumstances – their consumption-labour bundle – which does not, and cannot exist in any real economy. Even a world without envy would not be a Foley equitable world unless everyone in it knew all the relevant facts about everyone else's income, consumption and (perhaps) preferences. For these two reasons, it is unsurprising that Foley equitability is comprehensively unrealisable. It is not obvious why it should be thought to have any ethical appeal. Foley equitability will be violated if anyone prefers another's consumption-labour bundle *for whatever reason*. In ordinary moral thought and practice, however, the reasons an agent has for preferring another's situation are crucial in our evaluation of the justice or equitability of that preference. If the agent's preferences are animated by morally unacceptable norms or sentiments – if they are inspired by racism or express the vicious disposition of envy – then in ordinary moral life they are disqualified from consideration and have no, or little weight in policy. In allowing any preference to be relevant to the equitability of a distribution, no matter how that preference is formed or grounded, the notion of Foley equitability neglects the truth that the relevance of preferences to equity is itself bounded by considerations of equity – including, importantly, considerations having to do with the history of the distribution under assessment. This latter, I take it, is Nozick's point, when he argues[1] that how a distribution came about is (at the least) as important for its justice as its structure or pattern.

Foley equitability is as morally questionable as it is practically unrealisable. Contribution equitability focusses on individuals' skills rather than their preferences or utility. The authors tell us that the unique allocation in which contribution equitability is satisfied is the laissez-faire state. Several questions arise, however, as to this result. In the first place, it seems to depend upon the (surely arbitrary) redefinition of utility functions in terms of differential productivity. Secondly, and more profoundly, the notion of skill or productivity is very unclear. As we know from many criticisms of the Marxian labour theory of value, labouring abilities are vastly heterogeneous and insusceptible to scalar assessment. Again, as the authors themselves maintain, individuals may be expected to "optionally adjust their labour supply to the individual skill, taking account of the income taxation. Hence" they conclude "the individual optimum depending only on the

---

[1] See Nozick (1974), Chapter 7.

ability and no tax function – that leaves some incentive to work, can enforce an equitable allocation". In the most general terms, human abilities, skills or productive contributions are diverse and variable, they wax and wane with incentive structures and modes of human capital formation, and they are very imperfectly mapped on any formal model. The very idea of a productive contribution may, indeed, embody a vestige of the objectivist fallacy in respect of economic value while (as Hayek has argued[2]), the only criterion for the value of anyone's productive services is what others are willing to pay for them.

Neither Foley nor contribution equitability can give a satisfactory content to the demand for equity in income distribution, and, for that reason, neither can support or justify policies of progressive income taxation. Thus far, I am in effect following the lead of the authors, who conclude wisely that "the impossibility of an equitable income tax is deeply rooted in the whole philosophy of the taxation model". I wish to go further than they may well wish to do, by arguing that, whereas the ideal of equity in income and income taxation is an illusion, justice is not silent on the merits of progressive taxation, but rather condemns it. There are, to be sure, many weighty consequentialist arguments against progressive income taxation: its effects on incentives, its generation of a substantial parallel economy, its discouragement of risky enterprises and its tendency to undo the division of labour. I shall not develop these, since they are elaborated in other papers read at this conference, and they are clearly powerful and compelling. I want instead to look at effects of progressive income taxation which are condemnable, not only or primarily because of their consequences for general welfare, but because they violate ordinary canons of justice. Here Hayek has specified several such effects. First, progressive income taxation tends to restrict competition in an arbitrary way: "The system tends generally to favour corporate as against individual saving and particularly to strengthen the position of the established corporations against newcomers. It thus assists to create quasi-monopolistic situations".[3] Second, progressive income taxation tends to perpetrate entrenched inequalities by restricting the opportunities of the poorer classes to accumulate wealth. This in turn undermines the legitimacy of established wealth and so of private wealth as such; "the less possible it becomes for a man to acquire a new fortune, the more must existing fortunes appear as privileges for which there is no justification. ... A system based on private property and control of the means of production presupposes that such property and control can be acquired by any successful person. If this is made impossible, even the men who otherwise would have been the most eminent capitalists of the new generation are bound to become the enemies of the

---

[2] Hayek (1960), Chapter 6.
[3] Hayek (1960), p. 320.

established rich".[4] Thirdly, progressive income tax not only acts to freeze existing income inequalities, it is inherently discriminatory: "That a majority should be free to impose a discriminatory tax burden on a minority; that, in consequence, equal services should be remunerated differently; and that for a whole class, merely because its incomes are not in line with those of the rest, the normal incentives should be partially made ineffective – all of these are principles which cannot be defended on grounds of justice".[5] In addition to the many deleterious side-effects of progressive income taxation – including its corrupting effect on government, well theorized in the public choice tradition in Niskanen's paper, as well as its dis-coordinating impact on the market economy – there are injustices that are integral to its very nature which should lead us to reject it.

Thus far I have followed Hayek's argument against progressivity, which leads naturally (though perhaps not inevitably) to the demand for proportionality in income taxation. I want now to qualify the Hayekian argument, or to develop it further, by contending that accepting the injustice of progressive income taxa-tion does not entail that we accept that justice has nothing to say about income distribution. For, in the first place, as Hayek himself acknowledges,[6] substantial income redistribution may be achieved even in a system of proportional taxation, simply by the transfer system being weighted toward the poorer classes. Especially where poverty has been increased or caused by arbitrary governmental interven-tions, including progressive tax policies, there is a good case in justice for income redistributing policies on the spending side that seek to rectify previous injustices by enhancing opportunities at the bottom. Such policies of income redistribu-tion, though they need careful design and implementation, may well be demanded by justice and in any case do not have the levelling consequences that are most offensive to justice. They are accordingly entirely consilient with a Hayekian per-spective on progressivity.

The most fundamental concern of justice is, however, not with the distribu-tion of income at all, but with the allocation of assets from which income streams arise. It is here, in my view, that considerations of justice have their primary and proper application. The thesis which I would wish to maintain is that, once the allocation of initial holdings is just, the resultant stream of incomes cannot be unjust (except in unusual circumstances where rectification of earlier injustices is needed). But what are the principles in terms of which we are to assess the justice of the allocation of endowments? The most promising perspective on this question seems to me to be that developed by James Buchanan, in which a species

---

[4] Hayek (1960), p. 321.
[5] Hayek (1960), p. 322.
[6] Hayek (1960), p. 307.

A Political Philosopher's View of Equitable Taxation 105

of contractarian reasoning is applied which yields the prescription that these be Pareto-optimal redistributions from a status-quo baseline. One need not accept all of Buchanan's positions – for instance, one need not accept the arguments for confiscatory inheritance taxation he has elsewhere and independently developed – to accept his statement that "Attempts to mitigate distributional inequalities or injustice that may be due largely to pre-market inequalities should not take the form of interferences with the market process. ... Attempts to modify distributional results should be directed at the source of the undesired consequences, which is the distribution of pre-market economic power to create economic values".[7] It may well be, as I have myself argued elsewhere,[8] that contractarian reasoning can achieve only partly determinate results and cannot, therefore, specify any distribution of initial endowments as uniquely demanded by justice. Even if this is so, the contractarian method may prove useful in disqualifying certain distributions and in illuminating the truth that the inherited or historic distribution has no overriding ethical legitimacy. It is likely, indeed, that the contractarian method sponsored by Buchanan would yield the result that each and every citizen of a liberal order is entitled to a patrimony of a minimal capital endowment (together with provision for human capital formation through education). Further, given the vast assets presently held by the interventionist state, there is every reason why such redistribution should proceed by the privatisation of government assets and should then involve no entrenchment on private capital. If this programme could be worked out, then justice would have been done without any cost to economic liberty – and the quest for a delusive standard of equity in income distribution, together with the injurious and unjust policies of progressive income taxation which it has spawned, could both be consigned to an Orwellian memory hole.

References

Buchanan, J. (1986): *Liberty, Market and State*. Brighton: Wheatsheaf Books.

Gray, J. (forthcoming): "Contractarian Method, Private Property and the Market Economy." Nomos: Justice and Markets.

Hayek, F.A. (1960): *The Constitution of Liberty*. London: Routledge & Kegan Paul.

Nozik, R. (1974): *Anarchy, State and Utopia*. Oxford: Basil Blackwell.

---

[7] Buchanan (1986), p. 138.
[8] See Gray (forthcoming).

An Economists' View of Equitable Taxation

Dieter Bös and Georg Tillmann, Bonn, West Germany

A political philosopher and an economist apparently approach any given topic in very different ways. The political philosopher wants to start from a very general approach including "human abilities ... which are diverse and variable, which wax and wane with incentive structures and modes of human capital formation." (p. 103) The economist is much more modest. For him progress in economic knowledge is a step by step procedure and he first wants to make clear the basic principles. So before dealing with abilities which wax and wane, one should deal with given abilities to get a feeling for the way in which abilities are relevant for income formation and taxation. Before including all possible effects of progressive taxation, one should carefully deal with different single aspects. Models, which make everything endogenous, have not brought very much progress in economic analysis. Economists have learned that small models are useful to achieve precise results on particular interrelationships, and this information can be used to evaluate more complex phenomena.

In our paper there is yet another reason for choosing a simple model. Remember our argumentation about differences in productivities and preferences: if individuals differ with respect to both productivities and preferences, in large economies Foley fairness never exists, and contribution fairness exists only in the laissez-faire state. It is clear, then, that the assumption of a many-dimensional productivity vector would only strengthen these results, and a negative result is more distressing the simpler the model.

Such mathematically simple economic models are, of course, not a realistic description of economic reality. However, they allow us to learn something about how the economy works. And this is often not the case in large models where there are too many countervailing effects.

We come to our next point. On p. 103, Mr. Gray states that "the effects of progressive income taxation are condemnable". We dislike the use of the word "condemnable". Here one important advantage of mathematical economics must be accentuated. The topic of equity, envy, and progressive taxation is loaded with value judgements. A mathematical definition of equitability is the best possibility to make a clear statement of what a policy maker may mean when speaking of equity. Given such a definition of equitability as the starting point of an analysis, by simple logical operations we can determine whether income taxation is a good instrument to achieve equitability or not. In such an analysis there is no need of "condemning" the effects of income taxation. Rather, we clearly show that taxation cannot achieve a fair allocation.

That is precisely where our paper fits nicely into the general tendencies presented in other papers at this conference. What we show is the following: if we start from meaningful criteria of equitability, it is impossible to have an income tax which leads to a fair allocation. Hence, we present a general impossibility theorem for income taxation. Our result is even stronger than Hayek's because we do not only include progressive income taxation, but also proportional and regressive income taxation. Given our negative results on income taxation, Mr. Gray should have embraced us instead of rejecting our approach for not using Hayek's arguments.

Before concluding, we would like to address some minor points in Mr. Gray's comments. We cannot go into details, but we would like to mention the following three points:

1) Mr. Gray accentuates the informational requirements of achieving equitability. However, on p. 105 of his comment he praises Buchanan's contractarian approach "to obtain Pareto-optimal redistributions from a status-quo baseline". However, for such an approach knowledge of all preferences and total endowments is necessary. Therefore, this approach requires as much information as our approach.

2) According to Mr. Gray, progressive taxation has condemnable effects, but this is not the case for proportional income taxation,[1] so "substantial income redistribution" could be performed by taking the revenues from a proportional income tax and using it for a transfer system weighted toward the poorer classes. (p. 104) Now assume a 95 percent proportional income tax which is redistributed by transfers. Surely such a proportional tax would have negative effects similar to those of a progressive income tax.

3) Finally, on p. 102 Mr. Gray states: "If the agent's preferences are animated by morally unacceptable norms or sentiments – if they are inspired by racism or express the vicious disposition of envy – then in ordinary moral life they are disqualified from consideration and have no, or little weight in policy." Here the basic difference between the political philosopher and the economist becomes very clear. The economist typically starts from an individual utility function,

---

[1] This paragraph follows Mr. Gray in denoting a tax as progressive if the *marginal* tax rate increases with income. This is not the most usual definition in public economics, however.

which depends on the quantities consumed by that consumer. Labor supply may be explicitly included. Only utility functions of that type are contained in our paper and all possible preferences using these arguments are allowed. There is no vicious disposition of envy included in our paper. In footnote 5 on p. 76 we explicitly mention that Varian's choice of the word "envy" in connection with the equitability relation is unfortunate. Therefore, we do not feel attacked by Mr. Gray's statement.

However, his statement reveals two dangerous tendencies:

i)   the indirect insinuation that envy is something like racism, and

ii) the general idea that there are particular preferences which are excluded from consideration on the basis of moral a priori disqualification by a policy maker or by a political philosopher.

We feel uneasy with any such position.

Capital Markets, Entrepreneurship and Progressive Taxation

Peter Swoboda and Peter Steiner, Graz, Austria

1. Introduction

The theory of finance is composed of rather distinct branches. In most of these branches taxes play an important role. One branch of literature is concerned with the influence of taxes on the behavior of individual investors (entrepreneurs). In a second branch of the literature taxes have been considered with respect to portfolio theory and the theory of capital market equilibrium. A third body of literature concentrates on the capital structure choice of firm where taxes again are decisive parameters. Finally, in a rather new branch in the theory of finance agency theory is applied to financial problems. Since the relation of the tax authority to the taxpayer can be interpreted as a principal-agent relation, taxes are included also in these studies.

Our paper is influenced by this development in financial theory. Rather than selecting only one of these branches, we give an overview of the role of taxes in all four. In Section 2 we concentrate on the relation between the tax scheme and the risk-taking of individuals (entrepreneurs). In Section 3, we introduce a progressive tax scheme in a capital asset pricing model in order to study the implications for the portfolio choice of investors and the capital market equilibrium. The influence of a progressive taxation on the capital structure of firms and the resulting clientele effects are analysed in Section 4. Within this section, we derive in detail the interesting clientele effects with respect to equity capital and risky debt. Finally, Section 5 offers some preliminary ideas about taxation as an agency relation.

2. Progressive Taxation and Risk-Taking of Individuals

In the first part of this paper we will concentrate on the case of a sole owner-manager of a firm (entrepreneur). The effect of progressive tax rates on the risk-taking of the entrepreneur depends on his utility function. Numerous authors have dealt with this problem and have shown that the relationship between (progressive)

D. Bös and B. Felderer (Eds.)
The Political Economy of Progressive Taxation
© Springer-Verlag Berlin Heidelberg 1989

taxation and risk-taking is very ambiguous (Atkinson–Stiglitz, 1980; Bamberg–Richter, 1984; Bamberg–Richter, 1985; Buchholz, 1985, 1986, 1987a,b; Feldstein, 1969; Schneider, 1977, 1980; Stiglitz, 1969). The most advanced research is due to Buchholz. We start with a variation of a basic model by Buchholz in order to analyse the effects of a progressive taxation if losses may be incurred. Second, we summarize the results of Buchholz's work. We deal only with the either/or case: the entrepreneur has to decide between a risky and a riskless alternative.

We define the variables as follows:

w, v = return on the risky asset before taxes in the favorable and unfavorable state; both states are realized with a probability of 0.50
r = return on the riskless asset
$N(\cdot)$ = return after taxes
$T(\cdot)$ = income tax
n = 1 minus tax rate on the riskless return
τ = marginal tax rate

Although we apply the methodology of Buchholz (1985), Buchholz actually studied projects with $v, w > 0$. We, however, will concentrate on the case where $w > 0$, $v < 0$.

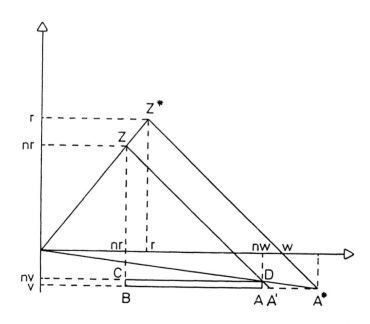

Figure 1

Capital Markets, Entrepreneurship and Progressive Taxation 113

In Fig. 1, $Z^*(A^*)$ represents the outcome of the riskless (risky) project before taxes in the two states. Z shows the result of the riskless asset after taxes. We assume that the marginal tax rate $\tau \leq 1$ and that it is weakly increasing with income

$$nr \leq N(w) \leq nw, \tag{1a}$$

$$v \leq N(v) \leq nv. \tag{1b}$$

Thus the return of the risky asset after taxes must lie in the area ABCD. When there is no loss offset $(N(v) = v)$, the feasible combinations lie on AB.

With a progressive tax the condition

$$\frac{N(w)}{w} \leq \frac{N(r)}{r} \leq \frac{N(v)}{v} \tag{2}$$

must also hold. Alternatively, (2) may be written

$$\frac{N(r) - N(v)}{r - v} \geq \frac{N(w) - N(r)}{w - r} \tag{2a}$$

or

$$\frac{N(r) - N(v)}{N(w) - N(r)} \geq \frac{r - v}{w - r}. \tag{2b}$$

But (2b) is clearly redundant since it would also include the point A', which is not feasible.

If we assume that the investor is indifferent between Z^* and A^*, then the project which is favored by taxation clearly depends on the relation between income and risk aversion. If the absolute risk aversion decreases with income, taxation will favor the riskless project. But if the relative or absolute risk aversion increases with income so that indifference curves nearer to the origin are steeper, the risky project might be preferred after taxation, even if there is no loss offset.

An example may demonstrate this result:

The utility function of the entrepreneur is $100z - z^2/2$. Pratt's measure of risk aversion, $-u''(z)/u'(z) = 1/(100 - z)$, shows increasing absolute (and also increasing relative) risk aversion. Further it is assumed that $w = 95$, $v = -5$ und $r = 26$. The tax rate on positive income is 0.25, and there is no loss offset.

Without taxation, the utility of the risky asset is

$$0.5(u(95)) + 0.5(u(-5)) = 0.5(4987.5) + 0.5(-512.5) = 2237.5$$

and thus smaller than the utility of the riskless asset

$$u(26) = 2262.$$

With taxation, the utility of the risky project is

$$0.5(u(71.25)) + 0.5(u(-5)) = 2037.5$$

while the utility of the riskless project is clearly smaller

$$u(19.5) = 1759.88.$$

We obtain non-ambiguous results only if a linear utility function is assumed and if, without taxation, the risky project is inferior to the riskless project, or if the investor is indifferent between the two projects. In this case a strictly progressive taxation (in the sense that τ is increasing) will make the risky project still more unfavorable.

In Buchholz (1987a) the following conditions are derived under which progressive taxation generally favors a risky project over a riskless project (all incomes are greater than zero):

$N(r) < r,$

$N(z)/z$ is decreasing in z,

$N'(z)$ is increasing in z and

the relative risk aversion$(-u''(z)z/u'(z))$ increases in z.

These conditions imply that the marginal tax rate must *decrease* while the average tax rate increases. This may be possible for a section of the tax function, but not over the whole range.

Buchholz also derives the conditions under which progressive taxation generally favors a riskless project over a risky project:

$$N(r) \geq r,$$
$$N(z)/z \text{ is increasing in } z,$$
$$N'(z) \text{ is decreasing in } z \text{ and}$$

the relative risk aversion decreases in z.

Again, conditions 2 and 3 are not compatible over the whole range of the tax function. Also, condition 1 is not very realistic.

An example may illustrate the first case. We assume: up to an income of 100 the tax rate is zero; for returns from 100 to 200, $\tau = 0.20$; and for the income range of 200 to 300, $\tau = 0.15$.

z	T(z)	T(z)/z	N(z)/z
100	0	0	1
200	20	.10	.90
300	35	.1167	.8833

Although the marginal tax rate decreases, the average tax rate increases over the income range 100 to 300. An investor subject to this tax function may have to choose between a riskless project ($r = 200$) and a risky project ($v = 100, w = 300$, equal probabilities). Before taxation, the expected returns of the two alternatives are equal. After taxation, $N(r) = 180, N(v) = 100$ and $N(w) = 265$. Therefore, the expected return of the risky asset (182.5) is now higher than the return of the riskless asset (180). This is the result of assumptions 2 and 3. Also the risk of the risky asset, measured, for example, by the standard deviation, becomes smaller. Combined with the lower risk aversion, this would indicate that the risky project must be favored.

Buchholz (1986) also investigated in what sense a tax function $T_2(z)$ must be more progressive than a tax function $T_1(z)$ to guarantee that a transition from $T_1(z)$ to $T_2(z)$ preserves a second degree stochastic dominance between investment projects. A riskless project is second degree stochastic dominant over a risky project if its return is higher than the expected return of the risky asset. This stochastic dominance is preserved if $N_2(z)$ can be derived by multiplying $N_1(z)$ by a strictly increasing, concave function $N(z)$

$$N_2(z) = N(N_1(z)) \text{ for all returns greater than zero.}$$

However, this does not answer the question under which conditions a risky project remains the better alternative if the tax function $T_1(z)$ is changed to $T_2(z)$. This is the case if the so called residual progressivity of $T_2(z)$ is lower than that of $T_1(z)$

$$T_2'(z)/N_2(2) \leq T_1'(z)/N_1(z),$$

and the relative risk aversion is strictly decreasing (see also Atkinson and Stiglitz, 1980, p. 111); or if the absolute risk aversion is strictly decreasing and if $T_2'(z) < T_1'(z)$.

In Buchholz (1987b) the general question is posed as to which tax functions are neutral (do not affect the decision between riskless and risky projects) with respect to given utility functions. Thus Buchholz is following up the pioneering article by Feldstein (1969). Also the reverse question is analysed: which utility functions are neutral with respect to a given tax function. A basic result is that a tax function can only be neutral with respect to a given utility function if the utility of the income after tax is a linear function of the utility of the income before tax. In order that the neutral tax functions are progressive (in the sense of an increasing average tax rate), it is important that the utility function is at least as risk averse as $ln(\cdot)$. But this condition alone is not sufficient for progressivity. Neutral progressive tax functions in the sense of not decreasing marginal tax rates are guaranteed if the assumption of non-decreasing relative risk aversion is added. With respect to utility functions with a constant relative risk aversion and if the relative risk aversion is smaller than or equal to one, neutrality can only be achieved by a proportional tax. If the relative risk aversion is greater than one, strictly progressive tax functions may also be neutral. The results stated up to now are related to cases where the possibility of losses is excluded. For the case where losses are allowed the following results are derived: a proportional tax with full loss offset can only be neutral with respect to a linear utility function. A proportional tax without full loss offset cannot be neutral with respect to any concave or linear utility functions.

3. Portfolio Decisions, Capital Market Equilibrium and Progressive Taxation

In this section the effect of progressive taxation on the portfolio decisions of investors and capital market equilibrium is analysed. Our arguments are taken from the context of the capital asset pricing model by Sharpe–Lintner–Mossin. Important previous work on the inclusion of (progressive) taxation in the CAPM is due to Brennan (1970), Litzenberger and Ramaswamy (1979) and Modigliani (1982). Brennan (1970) derived an after-tax version of the CAPM on the basis of a progressive tax scheme, but with constant tax rates for each investor. Litzenberger and Ramaswamy (1979) extended Brennan's model by incorporating constraints on individual borrowing. Modigliani (1982) concentrated on the individual's portfolio decision when individuals were subject to a progressive tax.

The model presented in this paper may be regarded as a combination of the Litzenberger–Ramaswamy approach and the basic ideas of the paper by Modigliani. Particular attention will be paid to the portfolio composition of investors under different dividend policies of the firm. Our problem is to determine how sensitive investment decisions are to different income tax schemes, given the dividend policy of firms and the tax revenue of the government.

The following assumptions are made:

(A1)   Individuals' utility functions are monotonic increasing concave functions of after-tax end-of-period wealth.

(A2)   Rates of return are multivariate normal distributed.

(A3)   There are no transaction costs, no restrictions on short sales of securities and individuals are price-takers.

(A4)   Individuals have homogeneous expectations with respect to the probability distribution of future rates of return.

(A5)   There exists a riskless asset with a rate of return r_f.

(A6)   Dividends are paid at the end of the period and are known with certainty at the beginning of the period.

(A7)   Income taxes are progressive and the marginal tax rate is a continuous function of taxable income.

(A8)   There are no taxes on capital gains.

The expected before-tax rate of return is

$$E(\tilde{R}_i) = E(\tilde{r}_i) + d_i. \tag{3}$$

$$
\begin{aligned}
d_i &= \text{dividend yield of security } i, \\
\tilde{R}_i &= \text{before-tax rate of return of security } i, \\
\tilde{r}_i &= \text{rate of capital gain (loss) of security } i.
\end{aligned}
$$

The ordinary income Y^k of the k-th individual is

$$Y^k = W^k(\sum_i x_i^k d_i + x_f^k r_f). \tag{4}$$

$$
\begin{aligned}
x_i^k &= \text{the fraction of the k-th individual's wealth invested in the i-th} \\
      &\quad \text{risky asset,} \\
x_f^k &= \text{the fraction of the k-th individual's wealth invested in the safe asset,} \\
W^k   &= \text{the k-th individual's initial wealth.}
\end{aligned}
$$

The expected after-tax rate of return μ^k of the individual's portfolio is

$$
\begin{aligned}
\mu^k &= \sum_i x_i^k(d_i + E(\tilde{r}_i)) + x_f^k r_f(1 - t^k) - t^k \sum_i x_i^k d_i = \\
      &= \sum_i x_i^k E(\tilde{R}_i) + x_f^k r_f - t^k Y^k / W^k.
\end{aligned}
\tag{5}
$$

$t^k = $ the k-th individual's average tax rate.

The variance σ_k^2 of the after-tax rate of return is

$$
\begin{aligned}
\sigma_k^2 &= \sum_i \sum_j x_i^k x_j^k cov(\tilde{R}_i - t^k d_i, \tilde{R}_j - t^k d_j) = \\
           &= \sum_i \sum_j x_i^k x_j^k cov(\tilde{r}_i, \tilde{r}_j) = \sum_i \sum_j x_i^k x_j^k \sigma_{ij}.
\end{aligned}
\tag{6}
$$

The k-th individual's utility function u^k is defined over the mean and variance of the after-tax portfolio rate of return $(f^k(\mu^k, \sigma_k^2))$ and can be described by the risk-return preference rate Φ^k. Since the individual's global risk tolerance at the optimum (see Rubinstein, 1973) is defined as

$$\theta^k := -W^k \frac{\delta(f^k(\cdot))/\delta\mu}{\delta(2f^k(\cdot))/\delta\sigma^2} = -\frac{E((u^k)')}{E((u^k)'')}, \tag{7}$$

an appropriate measure for the risk-return preference rate (or the risk tolerance) is

$$\Phi^k := \frac{2\theta^k}{W^k}. \tag{8}$$

The k-th individual's optimization problem is represented by the following Lagrangian:

$$L^k = f^k(\mu^k, \sigma_k^2) + \lambda^k(1 - \sum_i x_i^k - x_f^k) =$$
$$= \Phi^k \mu^k - \sigma_k^2 + \lambda^k(1 - \sum_i x_i^k - x_f^k). \tag{9}$$

The first order conditions are

$$\frac{\partial L^k}{\partial x_i^k} = \Phi^k(E(\tilde{R}_i) - Y^k(t^k)'/W^k - t^k(Y^k)'/W^k) - 2\sum_j x_j^k \sigma_{ij} - \lambda^k = 0 \tag{10a}$$

$$\frac{\partial L^k}{\partial x_f^k} = \Phi^k(r_f - Y^k(t^k)'/W^k - t^k(Y^k)'/W^k) - \lambda^k = 0 \tag{10b}$$

$$\frac{\partial L^k}{\partial \lambda^k} = 1 - \sum_i x_i^k - x_f^k = 0. \tag{10c}$$

Since the average tax rate t is a function of the taxable income Y, and $t = g(Y)$,

$$t' = \frac{\partial t}{\partial x_i} = g'(Y)Y' = g'(Y)W d_i, \text{ and} \tag{11a}$$

$$t' = \frac{\partial t}{\partial x_f} = g'(Y)W r_f, \text{ respectively.} \tag{11b}$$

The marginal tax rate τ can be written as

$$\tau = \frac{d(tY)}{dY} = t'Y + Y't = t + Yg'(Y). \tag{12}$$

The first order conditions can then be simplified to

$$\frac{\partial L^k}{\partial x_i^k} = \Phi^k(E(\widetilde{R_i}) - d_i \tau^k) - 2 \sum_j x_j^k \sigma_{ij} - \lambda^k = 0 \qquad (13a)$$

$$\frac{\partial L^k}{\partial x_f^k} = \Phi^k(r_f - r_f \tau^k) - \lambda^k = 0 \qquad (13b)$$

$$\frac{\partial L^k}{\partial \lambda^k} = 1 - \sum_i x_i^k - x_f^k = 0. \qquad (13c)$$

To obtain the expected before-tax rate of return on security i we have to substract (13b) from (13a):

$$\frac{\partial L^k}{\partial x_i^k} - \frac{\partial L^k}{\partial x_f^k} = \Phi^k\{E(\widetilde{R_i}) - r_f - (d_i - r_f)\tau^k\} - 2 \sum_j x_j^k \sigma_{ij} = 0. \qquad (14)$$

Rearranging terms, noting that $\sum_j x_j^k \sigma_{ij} \equiv cov(\widetilde{r_i}, \widetilde{r}_{PF})$, and resubstituting for Φ^k leads to the same result as in Litzenberger–Ramaswamy, provided there are no constraints on individuals' borrowings. Let $\widetilde{r}_{PF}^k$ = rate of return of the k-th individual's portfolio:

$$E(\widetilde{R_i}) = r_f(1 - \tau^k) + d_i \tau^k + \frac{W^k}{\theta^k} cov(\widetilde{r_i}, \widetilde{r}_{PF}^k). \qquad (15)$$

Market equilibrium requires that relation (15) holds for all individuals, since homogeneous expectations are assumed. Furthermore, the market clearing condition requires that the value weighted average of all individuals' portfolio is equal to the market portfolio:

$$W^m := \sum_k W^k \text{ (the wealth of the market)} \qquad (16a)$$

$$\widetilde{R}_m := \sum_k \frac{W^k}{W^m} \widetilde{R}_{PF}^k \qquad (16b)$$

$$\theta^m := \sum_k \theta^k. \qquad (16c)$$

Multiplying relation (15) by θ^k, summing over all individuals, noting that $\sum_k cov(\widetilde{R}_i, W^k \widetilde{R}^k_{PF}) \equiv cov(\widetilde{R}_i, W^m \widetilde{R}_m)$ (from (16b)), $\beta_i := cov(\widetilde{R}_i, \widetilde{R}_m)/var(\widetilde{R}_m)$, and rearranging terms yields

$$E(\widetilde{R}_i) = r_f + \frac{\sum_k \theta^k \tau^k}{\theta^m}(d_i - r_f) + \frac{W^m}{\theta^m}\beta_i var(\widetilde{R}_m), \tag{17}$$

where $\frac{W^m}{\theta^m}$ is called the global market relative risk aversion.

The next step is to calculate the fractions x_i^k, x_f^k of the k-th individual's optimal portfolio. The following $(n+2)$ equations have to be solved (see (13a), (13b) and (13c); $\overline{R} = E(\widetilde{R})$):

$$\begin{pmatrix} \Phi^k(\overline{R}_1 - d_1\tau^k) \\ \vdots \\ \Phi^k(\overline{R}_n - d_n\tau^k) \\ \Phi^k(r_f - r_f\tau^k) \\ 1 \end{pmatrix} = \begin{pmatrix} & & & 0 & 1 \\ & 2\sigma_{ij} & & \cdot & \cdot \\ & & & \cdot & \cdot \\ 0 & \cdots & 0 & 1 \\ 1 & \cdots & 1 & 0 \end{pmatrix} \times \begin{pmatrix} x_1^k \\ \vdots \\ x_n^k \\ x_f^k \\ \lambda^k \end{pmatrix}. \tag{18}$$

If the inverse elements of the extended $2var - cov$ matrix are designed as $a_{i,j}$, $i,j = 1, \ldots, n+1$, the problem above has the following solution:

$$\begin{pmatrix} x_1^k \\ \vdots \\ x_n^k \\ x_f^k \\ \lambda^k \end{pmatrix} = \begin{pmatrix} a_{11} & \cdots & a_{1n} & a_{1,n+1} & 0 \\ \vdots & & \vdots & \vdots & \vdots \\ a_{n1} & \cdots & a_{nn} & a_{n,n+1} & 0 \\ a_{n+1,1} & \cdots & a_{n+1,n} & a_{n+1,n+1} & 1 \\ 0 & \cdots & 0 & 1 & 0 \end{pmatrix} \times \begin{pmatrix} \Phi^k(\overline{R}_1 - d_1\tau^k) \\ \vdots \\ \Phi^k(\overline{R}_n - d_n\tau^k) \\ \Phi^k(r_f - r_f\tau^k) \\ 1 \end{pmatrix}. \tag{19}$$

For a more extensive analysis the following properties are useful

$$a_{ij} = a_{ji}, \ i,j = 1, \ldots, n+1 \tag{20}$$

$$\sum_{i=1}^{n+1} a_{ij} = \sum_{j=1}^{n+1} a_{ij} = 0. \tag{21}$$

For the fractions x_i^k and x_f^k the following relations hold:

$$x_i^k = \Phi^k(\sum_{j=1}^{n} a_{ij}(\overline{R}_j - d_j\tau^k) + a_{i,n+1}r_f(1 - \tau^k)) \tag{22a}$$

$$x_f^k = 1 + \Phi^k(\sum_{j=1}^{n} a_{n+1,j}(\overline{R}_n - d_j\tau^k) + a_{n+1,n+1}r_f(1 - \tau^k)) =$$
$$= 1 - \Phi^k \sum_{i=1}^{n} x_i^k \tag{22b}$$

$$\lambda^k = \Phi^k r_f(1 - \tau^k). \tag{22c}$$

For an extreme risk averse investor Φ becomes zero and he/she invests only in the riskless asset.

For simplification let

$$c_i := \sum_{j=1}^{n} a_{ij}\overline{r}_j$$

$$c_o := \sum_{j=1}^{n} a_{n+1,j}\overline{r}_j.$$

Then

$$x_i^k = \Phi^k(c_i + \sum_{j=1}^{n} a_{ij}d_j(1 - \tau^k) + a_{i,n+1}r_f(1 - \tau^k)) \tag{23a}$$

$$x_f^k = 1 + \Phi^k(c_o + \sum_{j=1}^{n} a_{n+1,j}d_j(1 - \tau^k) + a_{n+1,n+1}r_f(1 - \tau^k)). \tag{23b}$$

If we denote the terms in the cornered brackets as the k-th individual's terms c_i^k and c_o^k we can write

$$x_i^k = \Phi^k c_i^k \tag{24a}$$

$$x_f^k = 1 + \Phi^k c_o^k \tag{24b}$$

and

$$\Phi^k \sum_{i=1}^{n} c_i^k = -\Phi^k c_o^k \tag{25}$$

must hold, since the sum of all weights must be 1.

Capital Markets, Entrepreneurship and Progressive Taxation 123

If the dividend rates of all firms are equal (23a) and (23b) (see equation (21)) can be written as:

$$x_i^k = \Phi^k(c_i - a_{i,n+1}(d - r_f)(1 - \tau^k)) \tag{26a}$$

$$x_f^k = 1 + \Phi^k(c_o - a_{n+1,n+1}(d - r_f)(1 - \tau^k)). \tag{26b}$$

For two investors with different risk-return preferences Φ^ℓ and Φ^m, but identical marginal tax rates τ^k, the structure of their *risky* portfolio is identical, since

$$\frac{x_i^\ell}{x_j^\ell} = \frac{x_i^m}{x_j^m} = \frac{c_i^k}{c_j^k} = const.$$

Only the relation between risky assets and the riskless asset differs, because

$$\frac{\Phi^\ell \sum_i c_i^k}{1 + \Phi^\ell c_o^k} \neq \frac{\Phi^m \sum_i c_i^k}{1 + \Phi^m c_o^k}.$$

The first derivative of this relation with respect to Φ is always negative:

$$\delta\left(\frac{-\Phi c_o^k}{1 + \Phi c_o^k}\right)/\delta\Phi = -\frac{1}{(1 + \Phi c_o^k)^2} = -\frac{1}{(x_f^k)^2}. \tag{27}$$

Therefore, if the risk-return preference rate Φ increases (the investor becomes less risk averse), the fraction invested in the riskless asset decreases.

We are particularly interested in the relation between the composition of the portfolio and the marginal tax rate. If we assume that Φ is independent of income, the first derivative of the portfolio components with respect to τ yields

$$\frac{\partial x_i}{\partial \tau} = -\Phi\left(\sum_j a_{ij}d_j + a_{i,n+1}r_f\right) \tag{28a}$$

$$\frac{\partial x_f}{\partial \tau} = -\Phi\left(\sum_j a_{n+1,j}d_j + a_{n+1,n+1}r_f\right). \tag{28b}$$

With constant dividend rates we obtain

$$\frac{\partial x_i}{\partial \tau} = \Phi a_{i,n+1}(d - r_f) \tag{28c}$$

$$\frac{\partial x_f}{\partial \tau} = \Phi a_{n+1,n+1}(d - r_f). \tag{28d}$$

It can be shown that $a_{n+1,n+1}$ is always positive. Thus the fraction invested in the riskless asset decreases if the tax rate increases, provided that the dividend yield is smaller than the riskless rate of return. These conditions imply that progressive taxation makes risky assets more attractive. Only if the dividend yield is equal to the riskless rate of return the structure of the portfolio is invariant to the tax rates of the investors. If we assume that Φ is also a function of τ the first derivative of x_f with respect to τ leads to

$$
\frac{\partial x_f}{\partial \tau} = \frac{\partial \Phi(\tau)}{\partial \tau} \cdot [c_o - a_{n+1,n+1}(d - r_f)(1 - \tau)] + \\
+ \Phi(\tau) \cdot a_{n+1,n+1}(d - r_f). \tag{28e}
$$

Since the expression in the cornered bracket must be less than or equal to zero, we can conclude that a higher tax rate (which implies a lower taxable income) can only lead to a higher share of the riskless asset if $\partial \Phi(\tau)/\partial \tau$ is *sufficiently negative*. Therefore, increasing relative risk aversion is a necessary, but not sufficient condition for an increase in the riskless asset.

If a linear tax is replaced by a progressive tax and if the tax receipts of the government are held constant, not only the individual portfolio composition, but also asset prices and the rate of interest may change. Investors with high marginal tax rates will tend to increase their holdings of assets with a low dividend yield and to decrease their bond holdings or to increase their debt. We illustrate these effects by means of an example in the Appendix. But the clientele effect is not as radical as shown in the next section when we introduce a progressive tax in a state-preference model.

4. Progressive Taxation and Optimal Capital Structure

4.1 The Clientele Effect of Progressive Taxation with Respect to Equity and Debt Financing

Until the seminal work by Miller (1977), the literature on optimal-capital structure did not have any problems with progressive taxation: without a corporation tax and with a progressive income tax on profits and interest income, the capital structure would be irrelevant. With a corporation tax and an income tax on dividends and interest income, assuming that profits are distributed to shareholders, full debt financing would be optimal, regardless of whether the income tax was linear or progressive (Modigliani–Miller, 1963).

It was Miller who discovered the flaw in the capital structure studies prior to 1977: firms which are subject to a corporation tax would not distribute profits. Therefore, profits would only be subject to the corporation tax and to the capital gains tax. An investor (= marginal investor) with a marginal tax rate τ_i^* equal to the combined corporation tax rate and capital gains tax rate would be indifferent between buying stock or bonds (Miller, 1977):

$$
\begin{aligned}
(1 - \tau_c)(1 - \tau_g) &= 1 - \tau_i^*, \\
\tau_i^* &= \tau_c + \tau_g - \tau_c\tau_g,
\end{aligned}
\tag{29}
$$

$\tau_g =$ capital gains tax rate,
$\tau_c =$ corporation tax rate.

Investors faced with a marginal tax rate higher (lower) than τ_i^* would invest in stocks (bonds).

For the firm the capital structure is irrelevant. Since in equilibrium it must offer the same rate of return net of taxes on equity and debt capital to the marginal investor, the cost of capital before taxes is equal for equity and debt capital. Furthermore, if interest payments from private credit arrangements are fully taxable (tax deductible) and capital gains tax rates are constant, equilibrium will be characterized by equal marginal tax rates for all investors: if the tax rate of investor $A(B)$ is higher (lower) than τ_i^*, A would take a credit from B and buy shares from B short. So the net capital exposure of both partners would be 0. Thus A could deduct the interest payments and save on income tax at a rate higher than τ_i^*. B would pay tax on the interest income at a rate lower than τ_i^*. The capital gains tax for A would cancel out the tax refunded for capital losses of B. This process would continue until the marginal tax rates of A and B were equal.

Dybvig and Ross (1986) have distinguished between three cases. In the marginalist case, all agents have the same marginal tax rates in all states and there are no clientele effects. In the marginal investor case, at least one real or hypothetical agent is marginal on all assets. With respect to his marginal tax rate, all assets promise the same net rate of return. There is a clientele effect in quantities (investors in general have different portfolios), but not in prices. In the third case, no agent is marginal on all assets and there are clientele effects both in quantities and prices.

Miller's theorem applies to the case of certainty, i.e. the debt payments must be certain and the profits of the firm must be at least as high as the interest payments so that the interest payments are not redundant tax shields. A number of authors have dealt with the case where debt and debt-related tax savings are uncertain (DeAngelo–Masulis, 1980, Talmor et al., 1985, Zechner–Swoboda, 1986). Two tendencies have to be taken into consideration: first, uncertainty reduces the probability that interest payments can be used as a tax shield. Second, because of the probability of default, creditors must be promised a higher rate of interest. This increases the tax shield of the firm as well as the income tax payments of the investors in favorable states. It can be shown that with very low and very high debt levels the critical implicit income tax rate is equal to the combined corporation and capital gains tax rate, as in the Miller model, but it is lower for values between these two ranges. The conclusion is, therefore, that if the tax rate of the marginal investor (or all investors) is equal to the combined corporation and capital gains tax rate, very low or very high debt levels would be optimal (Zechner–Swoboda, 1986).

4.2 The Clientele Effect of Progressive Taxation with Respect to Risky Debt

4.2.1 Exploration of the Clientele Effect

To study how the clientele effect with respect to risky debt depends on the existence of a capital gains tax, on the risk of default and on whether the risk of default is compensated by an increase in the interest rate or by issuing the bond at a discount, the following assumptions are made:

$D =$ repayment value of the riskless and the risky bond if fully repaid or the issuing price of the riskless bond

$D_d =$ repayment value of the risky bond if only partly repaid

$P^* =$ price of the risky bond at $t = 0$

$C =$ interest payments (coupon) of the riskless bond

$C^* =$ interest payments of the risky bond if fully paid

$C_d =$ interest payments of the risky bond if only partly paid

$\pi_1, \ldots, \pi_4 =$ probability of states 1 to 4

$\tau =$ income tax rate

$\tau_g =$ capital gains tax rate (losses are deductible)

In state 1, D and C^* are paid. In state 2, D and a part of the interest payments (C_d) are paid. In state 3, only a part of the debt (D_d) is repaid. In state 4, the debtor defaults completely. We assume risk neutrality in all states.

Capital Markets, Entrepreneurship and Progressive Taxation 127

A risk neutral investor with (marginal) tax rates τ and τ_g will be indifferent between a risky and a riskless bond with the same D if

$$\{[C^*(1-\tau) + D - (D - P^*)\tau_g]\pi_1 + [C_d(1-\tau) + D - (D - P^*)\tau_g]\pi_2 + \\ + [D_d - (D_d - P^*)\tau_g]\pi_3 + P^*\tau_g\pi_4 - P^*\}/P^* = C(1-\tau)/D \tag{30}$$

$$= \{[C^*(1-\tau) + D(1-\tau_g)]\pi_1 + [C_d(1-\tau) + D(1-\tau_g)]\pi_2 + \\ + [D_d(1-\tau_g)]\pi_3 - P^*(1-\tau_g)\}/P^* = C(1-\tau)/D. \tag{30a}$$

In our study we distinguish between two cases. In case 1 the risk of default is compensated by a higher rate of interest. In case 2 the bond is issued at a discount. In both cases π_1 is strictly positive.

Case 1

In case 1 C^* reflects the default risk and $P^* = D$. In this scenario

$$C^* = \{C(1-\tau) + D - [C_d(1-\tau) + D]\pi_2 - D_d\pi_3 - \\ - (D - D_d)\tau_g\pi_3 - D\tau_g\pi_4 - D\pi_1\}/(1-\tau)\pi_1. \tag{31}$$

A clientele effect is effective if C^* depends on τ. Therefore the first derivative of C^* with respect to τ is computed.

$$\partial C^*/\partial\tau = \{[1 - \tau_g - (1-\tau)(\partial\tau_g/\partial\tau)][D\pi_4 + (D - D_d)\pi_3]\}/(1-\tau)^2\pi_1. \tag{32a}$$

For $\tau_g = 0$ (no capital gains tax) equation (32a) reduces to

$$\partial C^*/\partial\tau = [D\pi_4 + (D - D_d)\pi_3]/(1-\tau)^2\pi_1. \tag{32b}$$

(32b) is positive if $\pi_3 + \pi_4 > 0$. This implies that there is a clientele effect only when a part of the principal is risky. The positive sign of $\partial C^*/\partial\tau$ shows that investors with higher tax rates must be offered a higher rate of interest to be indifferent between a risky and a riskless bond. If only the interest payments are risky, no clientele effect arises ($\pi_1 + \pi_2 = 1$). The reason for this is that if investors receive lower interest payments, they also save taxes at their marginal rate. Therefore, the *relative* losses of all investors are equal and there is no tax clientele effect. On the other hand, if there are capital losses, investors only save the capital gains tax, if any. For investors with higher tax rates, capital losses net of taxes are, therefore, higher with respect to their expected income than for investors with lower income tax rates.

If τ_g is a constant, equation (32a) reads

$$\partial C^*/\partial \tau = \{(1 - \tau_g)[D\pi_4 + (D - D_d)\pi_3]\}/(1 - \tau)^2\pi_1. \tag{32c}$$

$\partial C^*/\partial \tau > 0$, if $\tau_g < 1$ and $\pi_4 + \pi_3 > 0$.

If τ_g is linear dependent on $\tau(\tau_g = \lambda\tau)$, equation (32a) reads

$$\partial C^*/\partial \tau = \{(1 - \lambda)[D\pi_4 + (D - D_d)\pi_3]\}/(1 - \tau)^2\pi_1. \tag{32d}$$

$\partial C^*/\partial \tau > 0$, if $\lambda < 1$ and $\pi_4 + \pi_3 > 0$.

There is again a clientele effect in the sense that investors with higher tax rates will prefer riskless bonds, if $\pi_4 + \pi_3 > 0$ and if the tax rate for the capital gains tax is smaller than 100 percent (if constant), or smaller than the tax rate for ordinary income (if dependent on the income tax rate). A capital gains tax, however, clearly decreases the clientele effect.

Case 2

In case 2 P^*, the price at which the bond is issued, reflects the risk of default and $C^* = C$. Under this assumption (30) is to be solved for P^*.

$$P^* = D\{[C(1 - \tau) + D]\pi_1 + [C_d(1 - \tau) + D]\pi_2 + D_d\pi_3 - \\ - \tau_g[D(\pi_1 + \pi_2) + D_d\pi_3]\}/[C(1 - \tau) + D(1 - \tau_g)], \tag{33}$$

$$\partial P^*/\partial \tau = \{D[1 - \tau_g - (1 - \tau)(\partial\tau_g/\partial\tau)][D(C - C_d)\pi_2 + D_dC\pi_3]\}/ \\ /[C(1 - \tau) + D(1 - \tau_g)]^2. \tag{34a}$$

If $\tau_g = 0$ (no capital gains tax)

$$\partial P^*/\partial \tau = D[D(C - C_d)\pi_2 + D_dC\pi_3]/[C(1 - \tau) + D]^2. \tag{34b}$$

$\partial P^*/\partial \tau > 0$, if $\pi_2 + \pi_3 > 0$! If only π_1 and π_4 (complete default) is positive, there is no clientele effect in case 2! Also, the clientele effect is commutative: a positive value for $\partial P^*/\partial \tau$ implies that to investors with a higher tax rate, bonds can be sold at a higher price or a lower rate of return. In other words, investors with higher tax rates will prefer risky bonds to riskless bonds if the implied rates of return before taxes are equal!

This result can be explained as follows: in favorable states of the world investors realize capital gains. Capital gains, however, are more favorable for investors with high income tax rates than for investors with low income tax rates. The higher the risk of the bond, the higher are the capital gains in the favorable states, and the more interested are investors with high income tax rates in this bond.

If $\tau_g = \text{constant}$

$$\partial P^*/\partial \tau = \{D(1 - \tau_g)[D(C - C_d)\pi_2 + D_d C \pi_3]\}/[C(1 - \tau) + D(1 - \tau_g)]^2. \quad (34c)$$

$\partial P^*/\partial \tau > 0$, if $\pi_2 + \pi_3 > 0$ and $\tau_g < 1$.

If $\tau_g = \lambda \tau$

$$\partial P^*/\partial \tau = \{D(1 - \lambda)[D(C - C_d)\pi_2 + D_d C \pi_3]\}/[C(1 - \tau) + D(1 - \lambda \tau)]^2. \quad (34d)$$

$\partial P^*/\partial \tau > 0$, if $\pi_2 + \pi_3 > 0$ and $\lambda < 1$.

Concluding, we have derived the interesting result that investors with high tax rates will prefer risky bonds if the risk of default is reflected in the price for the bond, but riskless bonds, if the risk of default is reflected in the interest payments.

4.2.2 Incorporating the Clientele Effect with Respect to Risky Debt into the Theory of Optimal Capital Structure

The objective of this section is to integrate the effects of a progressive income tax on the debt-equity ratio (treated in Section 4.1) and the effects of a progressive income tax on debt instruments with different risk characteristics (treated in Section 4.2.1). The question is: which debt-equity ratio should a firm choose and which debt instruments should it issue if its optimal capital structure includes debt?

The model presented in this section builds on the work of Zechner–Swoboda (1986) and Zechner (1987).

The assumptions of this model are:

- risk neutrality;

- competitive security markets in the sense that investors perceive prices as given;

- short sales of securities (and therefore tax arbitrage) are prohibited;

- investors' taxable income is a function of their pre-tax income and is taxed at their state-dependent tax rate.

We define:

τ_{is} = investor i's marginal tax rate on taxable income from security $j, j = 0, \ldots, J$, in state s

τ_j = security j's implicit tax rate; (as defined in (35))

$\pi(s)$ = probability density of state s at t_1

$Y_j(s)$ = total pre-tax income received by the owners of security j in state s at t_1

$Y_j^T(s)$ = total taxable income received by the owners of security j in state s at t_1

V_j = total value of security j at t_o

α_{ij} = investor i's holdings of security j

W_i = investor i's wealth endowment at t_o.

Assume that security 0 is tax exempt such that $Y_o^T(s)$ is zero for all s. Security j's implicit tax rate, τ_j, is then defined as

$$r_o \equiv \frac{\int_s Y_o(s)\pi(s)ds}{V_o} = \frac{\int_s (Y_j(s) - \tau_j Y_j^T(s))\pi(s)ds}{V_{j,}}. \tag{35}$$

Thus, an investor with an average marginal tax rate τ_j is indifferent between holding the tax exempt security and security j.

Investor i's maximization problem at t_o is

$$\max_{\alpha_{ij}} \sum_i \alpha_{ij} \int_s (Y_j(s) - \tau_{is} Y_j^T(s))\pi(s)ds \tag{36}$$

$$\text{s.t.} \sum_j \alpha_{ij} V_j - W_i \leq 0 \tag{37}$$

$$\alpha_{ij} V_j \geq 0 \qquad \forall j. \tag{38}$$

Capital Markets, Entrepreneurship and Progressive Taxation   131

The first order conditions are

$$\int_s (Y_j(s) - \tau_{is}Y_j^T(s))\pi(s)ds - \lambda_i V_j - n_{ij}V_j = 0 \qquad \forall j \qquad (39)$$

$$\lambda_i > 0 \quad \alpha_{ij}V_j \geq 0 \ \forall j \quad n_{ij}\alpha_{ij}V_j = 0 \quad n_{ij} \leq 0. \qquad (40a-d)$$

λ_i and n_{ij} are Kuhn–Tucker multipliers associated with the budget constraint and the short sales constraint, respectively.

Dividing by V_j and using (35), the first order condition can be written ·

$$r_o - \lambda_i - n_{ij} + (\int_s (\tau_j - \tau_{is})Y_j^T(s)\pi(s)ds)/V_j = 0 \qquad \forall j \qquad (41a)$$

or

$$r_o - \lambda_i - n_{ij} + M_{ij} = 0 \quad \forall j \qquad (41b)$$

$$M_{ij} = (\int_s (\tau_j - \tau_{is})Y_i^T(s)\pi(s)ds)/V_j.$$

Since r_o is constant and λ_i and n_{ij} are shadow prices, an investor will hold that security which maximizes M_{ij}

$$j \in arg\,max\, M_{ij}.$$

Let us turn now to the capital structure of the firm. We assume:

- equity income is realized in the form of capital gains or losses;

- capital gains (losses) are not taxable (tax deductible);

- in the case of default, the principal precedes interests;

- debt is issued at par, or, if issued at a discount, the discount must be amortized over the life of the bond, which in this case is one year;

- interest payments are the only tax shield.

Under these assumptions, the debt-related tax shields are

$$D_j^T(s) = max[D_j(s) - D_j, 0]. \qquad (42)$$

$D_j^T(s) =$ taxable income from firm j's debt in state s at t_1

$D_j(s) =$ pre-tax income from firm j's debt in state s at t_1

$D_j =$ value of firm j's debt at t_o

Further definitions are:

$X_j(s) =$ total pre-tax cash flow of the firm in state s at t_1

$B_j =$ total debt claim of the firm at $t = 1$ (interest plus principal).

Table 1
State contingent cash flows to debt and equityholders

tax shields $= max[D_j(s) - D_j, 0]$

$X_j(s)$	$D_j(s)$	$D_j^T(s)$	$E_j(s)$
$X_j(\underline{s}) \le X_j(s) < X_j(s^a) =$ $= \frac{D_j}{1-\tau_c}$	$X_j(s)(1 - \tau_c)$	0	0
$X_j(s^a) \le X_j(s) < X_j(s^b) =$ $= B_j \frac{\tau_c D_j}{1-\tau_c}$	$X_j(s) - \frac{\tau_c D_j}{1-\tau_c}$	$X_j(s) - \frac{D_j}{1-\tau_c}$	0
$X_j(s^b) \le X_j(s) \le X(\bar{s})$	B_j	$B_j - D_j$	$X_j(s) - \tau_c(X_j(s)- -B_j + D_j) - B_j$

Table 1 shows the bondholders and equity holders taxable income in different states. Substituting the bondholders' taxable income from Table 1 for Y_j^T in equation (41b), M_{ij} now reads

$$M_{ij} = \frac{\int\limits_{s^a}^{s^b}(\tau_j - \tau_{is})(X_j(s) - \frac{D_j}{1-\tau_c})\pi(s)ds + \int\limits_{s^b}^{\bar{s}}(\tau_j - \tau_{is})(B_j - D_j)\pi(s)ds}{D_j} \tag{43a}$$

or

$$M_{ij} = \tau_j \frac{\int\limits_{s^a}^{s^b} (X_j(s) - \frac{D_j}{1-\tau_c})\pi(s)ds + \int\limits_{s^b}^{\bar{s}} (B_j - D_j)\pi(s)ds}{D_j} -$$

$$- \frac{\int\limits_{s^a}^{s^b} \tau_{is}(X_j(s) - \frac{D_j}{1-\tau_c})\pi(s)ds + \int\limits_{s^b}^{\bar{s}} \tau_{is}(B_j - D_j)\pi(s)ds}{D_j}. \tag{43b}$$

There is a clear result only if τ_{is} is constant. Then (43b) reduces to

$$M_{ij} = (\tau_j - \tau_i) \frac{\int\limits_{s^a}^{s^b} (X_j(s) - \frac{D_j}{1-\tau_c})\pi(s)ds + \int\limits_{s^b}^{\bar{s}} (B_j - D_j)\pi(s)ds}{D_j}. \tag{43c}$$

It can be shown that $\frac{\partial(Y_T/D_j)}{\partial B_j} > 0$. Therefore, if $\tau_j \geq \tau_i$, $\frac{\partial M_{ij}}{\partial B_j} > 0$. Now assume that the firm increases B. If τ_j stays constant, investors previously indifferent between firm j's debt and other bonds would now prefer firm j's debt.

This will bid up the price of bond j. Hence, market equilibrium requires that $\frac{\partial \tau_j}{\partial B_j} < 0$.

We can now analyse the impact of tax clienteles on a firm's capital structure decision. The value of a firm is given by

$$V_j = r_o^{-1}\{\int_s D_j(s)\pi(s)ds - \tau_j \int_s D_j^T(s)\pi(s)ds + \int_s E_j(s)\pi(s)ds\}. \tag{44}$$

Using the cash flows defined in Table 1 and taking the first derivative with respect to B_j, we get

$$\frac{\partial V_j}{\partial B_j} = r_o^{-1}(\tau_c - \tau_j)K - \frac{\partial \tau_j}{\partial B_j}K^+ \tag{45}$$

where

$$K = \int\limits_{s^b}^{\bar{s}} \pi(s)ds - \frac{\partial D_j}{\partial B_j}(\int\limits_{s^b}^{\bar{s}} \pi(s)ds + \frac{1}{1-\tau_c}\int\limits_{s^a}^{s^b} \pi(s)ds)$$

$$K^+ = \int\limits_{s^a}^{s^b} X(s)\pi(s)ds + B_j \int\limits_{s^b}^{\bar{s}} \pi(s)ds - D_j(\int\limits_{s^b}^{\bar{s}} \pi(s)ds + \frac{1}{1-\tau_c}\int\limits_{s^a}^{s^b} \pi(s)ds).$$

K and K^+ can be shown to be positve. Since $\frac{\partial \tau_j}{\partial B_j}$ must be negative, the third term in equation (45) is positive. After an increase in leverage, the debt will be held by investors in lower tax brackets. Now, without considering the clientele effect, the firm will issue debt capital if the personal tax rate implicit in bond prices τ_j is smaller than or equal to the corporate tax rate τ_c. But in this case $\frac{\partial V_j}{\partial B_j} > 0$, so that the optimal debt level must be a corner solution.

The resulting distribution of firms' optimal capital structures is bimodal: firms that are risky enough to attract investors in tax brackets below the corporate tax rate would be debt-financed. Firms for which $\tau_j(B_j^{max})$ is greater than the corporate tax rate, will be all equity financed.

Let us return to the general case in equation (43b). τ_{is}, the state dependent tax rate, can be smaller or greater than τ_j. M_{ij} is positive, if the weighted average of τ_{is} is smaller than τ_j. Whether this will be the case also depends on the correlation between τ_{is} and Y^T. If M_{ij} is positive and if the expected tax payments from the interest income are smaller than the expected taxable interest income, $\frac{\partial M_{ij}}{\partial B_j} > 0$. Therefore, in this case market equilibrium also requires that $\frac{\partial \tau_j}{\partial B_j} < 0$. The implications for the firm's optimal capital structure are thus the same as with constant τ_i.

Zechner (1987) extended this model to two periods. At the end of period 1 investors and firm receive new information about the value of the firm at the end of period 2. The market value of debt and equity then adjusts to the new information. As can be derived from our discussion in Section 4.2.1, investors with a high marginal tax rate will be interested in bonds which will sell at a discount. Those will be bonds of firms which experience an unfavorable state in t_1. The implicit tax rate of these bonds will be high. On the other hand, bonds which trade at a premium will be demanded by investors in low tax brackets. If this clientele effect at t_1 is incorporated into the capital structure decision at t_o, it can be shown that firms can have an optimum interior capital structure.

5. The Agency Effects of Progressive Taxation

An agency relation exists if the actions of a person (= agent) not only affect his/her own welfare, but also the welfare of another person (group) (= principal). This principal normally has the right to prescribe payoff rules for the result of the actions of the agent (Arrow, 1985, p. 38). The relation between the tax authority and the taxpayer is clearly an agency relation, the taxpayer being the agent and the tax authority being the principal. In the previous sections of this paper only one side of this agency relationship, the reactions of the agent to given sharing rules, was analysed. In this last section, this agency setting shall be viewed more globally. A thorough analysis of progressive taxation as a form of risk-sharing in an agency setting has not yet been addressed in the literature and is well beyond the scope of this paper. We will only discuss whether the agency problems dealt with in the literature can tell us something about the optimality of linear or progressive tax rates.

If an agent could costlessly be induced to internalize the principal's objective, the agency relation would be without relevance. But this is not the case with respect to taxation. The reason is asymmetric information, either with respect to the alternatives open to the agent (case of hidden information) or with respect to the actions taken by the agent (case of hidden action) (Arrow, 1985). The case of hidden action subsumes the case of hidden information (Hart–Holmstrom, 1986, p. 9). With respect to taxation, the case of hidden information is more important than the case of hidden action. Therefore, tax basis, tax rate, tax auditing and the sanctions for not observing tax rules should be designed as an incentive scheme to minimize agency costs. The agency costs include the cost of tax administration and the welfare losses of second best actions.

As to the linearity of tax rates, Hart–Holmstrom (1985, pp. 30/31) show that optimal *linear* sharing rules are the result of rather special assumptions, even in very basic models. If it is assumed that the marginal disutility of effort increases with additional expected income, marginal income tax rates would have to be degressive in order not to distort incentives. The popularity of linear rules is hardly explained by meeting the necessary assumptions in reality. Hart–Holmstrom believe, however, that linear schemes in many cases work because "incentive schemes need to perform well across a wider range of circumstances than specified in standard agency models". The more options an agent has, the poorer complicated schemes will work. Hart–Holmstrom give an example for the optimality of linear rules which is directly relevant for taxation: if arbitrage is possible, "linear schemes are optimal because they are the only ones that are operational".

In their famous paper, Jensen–Meckling (1976) argue that if the owner-manager of a firm sells equity claims, the incentive to enjoy fringe benefits and to decrease his effort will increase, since he will then bear only a fraction of the costs of fringe benefits and the lower profit due to decreased effort. An increase in income tax rates has the same effect. In the case of partnerships, the manager-owner is interested in binding himself by contract to a maximum amount of fringe benefits and a minimum amount of effort to realize a higher price for the equity claims he wants to sell. With respect to taxation, however, private agreements to limit fringe benefits or efforts to attain lower tax rates would not work since tax rules affect not only one, but all firms. Therefore, only general limits on fringe benefits for all taxable firms are possible.

The agency problem of taxation is complicated by the fact that, except in the case of the sole owner of a firm, the agency relation between manager and (other) owners is interwoven with the agency relation between manager and tax authority. The manager shares his or her profits with the owners and the tax authority. For example, a progressive share in the profits together with progressive taxation can result in a linear scheme. Therefore, the contracts between owners and managers can react to the specific tax rules and thus eliminate negative incentives from the tax rules.

A further unexplored problem is the non-coincidence between tax period (1 year) and decision period (much shorter). It makes a difference whether an agent has to take one decision in a tax period or many successive decisions. For example, the decision to put in another big effort in December may depend on the income already realized prior to November and the progressivity of the tax tariff. As Hart–Holmstrom (1985, pp. 32/33) point out, a linear scheme will lead to a more uniform choice of effort over the year. If the agent knows the result of his or her actions only at the end of the period and if his or her utility function is exponential, a linear sharing rule, leading to a constant effort, would be optimal.

6.   Summary

The main conclusion drawn in this paper is that the effects of progressive taxation on the risk-taking of individuals (entrepreneurs) are very indeterminate. Whether progressive taxation enhances or hinders risk-taking depends essentially on the utility function of the individual. Introducing a progressive tax scheme into a capital asset pricing model shows that investors will adjust the composition of their portfolios. Investors who are subject to a high tax rate will decrease their holdings of bonds (or increase their debt) and will prefer shares of firms with low dividend yields. But the effects do not seem to be very dramatic. However, in a state-preference model or under assumptions of risk neutrality, the clientele effects become very important. There exists not only a clientele effect with respect to the choice between equity and debt capital, but also with respect to risky debt. We showed that the direction of the clientele effect with respect to risky debt depends on whether the default risk is compensated by a higher rate of interest or a lower price of the bond. In the last section we demonstrated that taxation gives rise

Capital Markets, Entrepreneurship and Progressive Taxation

to an important agency relation. Under which conditions a linear or progressive tax scheme would be an optimal way of risk-sharing among principal and agent remains to be analysed.

7.   Appendix

Example:

A market is represented by three firms and three individuals. The relevant data are

Firm	Value	Beta
F^1	4200	.65
F^2	3168	1.14
F^3	2632	1.39
Market	10000	$var(\widetilde{r}_m) = .024; \ r_f = .06$

Investor	Wealth	Φ
I^1	2200	.150
I^2	3400	.300
I^3	4400	.375

Since $\theta^k = W^k \Phi^k / 2$ we obtain

$$\theta^1 = 165, \quad \theta^2 = 510, \quad \theta^3 = 825, \quad \text{and} \ \theta^m = 1500.$$

Scenario 1:
The dividend yield of all firms is .02 and all investors are taxed by the same rate of .3.

From relation (17) we obtain

$$E(\widetilde{R}_1) = .152, \quad E(\widetilde{R}_2) = .2304, \quad \text{and} \ E(\widetilde{R}_3) = .2704.$$

Rearranging terms in (15) together with (17) and the market clearing condition

$$\sum_k x_i^k W^k = x_i^m W^m, \quad \forall i$$

we obtain x_i^k, the fraction of the k–th individual's wealth invested in the i–th firm (it is also possible to calculate x_i^k from relation (24a)):

$$x_i^k = \frac{\theta^k}{W^k} x_i^m \frac{E(\widetilde{R}_i) - r_f - \tau^k(d_i - r_f)}{\beta_i var(\widetilde{r}_m)} = x_i^m \frac{cov(\widetilde{r}_i, \widetilde{r}_{PF}^k)}{\beta_i var(\widetilde{r}_m)} = x_i^m \frac{cov(\widetilde{r}_i, \widetilde{r}_{PF}^k)}{cov(\widetilde{r}_i, \widetilde{r}_m)}.$$

Taking the relevant input data the optimal portfolio structure of each investor is given in Table 2a (RRPR = risk-return preference rate), and the tax payments and the shares which are held by the individuals are given in Table 2b.

Since $\sum_k x_i^k W^k$ = value of the i-th firm $\forall i$,
$\sum_k x_f^k W^k = 0$, and $x_i^k = x_i^m \cdot \sum_i x_i^k \; \forall i, k$
we have a market equilibrium in the sense of the CAPM and all individuals hold a fraction of the market portfolio.

Since we know the β_i's, the x_i^m's, and the variance of the market portfolio, we can construct a possible scenario of the σ_{ij}'s. The following relations must hold:

$$\beta_1 x_1^m var(\widetilde{r}_m) = (x_1^m)^2 \sigma_{11} + (x_1^m x_2^m)\sigma_{12} + (x_1^m x_3^m)\sigma_{13}$$

$$\beta_2 x_2^m var(\widetilde{r}_m) = (x_2^m)^2 \sigma_{22} + (x_1^m x_2^m)\sigma_{12} + (x_2^m x_3^m)\sigma_{23}$$

$$\beta_3 x_3^m var(\widetilde{r}_m) = (x_3^m)^2 \sigma_{33} + (x_1^m x_3^m)\sigma_{13} + (x_2^m x_3^m)\sigma_{23}.$$

Table 2a

RRPR	X1 %	X2 %	X3 %	XF %
.150	21.00	15.84	13.16	50.00
.300	42.00	31.68	26.32	.00
.375	52.50	39.60	32.90	−25.00

Table 2b

Invest	Taxes	Firm 1	Firm 2	Firm 3	Riskless
Indiv 1	26.40	462.00	348.48	289.52	1100.00
Indiv 2	20.40	1428.00	1077.12	894.88	.00
Indiv 3	13.20	2310.00	1742.40	1447.60	−1100.00
Market	60.00	4200.00	3168.00	2632.00	.00

Capital Markets, Entrepreneurship and Progressive Taxation

Table 3a

RRPR	X1 %	X2 %	X3 %	XF %
.150	20.60	15.67	13.04	50.70
.300	43.62	32.37	26.79	−2.78
.375	61.70	43.56	35.60	−40.86

Table 3b

Invest	Taxes	Firm 1	Firm 2	Firm 3	Riskless
Indiv1	22.15	453.12	344.66	286.92	1115.31
Indiv2	25.69	1482.92	1100.74	910.97	−94.64
Indiv3	12.16	2714.91	1916.54	1566.26	−1797.71
Market	60.00	4650.95	3361.94	2764.15	−777.04

For simplicity we set $\sigma_{ii} = \beta_i var(\tilde{r}_m)/x_i^m$, $i = 1, 2, 3$, which implies $\sigma_{ij} = 0$, $i, j = 1, 2, 3$.

Now we can show, e.g. for individual 3, that his/her portfolio is optimal:

$$
\begin{pmatrix} & & & 0 & 1 \\ & 2\sigma_{ij} & & 0 & 1 \\ & & & 0 & 1 \\ 0 & 0 & 0 & 0 & 1 \\ 1 & 1 & 1 & 1 & 0 \end{pmatrix}^{-1} = \begin{pmatrix} \frac{175}{13} & 0 & 0 & -\frac{175}{13} & 0 \\ 0 & \frac{110}{19} & 0 & -\frac{110}{19} & 0 \\ 0 & 0 & \frac{1645}{417} & -\frac{1645}{417} & 0 \\ -\frac{175}{13} & -\frac{110}{19} & -\frac{1645}{417} & 23.20 & 1 \\ 0 & 0 & 0 & 1 & 0 \end{pmatrix}
$$

$$
x_1^3 = .375(\frac{175}{13})(.132 + .7(.02 - .06)) = .525
$$

$$
x_2^3 = .375(\frac{110}{19})(.2104 + .7(.02 - .06)) = .396
$$

$$
x_3^3 = .375(\frac{1645}{417})(.2504 + .7(.02 - .06)) = .329; \quad x_f^3 = -.25.
$$

Scenario 2:

The dividend yield is held constant; the linear taxation is replaced by a progressive taxation in such a way that the sum of the tax payments is held constant; a possible solution is $\tau^1 = .25$, $\tau^2 = .40$, and $\tau^3 = .755743$. (In this comparative static analysis we have assumed that the expected rates of return do not change.)

The results are given in Table 3a and 3b.

The main result is that individual 3 with the high tax rate *takes more risk*. He/she invests more of his/her wealth in the risky assets and pay even less taxes (12.16 compared to 13.20)! On the other hand, individual 2 pays more taxes because he/she is too risk averse to invest a higher fraction of his/her wealth in the risky assets.

As a consequence of the comparative static analysis we have now a disequilibrium. The progressive taxation causes an increase of the firm values (since the dividend yield is less than the riskless rate of return) and we have more lending than borrowing. To reach equilibrium, the riskless rate of return and the expected rates of return of the risky assets would have to be adjusted. This would also affect the betas of the firms. But this would not alter the above conclusions.

8. References

Arrow, K.J. (1985): "The Economics of Agency." In *Principals and Agents: The Structure of Business,* edited by J.W. Pratt and R.J. Zeckhauser. Boston: Harvard Business School Press.

Atkinson, A.B., and **Stiglitz, J.E.** (1980): *Lectures on Public Economics.* London et al.: McGraw-Hill.

Bamberg, G., and **Richter, W.F.** (1984): "The Effects of Progressive Taxation on Risk-Taking." *Zeitschrift für Nationalökonomie 44*: 93–102.

Bamberg, G., and **Richter, W.F.** (1985): "Three Effects of Progressive Taxation on Risk-Taking." Manuscript.

Brennan, M.J. (1970): "Taxes, Market Valuation and Corporate Financial Policy." *National Tax Journal 23*: 417–427.

Buchholz, W. (1985): "Die Wirkung progressiver Steuern auf die Vorteilhaftigkeit riskanter Investitionen." *Zeitschrift für betriebswirtschaftliche Forschung 37*: 882–890.

Buchholz, W. (1986): "Der Einfluß des Steuerprogressionsgrades auf die Bewertung riskanter Investitionsprojekte." In *Operations Research Proceedings 1985.* Berlin-Heidelberg: Springer-Verlag, 450–457.

Buchholz, W. (1987a): "Risikoeffekte der Besteuerung." Manuscript, University of Tübingen.

Buchholz, W. (1987b): "Neutral Taxation of Risky Investment." Manuscript, University of Tübingen.

DeAngelo, H., and **Masulis, R.W.** (1980): "Optimal Capital Structure under Corporate and Personal Taxation." *Journal of Financial Economics 7*: 3–29.

Dybvig, P.H., and **Ross, S.A.** (1986): "Tax Clienteles and Asset Pricing." *The Journal of Finance 41*: 751–762.

Feldstein, M.S. (1969): "The Effects of Taxation on Risk-Taking." *Journal of Political Economy 77*: 755–764.

Hart, O., and **Holmstrom, B.** (1985): "The Theory of Contracts." Paper presented at the World Congress of the Econometric Society. Cambridge, Massachusetts.

Jensen, M.C., and **Meckling, W.H.** (1976): "Theory of the Firm: Managerial Behavior, Agency Costs and Ownership Structure." *Journal of Financial Economics 3*: 305–360.

Litzenberger, R.H., and **Ramaswamy, K.** (1979): "The Effect of Personal Taxes and Dividends on Capital Asset Prices." *Journal of Financial Economics 7*: 163–195.

Miller, M.H. (1977): "Debt and Taxes." *The Journal of Finance 32*: 261–275.

Modigliani, F. (1982): "Debt, Dividend Policy, Taxes, Inflation and Market Valuation." *The Journal of Finance 37*: 255–273.

Modigliani, F., and **Miller, M.H.** (1963): "Corporate Income Taxes and the Cost of Capital: A Correction." *The American Economic Review 53*: 433–443.

Park, S.Y., and **Williams, J.** (1985): "Taxes, Capital Structure and Bondholder Clienteles." *Journal of Business 58*: 203–224.

Ross, S.A. (1984): "Debt and Taxes and Uncertainty." Manuscript. Yale University.

Rubinstein, M.E. (1973): "A Comparative Statics Analysis of Risk Premiums." *Journal of Business 46*: 605–615.

Schaefer, S.M. (1982): "Tax-Induced Clientele Effects in the Market for British Government Securities." *Journal of Financial Economics 10*: 121–159.

Schneider, D. (1977): "Gewinnbesteuerung und Risikobereitschaft: Zur Bewährung quantitativer Ansätze in der Entscheidungstheorie." *Zeitschrift für betriebswirtschaftliche Forschung 29*: 633–666.

Schneider, D. (1980): "The Effects of Progressive and Proportional Income Taxation on Risk-Taking." *National Tax Journal 33*: 67–76.

Stiglitz, J.E. (1969): "The Effects of Income, Wealth and Capital Gains Taxation on Risk-Taking." *Quarterly Journal of Economics 83*: 262–283.

Stiglitz, J.E. (1985): "The General Theory of Tax Avoidance." *National Tax Journal 38*: 325–337.

Talmor, E., Haugen, R., and **Barnea, A.** (1985): "The Value of the Tax Subsidy on Risky Debt." *Journal of Business 58*: 191–202.

Zechner, J. (1987): "The Impact of Heterogeneous Personal Taxes on Asset Pricing and Optimal Capital Structure." Manuscript. University of British Columbia.

Zechner, J., and **Swoboda, P.** (1986): "The Critical Implicit Tax Rate and Capital Structure." *Journal of Banking and Finance 10*: 327–341.

Taxing Entrepreneurs: Models and Reality

Thomas W. Hazlett, Davis, California, USA

Professors Swoboda and Steiner have prepared a formidable paper for this conference, which carefully works through various aspects of the question: does progressivity of the income tax code affect optimal allocation of resources? In general, the answer is one familiar to those who have dwelled in financial economics: it depends upon the relevant utility function. This is wholly counter-intuitive to the general view of taxation, however. To most it appears instantly obvious that steeper tax scales limit risk-taking and, hence, lower productivity and welfare. The situation is a bit more complex than it appears; progressive tax rates can have relatively little consequence for the behavior of investors if, e.g., the utility function of the individual increases its level of risk aversion more quickly than the marginal tax rate rises. The contribution of their paper is to show and consider the consequence of the possible welfare effects of this sort of hedging via the tax code.

In general, the authors note, the conditions under which a linear (or "flat") tax implies the most efficient code comprise simply a set of special cases. We can hypothesize circumstances where, under standard assumptions, a progressive rate will promote the least burden (with investors whose risk aversion rises with income), and those where a regressive tax is least distortive (on wage-earners whose disutility of labor rises with income). Why should the common intuition, then, that flat taxes promote efficiency, be so widespread a view when it is simply the manifestation of one utility function among many?

I believe that the answer is to be found in two considerations in which a linear tax rate offers distinct advantages over a progressive rate. First, a progressive code biases the taxpayer sample. In that the tax base is not entirely inelastic with respect to the tax code, a progressive rate will do more than shuffle utility gains and losses between taxpayers. It will cause substitution effects, by in effect lowering taxes on those who perceive the lowest mean returns, and raising them on those perceiving the highest, irrespective of attitudes towards risk. Such a policy leaves any one country (we assume that tax codes are specific to nations) pursuing a high degree of progressivity in the position of perpetual battle with its most optimistic and (we might therefore assume) its most productive citizens (and their capital accounts). It should also be noted that such citizens are likely to be most elastic with respect to geography – owing to their financial resources and human capital – and should be equipped to put up a very good fight, indeed.

146   Thomas W. Hazlett

Secondly, the introduction of nonlinearity in the tax code inevitably leads to accounting "investments", substitutes for economic investments which are private goods but social costs. Whenever income can be moved forward or backwards, or shifted into different taxpayer accounts, or qualified as a distinct sort of income to gain more favorable treatment, such activity will be pursued by rational maximizers. This can become quite costly. Indeed, it has formed the essence of the argument for simplifying the U.S. tax code:

> The American people have lost their faith in the nation's tax system. The hideous complexity of the income tax is driving taxpayers to exasperation. Staggering resources go into preparing tax returns, checking and auditing them, making arrangements to minimize taxes through legal avoidance schemes, and into outright evasion of taxes (Hall and Rabushka, 1983, p. iii).

The very tenuous nature of predictions as to the distortive effects of tax progressivity ("The effects of progressive taxation on the risk taking of individuals (entrepreneurs) are very indeterminate" (Swoboda and Steiner, 1989, p. 136).), leads one to weight the certain costs of progressivity highly. Given that individuals are capable of adjusting their mean-variance positions without reliance on the tax code (i.e. other financial instruments are abundantly available, enabling portfolios to be placed along the risk-return frontier at the bidding of the individual), the search for interactions between tax codes and utility functions appears distracting to the pursuit of relationships better understood and more reliable. As Swoboda and Steiner demonstrate, the welfare effects of progressivity are complicated and indeterminate. Let us turn our attention to those effects of the tax code which boast of greater tractability. As we know that progressivity (or any nonlinearity) will produce costly tax avoidance activity as assets flow to where the lowest rates obtain, this unambiguous resource loss should be weighted quite highly in any policy debate.

A final consideration concerns the entrepreneurs mentioned in the title of the paper. To the extent that such actors are distinct from investors, one would think that they would be agents whose capital is relatively undiversified human capital, and whose behavioral sine qua non is the correction of unobserved market errors. As Kirzner (1973) defines the entrepreneur, he is the essentially important actor whose task it is to bring new forms, products, and exchanges to the marketplace, thusly bringing the world a step closer to equilibrium. (Contrast this view with Schumpeter's (1942) model of the entrepreneur as disrupter of equilibria, as in the "perennial gale of creative destruction".) As dynamic economic change is entirely the product of such behavior, the entrepreneur assumes central social importance.

Understanding this, it is problematic to see the entrepreneur reduced to the status of mere utility-maximizing investor. The entrepreneur may have a diversified investment portfolio, but in his role as economic discoverer he is inherently a risk-taker, embarking on the new and untried, and relatively undiversified. Again, the conventional wisdom would see the entrepreneur as an actor instantly harmed by progressive taxation, relative to the policy alternatives, and the distinctly, entrepreneurial function as one which would be discouraged under such a regime. Here, it looks as if the conventional wisdom may actually be correct.

In conclusion, the consideration of progressivity should not be unduly isolated so as to focus only upon the direct margin between the tax rate and expected utility. Indirect effects (the tax scales impact upon income which affects utility) may well dominate, a result made operationally crucial by the complexity and ambiguity of the direct relationship. Nonlinear tax schedules promote a host of effects which, while locally optimally, produce deadweight (tax-avoidance) costs for society as a whole. Indeed, the argument for a dramatically flatter code which prevailed in the 1986 U.S. tax reform relied solely upon these indirect linkages, and not at all upon the risk-aversion criterion. Moreover, what is of special interest in this particular discussion, is that entrepreneurs are the economic agents most likely to demonstrate risk-taking preferences and strategic tax-lowering behavior. On either count the effects of tax progressivity are to discourage entrepreneurship and, hence, to presumably lower social welfare.

References

Hall, R., and **Rabushka, A.** (1983): *Low Tax, Simple Tax, Flat Tax.* New York: McGraw Hill.

Kirzner, I. (1973): *Competition and Entrepreneurship.* Chicago: University of Chicago Press.

Schumpeter, J.A. (1942): *Capitalism, Socialism and Democracy.* New York: Harper and Row.

Swoboda, P., and **Steiner, P.** (1989): "Capital Markets, Entrepreneurship and Progressive Taxation." This volume, pp. 111–143.

The Consequences of Progressive Income Taxation for the Shadow Economy: Some Theoretical Considerations

Reinhard Neck, Friedrich Schneider, and Markus F. Hofreither,
Vienna, Linz, Austria[*]

1. Introduction

In recent years, both the public debate and the scientific literature have shown increased interest in the phenomenon of the shadow (underground, hidden) economy.[1] As a working definition, we may say that the shadow economy consists of those economic activities which contribute to value-added and should be included in GDP or national income according to the conventions of national-income accounting, but are at present not registered by the national measurement agencies. Political concern about the size and the growth of the shadow economy arises for various reasons: apart from the general undesirability of illegal activities, there are also economic problems associated with the underground economy. For example, it may be a result or a cause of allocative and distributive distortions; the effects of stabilization policies may be different when there is a considerable amount of hidden activities; and, in general, spillovers between the shadow and the official economy must not be neglected when policy measures are being planned and implemented. Moreover, if rising tax rates lead to an increase in the extent of the shadow economy, higher tax rates may cause lower instead of higher tax revenues for the government. This possibility of a falling portion of the Laffer curve has to be taken into account when budgetary policies are under consideration.[2]

Economists have dealt with the problems of the underground economy primarily from two perspectives. First, from a theoretical perspective, attempts have been made to explain the extent of the shadow economy, asking why people work

---

[*] We are indebted to J. Brunner, J. Falkinger and M. Winkler for their helpful discussions. Particular thanks are due to D. Bös, who has made many constructive suggestions for improvement on an earlier version of this paper. We are also grateful to F. Cowell for making available to us his unpublished work on tax evasion. Remaining errors and shortcomings are our responsibility.

[1] Cf., for instance, Frey and Pommerehne (1984), Gaertner and Wenig (1985) and Weck et al. (1984).

[2] Cf. the contribution of Alan Peacock to this volume.

D. Bös and B. Felderer (Eds.)
The Political Economy of Progressive Taxation
© Springer-Verlag Berlin Heidelberg 1989

in the hidden sector of the economy, sell and buy goods and services in black markets, etc. Second, an even greater number of empirical studies has been undertaken. Since the shadow economy, per definition, is not easily visible, the primary concern in this field is about the measurement of the size and the development of the underground sector, using either direct methods (based on data collected by tax authorities or through voluntary interviews) or indirect ones, such as the currency-demand approach or the model approach, among others. As soon as there is reliable information available about the extent of the shadow economy, empirical analyses of its determinants can be attempted, which may supplement theoretical considerations. These may employ different methodologies, such as econometric models, time-series analysis or experimental methods. Examples of such studies include those by Mork (1975), Spicer and Lundstedt (1976), Friedland et al. (1978), Lewis (1979), Clotfelter (1983), Geeroms and Wilmots (1985), Spicer and Hero (1985), Crane and Nourzad (1985, 1986, 1987), Poterba (1987), Dubin et al. (1987). Finally, the feedback effects from the shadow economy to the official economy can be studied empirically, as has been initiated by Schneider and Hofreither (1987) in simulation studies using an econometric model for Austria.

In the present paper, we pursue a theoretical approach and analyse some determinants of shadow economy activities of households and firms. Direct and indirect taxation are particularly studied, with special emphasis being given to the progression of the income tax. In Section 2, we formulate a simple microeconomic model including an official and an underground sector of the economy. Sections 3 and 4 contain investigations of the shadow economy activities of households and firms, respectively, within this model and derive some comparative-static results. In Section 5, an informal discussion of the equilibrium of the model is given, and the consequences for the influence of progressive income taxation on the shadow economy are outlined. Our results are preliminary in several respects: a unified approach is still lacking and we have not yet been able to integrate our partial-equilibrium results into a general-equilibrium model. Since our analytical results are in part ambiguous and are derived under special conditions, they have to be supplemented by numerically specified models in order to evaluate effects of changes in tax rates on the shadow economy. In the companion paper by Schneider et al. in this volume, results of some policy simulations are reported which show the impacts of changes in the marginal tax rate of wage-earners in reducing the incentives to work in the shadow economy, in indirect taxes, and in after-tax wages in the official economy on the endogenous variables of an econometric model containing an underground sector.

2. A Microeconomic Model of Shadow Economy Activities

Our aim in this paper is to give some "micro-foundations" for the supply and the demand of shadow economy activities. In order to do so, we start with a highly simplified microeconomic model. We consider two decision-making agents, the household and the firm. Households are characterized by von Neumann–Morgenstern expected utility functions; all households are regarded as identical with respect to their preferences and their endowments of time. Firms' production possibilities are described by production functions which are identical across firms. Therefore, in our model both the household and the firm qualify as representative agents within their respective class. Labor is the only variable factor of production in our short-run framework and there are no other sources of income for the household than those arising from selling its labor services.[3] The household supplies and the firm demands labor in perfectly competitive labor markets; the firm supplies and the household demands goods in perfectly competitive goods markets. The only activity of government considered is tax collection, including negative taxation (transfer payments to households). We have no explicit model of the public sector, and public goods and revenue constraints on the government are ignored.[4] The household maximizes expected utility subject to a budget constraint; the firm maximizes expected profit (i.e., it is risk-neutral) subject to its production function.

In order to concentrate on the problems of the official versus the shadow economy, we consider two kinds of labor, official (denoted by superscript o) and underground (superscript u). Moreover, we assume two goods, official and underground. Both kinds of labor and goods are assumed to be homogeneous within their class and to be perfect substitutes for each other, apart from different degrees of risk associated with them. The easiest way to conceive of this is an economy with just one good, which may be traded either in an official or in a black market; the same holds for the labor markets. Hence households and firms interact in four interrelated markets: two goods markets (official and underground) and two labor markets (official and underground). Official and underground markets differ from each other by the fact that transactions in official markets are subject to taxes (a direct income tax for the labor market, an indirect revenue tax for the goods market), at rates fixed by the government. Transactions in the underground markets, on the other hand, are hidden from the government. If this tax evasion is detected, then such transactions are subject to penalties, again at

---

[3] Different sources of income (labor and capital) are considered in the model by McCaleb (1976).

[4] Models of tax evasion which include public goods have been analysed by Cowell and Gordon (1988), Cowell (1989). In this case, an explicit model of government behavior is required.

rates fixed by the government. The government is assumed to detect tax evasion in goods and labor markets with fixed probabilities. Its objective function is not specified and strategic interactions between government and private sector agents are neglected.[5]

The household has the following options: it may work in the official labor market; it may work in the underground labor market; or it may be idle. Hence the problem of the household is to allocate its available time (called T and assumed to be fixed) to labor supply in the official economy (S^o), labor supply in the shadow economy (S^u), and leisure (L). $S(D)$ denotes hours of work per day supplied by the household (demanded by the firm) and L denotes the number of hours of leisure per day. Moreover, the household may spend its income derived from its labor supply decision for purchases of official-economy goods (d^o) or shadow economy goods (d^u). $s(d)$ denotes the quantity of goods supplied by the firm (demanded by the household). Hourly wage rates for official (W^o) and underground (W^u) labor are given to the household, and the same is true for prices of official (P^o) and underground (P^u) goods.

The difference between the official and the shadow economy for the household is most relevant in its labor supply decision: if the household works in the official economy, it receives income which is subject to direct income taxation. We assume a progressive tax system; for mathematical convenience, we restrict ourselves to a linear income tax.[6] That is, if the household works for S^o hours in the official labor market and gets pre-tax income $W^o S^o$, it has to pay income taxes $t_1 W^o S^o - t_o$, where t_1 is the marginal tax rate and $t_o > 0$ is a minimum income guaranteed by the government (a lump-sum transfer). On the other hand, if the household works for S^u hours in the shadow labor market, it gets an income of $W^u S^u$. If this is detected by the government, the household has to pay a penalty assumed to be proportional to the evaded income, namely, $t_2 W^u S^u$, where t_2 is the penalty tax rate. p is the probability of being detected for working in the[l] shadow economy; $p \in (0,1)$. The household's choice situation in the labor market is given in Appendix 1. Here y_i denotes disposable income from work in situation i, $i = 1, 2$, where situation 1 means that working in the shadow economy is not

---

[5] Optimal government policies maximizing a social welfare function in the presence of tax evasion have been investigated by Kolm (1973), Sandmo (1981), Slemrod and Yitzhaki (1987), Cowell (1987, 1989), among others. Interactions between government and taxpayers (and in some cases other agents) are the subject of game-theoretic models of tax evasion; see, e.g., Greenberg (1984), Graetz et al. (1986), Reinganum and Wilde (1985, 1986), Nitzan and Tzur (1987) and Cowell (1989).

[6] This simple tax schedule does not allow taking account of legitimate tax avoidance and sheltering, which, in a more general model, ought to be analysed together with tax evasion. On this, see for instance Cross and Shaw (1982), Cowell (1988).

The Consequences of Progressive Income Taxation for the Shadow Economy 153

detected, and situation 2 means that it is detected.

The firm, on the other hand, has the following possible choices: it may produce the official-economy good (s^o); it may produce the shadow economy good (s^u); or it may produce nothing at all. If it produces s^o, it sells it for $s^o P^o$, where P^o is the market price inclusive of indirect taxes. We assume that there is a proportional sales tax to be paid by the firm, with tax rate t, i.e., the firm has to pay $ts^o P^o$. Equivalently, if P^n is the price of the official-market good net of the indirect tax, then $P^o = P^n/(1-t)$ or $P^o = P^n(1+\tau)$, where $\tau = t/(1-t)$ is the indirect tax rate, expressed as a proportion of the price net of taxes (which is the common formulation, e.g. in tax laws). If the firm sells products in the underground market, its revenues are $s^u P^u$, and it does not pay taxes. However, if this activity is detected, the firm must pay a penalty proportional to the sales evaded from taxation, i.e., $t_3 s^u P^u$, where t_3 is the penalty tax rate for indirect tax evasion. The probability of being detected for selling in the shadow economy is $q \in (0,1)$. In our model, the firm does not pay direct taxes (such as the corporate income tax), hence it cannot evade direct taxation.[7]

The firm has to decide simultaneously about its goods supply and its factor demand. Labor is the only variable factor of production considered; all other inputs (denoted together by K) are fixed at a constant level, say $\overline{K}$, and have costs $C(\overline{K})$, assumed to be constant in the short run. The firm may demand labor in the official and the shadow economy, D^o and D^u, respectively. We assume that official-economy goods can be produced by official labor and underground economy goods by underground labor only. This separability assumption, which considerably simplifies the analysis of the firm's decision problem, may be justified by the presumption that tax authorities would be able to detect any "hidden" labor producing official goods and any "hidden" goods produced by official labor. The fixed inputs are used for both kinds of production in the same way, and they are common, i.e., they do not have to be allocated among the two uses. It is obvious that the separation between official and underground production is a severe restriction, as it excludes for instance joint production of the two goods considered; without this assumption, however, no meaningful results could be derived. The firm aims at maximizing its expected profit subject to the constraints given by the production functions for official and underground goods. Its choice situation is summarized in Appendix 2. Prices and wages are given for the firm.

---

[7] Allowing for direct taxation of the firm would considerably complicate our model; in this case, interactions between direct and indirect tax evasion could be analysed. For a model of the interaction between direct and indirect tax rates from the point of view of tax authorities under a budget constraint, see Büchner (1987).

3. Determinants of Household's Shadow Economy Activities

The problem of the household is similar to the one first studied by Allingham and Sandmo (1972), namely that of how much of its income to declare to the tax authorities. Similar models and modifications have been proposed in the literature by Yitzhaki (1974), Kolm (1973), Srinivasan (1973), and Singh (1973), among others. The influence of different tax schedules on tax evasion has been studied by Nayak (1978), Sproule et al. (1980), Christiansen (1980), and Koskela (1983, 1983a); for a comprehensive review of the literature, see Cowell (1989). The simultaneous decision on labor supply and declared income has been treated by Weiss (1976), Andersen (1977), Baldry (1979), Pencavel (1979), and Cowell (1981, 1985). Isachsen and Strøm (1980) were the first to study this problem within the context of an economy with an official and a shadow labor market.[8] We follow their analysis by considering the labor supply decision of the household first; however, instead of the proportional income tax assumed by Isachsen and Strøm, we consider a progressive linear income tax. The household's decision of allocating its income to purchases of different goods is not explicitly considered at first; that is, we assume the composite-commodity theorem to hold, and study the supply of labor and demand for goods separately.

The household's cardinal utility function U is assumed to depend (positively) on income and (negatively) on labor supplied in the official and the shadow market. By including both S^o and S^u instead of leisure as arguments of the utility function, differential disutilities of both kinds of labor can be incorporated. For instance, working in the underground economy may be considered to be more inconvenient if reputational considerations are taken into account. An alternative would consist in using leisure and a specific disutility term for working in the shadow economy as arguments of the utility function. The possibility of being detected for working in the hidden economy introduces an element of risk. The household maximizes its expected utility, which is given by

$$E[U] = (1-p)U(y_1, S^o, S^u) + pU(y_2, S^o, S^u), \tag{1}$$

with respect to S^o and S^u, where

$$y_1 = W^o S^o (1 - t_1) + t_o + W^u S^u, \tag{2}$$

---

[8] Further work with similar models has been done by Sandmo (1981), Wiegard (1984), Sproule (1985), Watson (1985).

$$y_2 = W^o S^o (1 - t_1) + t_o + W^u S^u (1 - t_2), \tag{3}$$

subject to

$$S^o + S^u \le T, \tag{4}$$

$$S^o \ge 0, \ S^u \ge 0. \tag{5}$$

Leisure L is the slack variable of the inequality constraint (4). To simplify the notation we define

$$t_2' = \begin{cases} 0 & \text{for } y = y_1 \text{ (non-detection)}, \\ t_2 & \text{for } y = y_2 \text{ (detection)}. \end{cases} \tag{6}$$

Denoting the Lagrangian function for the above nonlinear programming problem by $\mathcal{L}$ and the Lagrange multiplier for the constraint (4) by μ, we obtain the necessary Kuhn–Tucker conditions for an optimum (assuming differentiability of the utility function):

$$\mathcal{L}_{S^o} = E[U_y]W^o(1 - t_1) + E[U_{S^o}] - \mu \le 0, \tag{7}$$

$$\mathcal{L}_{S^u} = E[U_y W^u (1 - t_2')] + E[U_{S^u}] - \mu \le 0, \tag{8}$$

$$S^o \ge 0, \ S^o \cdot \mathcal{L}_{S^o} = 0; \ S^u \ge 0, \ S^u \cdot \mathcal{L}_{S^u} = 0, \tag{9}$$

$$\mathcal{L}_\mu = T - S^o - S^u \ge 0, \ \mu \ge 0, \ \mu \cdot \mathcal{L}_\mu = 0. \tag{10}$$

Partial derivatives are denoted by subscripts, and we define

$$E[U_y] = (1 - p)U_y(y_1, S^o, S^u) + pU_y(y_2, S^o, S^u), \tag{11}$$

and similarly for $E[U_{S^o}]$ and $E[U_{S^u}]$.

Consider first an interior solution. For $L > 0$ we have $\mu = 0$; for $S^o > 0$ and $S^u > 0$, we obtain:

$$E[U_y]W^o(1 - t_1) + E[U_{S^o}] = 0, \tag{12}$$

$$E[U_y W^u(1 - t_2')] + E[U_{S^u}] = 0. \tag{13}$$

The first condition can be written as

$$W^o(1 - t_1) = -E[U_{S^o}] \ / \ E[U_y], \tag{14}$$

meaning that the after-tax wage rate for official work must be equal to the ratio of the expected marginal disutility from official work to the expected marginal utility from income obtained both from official and underground work. The second necessary condition (13) gives:

$$W^u = -E[U_{S^u}] \ / \ E[U_y(1 - t_2')]. \tag{15}$$

This says that the wage rate for underground work must be equal to the ratio of the expected marginal disutility from underground work to the expected marginal utility from income obtained both from official and underground work weighted by the penalty rate to be paid to the tax authorities. This rate is zero if tax evasion is not detected, and t_2 if it is detected. Conditions (14) and (15) determine (implicitly) the two labor supply functions of the household:

$$S^o = S^o[W^o, W^u, t_o, t_1, t_2, p], \tag{16}$$

$$S^u = S^u[W^o, W^u, t_o, t_1, t_2, p]. \tag{17}$$

For a corner solution with $L = 0$ ($\mu > 0$), both functions additionally depend on T.

It is possible to derive comparative-static expressions from the above necessary conditions which show the dependence of the optimal labor supply in the official and the shadow economy on the parameters of the model. In general, however, these expressions do not provide definitive qualitative information as to the signs of these effects. The reason for this is that there are three distinct effects on these variables caused by changes in the parameters, namely a portfolio, an income and a leisure effect. The latter two are ambiguous unless additional restrictions are imposed on the utility function. This has been shown in the context of a fairly simple tax evasion model with labor supply by Baldry (1979), and carries over to our more complicated model. For particular utility functions, however, at least some of these effects can be shown to have unambiguous signs. For instance, Isachsen and Strøm (1980) analysed the influence of wages and the marginal tax rate on labor supply in the official and the underground economy for a model with a logarithmic utility function under some additional restrictions.

Here we refrain from specifying a particular functional form of the utility function, but use an additive separable one which is twice differentiable with respect to each argument. This is similar to the approach used by Andersen (1977), but differs from his analysis in its incorporation of two kinds of labor. That is, we assume

$$U_{yS^o} = U_{yS^u} = U_{S^oS^u} = 0, \tag{18}$$

together with usual concavity assumptions $U_y > 0$, $U_{yy} < 0$, $U_{S^o} < 0$, $U_{S^oS^o} < 0$, $U_{S^u} < 0$, $U_{S^uS^u} < 0$. Needless to say, the separability assumption is rather restrictive, in particular for the two kinds of labor, but without it (i.e., in the presence of mixed second-order partial derivatives) no sufficiently simple results can be derived.[9] For the following analysis we also assume $0 < t_1 < 1$ and $t_2 \leq 1$; the latter condition means that no more than the total income obtained from black-market activities must be paid as a penalty in case of detection. We consider only an interior maximum of the utility function. The necessary conditions (12) and (13), are simplified by replacing $E[U_{S^o}]$ and $E[U_{S^u}]$ by U_{S^o} and U_{S^u}, respectively. As is shown in Appendix 3, the sufficient conditions for a strict local maximum are fulfilled, hence the necessary conditions give a maximum indeed. Implicit differentiation of (12) and (13) with respect to any parameter gives the comparative-static effects of changing this parameter on labor supply in the official and the shadow economy, ceteris paribus.

---

[9] An attractive alternative is considered by Cowell (1985, 1989): by specifying another special utility function, he separates the leisure-work and the official-underground choice problems, which otherwise must be solved simultaneously for the household.

For the six parameters, we get the following results:

Effects on endogenous variables

Changes of parameters	S^o	S^u
p	$+$	$-^{*)}$
t_o	$-$	$-$
t_1	?	$+$
t_2	$+$	$-^{*)}$
W^o	?	$-$
W^u	$-$	?

$*)$ under additional assumptions, specified in Appendix 3

? implies ambiguity, due to different signs of substitution and income effects

The details of the resulting mathematical expressions are given in Appendix 3.

These results can be interpreted as follows: the amount of labor supplied in the official economy S^o is higher, ceteris paribus, the higher the probability of detection p, the lower the minimum-income transfer t_o, the higher the penalty rate t_2 and the lower the wage rate in the shadow economy W^u; the amount of labor supplied in the shadow economy S^u is higher, ceteris paribus, the lower the minimum-income transfer t_o, the higher the marginal tax rate t_1 and the lower the wage rate in the official economy W^o. For sufficiently high values of the penalty tax rate, an increase in the detection probability p or in the penalty rate t_2 will reduce the labor supply to the underground economy. The effects of the marginal tax rate and of the official-economy wage rate on official labor supply and the effects of the shadow economy wage rate on the underground labor supply are indeterminate due to the different signs of the substitution and income effects. It is remarkable that specific assumptions about risk aversion beyond those made about the concavity of the utility function are not helpful in obtaining more definitive results of comparative-static effects in the present model. In this respect the model differs from the simpler models of Allingham and Sandmo (1972) and Andersen (1977). This is due to the multidimensional nature of the problem, with y, S^o and S^u representing separate arguments in the utility function; therefore, the labor-supply decision and the portfolio-allocation problem between official (riskless) and underground (risky) activities cannot be separated (cf. Cowell, 1989). Although the risk aversion properties of the utility function are implicitly contained in the resulting comparative-static expressions, the direct

The Consequences of Progressive Income Taxation for the Shadow Economy 159

connection between them and decreasing or increasing (absolute and relative) risk aversion is eliminated. Our results thus confirm the conclusions obtained by other authors (Andersen, 1977; Baldry, 1979; Pencavel, 1979; Cowell, 1989) about the non-robustness of the Allingham–Sandmo results in the context of a model with a labor market.[10]

So far we have been concerned merely with the household's labor supply decision; however, within the framework of our model, it is also necessary to deal with the household's demand for official and shadow market goods. One possible way to do so is to regard the former decision as independent of the latter, as we have assumed so far. This amounts to a two-stage decision procedure of the household: at the first stage, the household decides how to allocate its time among labor supply in the official and the shadow economy and leisure. This is a decision problem under uncertainty, which results in disposable income y_1 or y_2, depending upon whether working in the underground economy is not or is detected. Given the actually realized income, at the second stage the household decides upon the allocation of that realized income between demand for official and underground goods. This is now a deterministic problem, because at this stage the household knows for certain both its income and the market prices of the two goods. Here we assume that the household will not be punished for buying underground goods, even if such a transaction is detected by the government; only firms will be held responsible in such a case. Therefore the second-stage decision problem of the household can be modeled as follows: the household has a utility function depending on the quantities consumed of each of the two goods. It maximizes this utility function, say V, with respect to the demand for official and underground goods, subject to a budget constraint which depends on its realized income. This, in turn, depends upon its labor supply decision from the first stage and upon whether its income tax evasion (working in the shadow economy) has been detected or not. This second-stage decision results in the household's demand for the two goods under consideration.

Therefore, in situation 1 (income tax evasion is not detected), the household maximizes

$$V[d^o, d^u] \tag{19}$$

with respect to d^o and d^u, for given S^o and S^u, subject to

---

[10] Under alternative model specifications, even opposite effects of the marginal tax rate on underground labor supply may be present, as is shown by Wiegard (1984) for a model which differs from ours only by a utility function defined over the total labor supply instead of the two different kinds of labor supply.

$$y_1 = W^o S^o (1 - t_1) + t_o + W^u S^u \geq d^o P^o + d^u P^u, \tag{20}$$

$$d^o \geq 0, \qquad d^u \geq 0. \tag{21}$$

As long as the household is not satiated with respect to either good, the marginal utilities are positive, hence the non-negativity constraints are not binding. This implies that some of at least one good is consumed and total income y_1 is spent. For given (constant) prices and given labor supplies, the necessary conditions for an optimum yield the familiar tangency condition for the consumer:

$$V_{d^o} / V_{d^u} = P^o / P^u, \tag{22}$$

meaning that the marginal rate of substitution between official and underground goods must be equal to the ratio of their prices. If the utility function V is concave, these necessary conditions are also sufficient for a global maximum.

From the necessary conditions we express the demand functions for situation 1 for given income y_1 as

$$d^o = d^o(P^o, P^u, y_1), \tag{23}$$

$$d^u = d^u(P^o, P^u, y_1), \tag{24}$$

given S^o and S^u. The particular form of the demand functions depends on the utility function V. Exactly the same reasoning leads to the necessary conditions for a utility maximum in situation 2, with (20) replaced by

$$y_2 = W^o S^o (1 - t_1) + t_o + W^u S^u (1 - t_2) = d^o P^o + d^u P^u. \tag{25}$$

The resulting demand functions have the same form as (23) and (24), with y_2 substituted for y_1. The comparative-static effects of P^o, P^u and the parameters of y_1 and y_2 (including S^o and S^u) on d^o and d^u can be determined in exactly the same way as in the usual theory of consumer's demand. Due to the familiar tension between the substitution and income effects, the signs of these expressions are undetermined in the general case and can be made unambiguous only by imposing additional restrictions on the utility function V, such as additive separability.

The two-step solution developed here may be criticized for not taking into account the simultaneous nature of the labor-supply and goods-demand decision of the household. In particular, one can argue that the household already considers its goods-demand decision when planning how to allocate its disposable time. If the

The Consequences of Progressive Income Taxation for the Shadow Economy   161

household in fact has a utility function $UV = UV(d^o, d^u, S^o, S^u)$, which depends on the quantities of both goods consumed separately instead of income (as we have assumed for U), and if the composite-commodity theorem is not applicable, then at the first step the household attempts to maximize $E[UV]$ with respect to S^o and S^u, subject to (4) and (5) and subject to its second-stage demand decision, which also depends upon whether income tax evasion is detected or not. If $d^o_i, d^u_i, i = 1, 2$, denote the demands for the two goods contingent upon whether situation 1 or 2 is realized, then, in addition to (4) and (5), the household has to take into account the constraints

$$d^o_1 = d^o_1(P^o, P^u, S^o, S^u), d^u_1 = d^u_1(P^o, P^u, S^o, S^u), \tag{26}$$

$$d^o_2 = d^o_2(P^o, P^u, S^o, S^u), d^u_2 = d^u_2(P^o, P^u, S^o, S^u), \tag{27}$$

which are given in implicit form (assuming an interior optimum for the consumption demand decision) by marginal conditions of the type (22) and the respective budget constraints for situations 1 and 2. The necessary conditions for the labor-supply decision together with (26) and (27) then determine the endogenous variables $S^o, S^u, d^o_i, d^u_i, i = 1, 2$, in implicit form.

Unfortunately, the solution to this combined optimization problem does not give much insight because of the ambiguity of the resulting comparative-static effects. Even for more specific utility functions, clear-cut results as to the signs of the effects of parameter changes on the endogenous variables are rarely obtained. The simultaneity of the household's consumption and labor-supply decisions thus complicates the determination of the labor-supply and goods-demand functions considerably. We have to conclude that the theoretically superior simultaneous solution leaves the influence of taxes, wages and prices on the extent of the household's shadow economy activities basically undetermined, although in the two-step treatment of its decision problem qualitative predictions of these effects can be made when involving some additional assumptions.

4. Determinants of Firm's Shadow Economy Activities

In examing the decision problem of the representative firm, we assume that the firm is a risk-neutral decision-maker, choosing simultaneously the demand for labor (both official and underground) and the supply of goods in both markets by maximizing its expected profit in the short run. The long-run problem of determining the demand for other factors of production (in particular, the capital stock) is neglected. By assuming the special production possibilities of the firm expressed by separate production functions for official and shadow economy goods, we can simplify the simultaneity problem arising here as well. In particular, we assume that the firm is faced with two production functions:

$$s^o = f(D^o, K), \tag{28}$$

$$s^u = g(D^u, K). \tag{29}$$

Denoting profit by π, from Appendix 2 it is easy to see that the firm's problem is to maximize $E[\pi]$ with respect to s^o, s^u, D^o, D^u, subject to (28), (29), and

$$D^o \geq 0, \ D^u \geq 0, \ s^o \geq 0, \ s^u \geq 0. \tag{30}$$

We assume the production functions $f(D^o, \overline{K})$, $g(D^u, \overline{K})$ to be twice differentiable with respect to their first arguments, and $f_{D^o} > 0$, $f_{D^o D^o} < 0$, $g_{D^u} > 0$, $g_{D^u D^u} < 0$, $f(0) = 0$, $g(0) = 0$, $f(D^o) > 0$ for $D^o > 0$, $g(D^u) > 0$ for $D^u > 0$.

Disregarding the possibility of corner solutions for the goods-supply decision at the moment, the problem becomes to maximize

$$E[\pi] = f(D^o, \overline{K})P^o(1-t) + g(D^u, \overline{K})P^u(1-qt_3) - W^o D^o - W^u D^u - C(\overline{K}) \tag{31}$$

with respect to D^o and D^u, subject to the non-negativity of the latter two variables. Necessary conditions are:

$$f_{D^o} P^o(1-t) - W^o \leq 0, \tag{32}$$

$$g_{D^u} P^u(1-qt_3) - W^u \leq 0, \tag{33}$$

$$D^o \geq 0, D^o \cdot \frac{\partial E[\pi]}{\partial D^o} = 0; \ D^u \geq 0, D^u \cdot \frac{\partial E[\pi]}{\partial D^u} = 0. \tag{34}$$

For an interior maximum, we must have

$$f_{D^o} = \frac{W^o}{P^o(1-t)}, \tag{35}$$

$$g_{D^u} = \frac{W^u}{P^u(1-qt_3)}. \tag{36}$$

These conditions say that the marginal productivity for official (underground) good production by official (underground) labor must be equal to the real wage rate in the official (underground) labor market, deflated by the (expected) after-tax price in the official (underground) goods market.

Sufficient second-order conditions for a maximum are

$$f_{D^o D^o} P^o (1 - t) < 0, \tag{37}$$

$$g_{D^u D^u} P^u (1 - q t_3) < 0. \tag{38}$$

Under our concavity conditions for the production function, (37) is equivalent to $1 - t > 0$, which is always fulfilled for finite indirect tax rates $\tau < \infty$, and (38) is equivalent to $1 - q t_3 > 0$, which means that the expected penalty for indirect-tax evasion is less than the revenue from selling underground goods. If the latter condition is not fulfilled, i.e., if $q t_3 > 1$, then $D^u = s^u = 0$, and the firm will not engage in underground activities at all. Thus, a sufficiently high probability of detecting black-market activities of the firm and/or a high penalty rate may prevent firms' shadow economy activities. In the following, we assume the interior solution to hold, i.e., the firm engages both in official and shadow activities.

In contrast to the model of the household, the model of the firm gives definite qualitative comparative-static results, given the above assumptions about the production functions (positive diminishing marginal productivities). This is due to the separation of the firm's decisions regarding the two markets. This would no longer be true if interactions between official and underground production were taken into account. The necessary conditions (35) and (36) are implicit expressions for the two labor-demand functions of the firm. Implicit differentiation with respect to the parameters establish the following comparative-static results, which are derived under the assumption $q t_3 < 1$:

Effects on endogenous variables

Changes of parameters	D^o	D^u	n
q	0	−	−
t	−	0	+
t_3	0	−	−
P^o	+	0	−
P^u	0	+	+
W^o	−	0	+
W^u	0	−	−

Here, $n = D^u / D^o$ is the relation of underground to official labor demanded, which is a measure of the relative extent of the shadow economy. The details of the resulting comparative-static expressions are given in Appendix 4. The same qualitative results are obtained if s^o is substituted for D^o, s^u for D^u, and s^u/s^o for n, respectively, where the latter ratio is an alternative (goods market) measure of the relative size of the shadow economy.

To check for the possibility of corner solutions, one must find positive values of D^o and D^u such that (35) and (36) are fulfilled, respectively; otherwise, $D^o = 0$ and $D^u = 0$, respectively. Finally, the firm's decision must fulfill the following conditions for $D^o > 0$ ($s^o > 0$) and $D^u > 0$ ($s^u > 0$):

$$f(D^o, \overline{K}) \quad P^o(1-t) - W^o D^o \geq 0, \qquad (39)$$

$$g(D^u, \overline{K}) \quad P^u(1-qt_3) - W^u D^u \geq 0. \qquad (40)$$

That is, in the short run (expected) revenues have to be no less than variable costs, otherwise the firm will close down the respective production activity and only incur losses of $C(\overline{K})$. For some special production functions, as for example the Cobb-Douglas production function, these conditions are equivalent to those for $D^o > 0$ and $D^u > 0$; in general, they must be fulfilled in addition to those already derived.

In economic terms, our results for the production sector can be interpreted as follows: if expected revenues cover at least the variable costs of the respective (official and underground) production, the firm always engages in the production of official goods in the short run in our model, and it engages in the production of shadow economy goods if and only if the expected penalty for indirect tax evasion is less than the revenue from its sales of underground goods. In this case, i.e., if we have an interior optimum for the firm's profit-maximization problem, the absolute and the relative extent of the firm's shadow economy activities (measured either by its demand for labor or its supply of goods in the underground sector) will be higher, ceteris paribus, the lower the detection probability q and the lower the penalty rate t_3 for indirect tax evasion, the lower the shadow economy wage rate W^u, and the higher the shadow economy price P^u. In addition, the relative extent of the firm's shadow economy activities as compared to its official economy activities will be higher, ceteris paribus, the lower the official economy price P^o, the higher the official economy wage rate W^o, and the higher the indirect tax rate t. All of these results hold only under our separability assumption and do not generalize to joint production functions for official and underground goods; moreover, they hold only in the short run, where no interaction between the two production activities via the determination of the other factors of production (K) can occur. Although all of the sensitivities which we have derived are consistent

5. Some Conclusions from the Theoretical Model

In Section 3 we investigated the determinants of the household's supply of underground labor and its demand for underground goods. Among other results, it has been shown that, at least under an additive-separable utility function and with the two-stage decision of the consumer, higher marginal income tax rates imply a higher supply of underground labor, and higher wage rates in the official economy imply a lower supply of underground labor. In Section 4, on the other hand, we have shown that the firm's demand for underground labor and supply of underground goods depend positively on the indirect tax rate and on the wage rate in the official economy, at least under the assumption of fixed non-human factors of production and separate production functions for official and underground goods. Disregarding other factors influencing the extent of the shadow economy, one can conjecture that in partial equilibrium higher indirect tax rates and higher marginal income tax rates tend to raise the amounts of labor and goods bought and sold in the underground sector. Official sector wage rate changes may have a positive or a negative influence on the equilibrium amount of underground labor, depending upon whether demand or supply changes dominate. In addition, the equilibrium quantities of shadow economy labor and goods also depend on other variables like penalty rates and detection probabilities for tax evasion, which are to some extent under the control of the government.

One must, however, be very careful not to draw premature policy conclusions from the present model. First, the qualitative comparative-static results have been derived only under special assumptions and do not generalize to arbitrary utility and production functions. Second, we have concentrated on the determinants of the quantities of goods and labor supplied and demanded by individual firms and households and have not presented a rigorous analysis of market equilibrium conditions. The present model ought to be closed by putting individual decision-makers into the context of a general equilibrium model, which in our case would consist of at least two labor markets and two goods markets, the official and shadow markets in each case. Only in such a theoretical framework could all spillovers be analysed appropriately, and prices and wages, which have been assumed to be given for the individual transactors, could then be determined endogenously. Obviously, the equilibrium conditions are

$$S^o = D^o, \ S^u = D^u, \ s^o = d^o, \ s^u = d^u. \tag{41}$$

A theoretical analysis would require determining the conditions for existence of a general equilibrium, where the possibility of corner solutions would complicate matters considerably. Even our very simple and special model does not give definite answers as to comparative-static effects of parameter changes on the general equilibrium values of prices and quantities in the goods and labor markets without further restrictive assumptions, in particular on the utility and production functions. Another reason to be cautious about the results obtained from the present model are the aggregation problems which arise if more than one representative household and firm are introduced. In particular, under a progressive income tax system such as ours, regarding all consumers as identical does not make much sense in a general equilibrium analysis, because one of the primary purposes of income tax progression is the redistribution of incomes between consumers of different living standards. From a theoretical point of view, further restrictions of our model are its ommision of strategic reactions of the decision-makers, especially to government actions, which will be relevant in a context involving illegal activities such as tax evasion, and its short-run, static character.

The foregoing remarks are especially important if one wants to study in more detail the effects of the progression of the tax system on the extent of the shadow economy. Our linear income tax is progressive as it implies average tax rates rising with income for all levels of income. As is well known, several alternative measures exist for the degree of progression of an income tax. Each of these may depend on the parameters of the tax function in a different way. Even for our simple linear income tax, it is not clear whether an increase in the marginal tax rate t_1 implies ceteris paribus lower, higher or unchanged progression. Under residual-income progression, which is most relevant for redistributive considerations (Jacobsson, 1976), a higher marginal tax rate means a higher degree of progression, ceteris paribus. Since such a change in our model implies a higher amount of shadow economy labor supply, one may be tempted to conclude that a higher degree of income tax progression will be associated with a higher extent of the shadow economy. This argument, however, neglects the possibility of changes in the degree of income tax progression by changes in t_o, which work in the opposite direction in our model. This ambiguity arises even if the household is considered in isolation, i.e., without taking into account general equilibrium feedbacks. The reason for this is the following: making the tax system more progressive by simultaneously increasing the marginal tax rate t_1 and the lump-sum transfer t_o, leads both to a labor supply effect (less labor is supplied, ceteris paribus) and to a portfolio allocation effect (more risky activities are demanded, i.e., the relative amount of labor supplied in the underground economy rises). Participating in the underground economy involves both of these effects (Cowell, 1989).

On a more general level, an analysis of the effects of the degree of progression on the shadow economy has to take into account differences of reactions across consumers with respect to their total and official economy labor supply. For a model with non-identical households, Sandmo (1983) has shown that under a linear income tax, in most (but not all) cases higher progression (in the sense of simultaneously higher t_1 and t_o) means lower total labor supply. However, the differential effects on official and underground labor supply so far seem to be an open question, which could be appropriately treated in a general equilibrium model with official and underground markets for labor and goods and with different types of consumers. A theoretical model of this kind is, however, not available at the present time.

To analyse the substitution, income and redistribution effects arising from changes in the tax rates, a general equilibrium model seems to be the first choice. Since some of these effects, such as those of changes in the wage rate, are unlikely to be unambiguously predictable using only theoretical considerations, an empirical model is desirable. While applied general equilibrium models based on microeconomic data have been used successfully to analyse tax policy problems in the United States (cf. Shoven and Whalley, 1984), they do not distinguish between the official and the underground markets; moreover, the data requirements for building such models are rather severe. As a "second-best" solution to this problem, studying the determinants of the shadow economy within a macroeconometric model may facilitate obtaining quantitative information about the effects of changes in the tax system, especially the progressive income tax, on the shadow economy and the feedback effects on the official economy. A macroeconometric model has also the advantage of being able to include sectors and relations which had to be neglected in the theoretical analysis, such as the foreign sector and investment. These advantages may outweigh the drawbacks of such a model, which include its inevitable ad-hoc character and the weak theoretical foundations for some empirically well-established relations. Such an analysis is presented in the paper by Schneider et al. in this volume.

6. Appendices

Appendix 1:
The Household's Choice Situation in the Labor and Goods Markets

	Situation 1: working in the shadow economy is not detected	Situation 2: working in the shadow economy is detected
probability	$1 - p$	p
disposable income from work	$W^o S^o + t_o - t_1 W^o S^o + + W^u S^u = y_1(S^o, S^u)$	$W^o S^o + t_o - t_1 W^o S^o + + W^u S^u - t_2 W^u S^u = = y_2(S^o, S^u)$
utility from labor market decision	$U[y_1, S^o, S^u]$	$U[y_2, S^o, S^u]$
utility from goods market decision	$V[d^o, d^u]$ $y_1 = y_1(S^o, S^u) \geq \geq d^o P^o + d^u P^u$	$V[d^o, d^u]$ $y_2 = y_2(S^o, S^u) \geq \geq d^o P^o + d^u P^u$

Appendix 2:
The Firm's Choice Situation

	Situation 1: selling goods in the shadow economy is not detected	Situation 2: selling goods in the shadow economy is detected
probability	$1 - q$	q
revenues	$s^o P^o + s^u P^u$	$s^o P^o + s^u P^u$
costs	$W^o D^o + t s^o P^o + + W^u D^u + C(\overline{K})$	$W^o D^o + t s^o P^o + W^u D^u + + t_3 s^u P^u + C(\overline{K})$
profit	$s^o P^o + s^u P^u - W^o D^o - - t s^o P^o - W^u D^u - C(\overline{K})$	$s^o P^o + s^u P^u - W^o D^o - - t s^o P^o - W^u D^u - - t_3 s^u P^u - C(\overline{K})$

The Consequences of Progressive Income Taxation for the Shadow Economy

Appendix 3:
Comparative-Static Effects of Changes in the Model Parameters on Labor Supplied in the Official and the Shadow Economy

The necessary first-order conditions (12) and (13) can be written as

$$F_1(S^o, S^u, \underline{\xi}) = 0, \tag{A1}$$

$$F_2(S^o, S^u, \underline{\xi}) = 0, \tag{A2}$$

where $\underline{\xi} = (p, t_o, t_1, t_2, W^o, W^u)$ is the vector of the parameters of the model. The principal minors of the Hessian matrix of this system alternate in sign, because

$$\partial F_1/\partial S^o = (W^o)^2(1 - t_1)^2 E[U_{yy}] + U_{S^o S^o} < 0, \tag{A3}$$

$$\partial F_2/\partial S^o = \partial F_1/\partial S^u = W^o(1 - t_1)W^u E[U_{yy}(1 - t_2')], \tag{A4}$$

$$\partial F_2/\partial S^u = (W^u)^2 E[U_{yy}(1 - t_2')^2] + U_{S^u S^u}, \tag{A5}$$

and

$$\begin{aligned} \Delta = (\partial F_1/\partial S^o) \cdot (\partial F_2/\partial S^u) - (\partial F_1/\partial S^u) \cdot (\partial F_2/\partial S^o) = \\ = p(1 - p)U_{yy}(y_1)U_{yy}(y_2)(W^o)^2(W^u)^2(1 - t_1)^2 t_2^2 + \\ + U_{S^o S^o}U_{S^u S^u} + (W^o)^2(1 - t_1)^2 U_{S^u S^u} E[U_{yy}] + \\ + (W^u)^2 U_{S^o S^o} E[U_{yy}(1 - t_2')^2] > 0. \end{aligned} \tag{A6}$$

The comparative-static effects of changes of an element of $\underline{\xi}$, say ξ, on labor supply in the official and the shadow economy are determined according to

$$\partial S^o/\partial \xi = (1/\Delta) \cdot [\partial F_1/\partial S^u \cdot \partial F_2/\partial \xi - \partial F_2/\partial S^u \cdot \partial F_1/\partial \xi], \tag{A7}$$

$$\partial S^u/\partial \xi = (1/\Delta) \cdot [\partial F_2/\partial S^o \cdot \partial F_1/\partial \xi - \partial F_1/\partial S^o \cdot \partial F_2/\partial \xi]. \tag{A8}$$

For the six parameters, we obtain the following results:

$$\begin{aligned} \partial S^o/\partial p = -(1/\Delta) \cdot W^o(1 - t_1)\{[U_y(y_2) - U_y(y_1)]U_{S^u S^u} + \\ + (W^u)^2 t_2[(1 - p)U_{yy}(y_1)U_y(y_2) + p(1 - t_2)U_{yy}(y_2)U_y(y_1)]\} > 0, \end{aligned} \tag{A9}$$

because $y_1 > y_2$;

$$\partial S^u/\partial p = -(1/\Delta) \cdot \{W^u[U_y(y_2)(1-t_2) - U_y(y_1)]U_{S^\circ S^\circ} - \\ - (W^\circ)^2 W^u(1-t_1)^2 t_2[(1-p)U_{yy}(y_1)U_y(y_2) + pU_{yy}(y_2)U_y(y_1)]\}, \tag{A10}$$

which is negative, at least for $t_2 > 1 - U_y(y_1)/U_y(y_2)$, but may be positive for "small" values of t_2;

$$\partial S^\circ/\partial t_o = -(W^\circ/\Delta) \cdot (1-t_1) \cdot \{(W^u)^2 t_2^2 p(1-p)U_{yy}(y_1)U_{yy}(y_2) + \\ + E[U_{yy}]U_{S^u S^u}\} < 0; \tag{A11}$$

$$\partial S^u/\partial t_o = -(W^u/\Delta) \cdot U_{S^\circ S^\circ} E[U_{yy}(1-t_2')] < 0; \tag{A12}$$

$$\partial S^\circ/\partial t_1 = (1/\Delta)\{(W^\circ)^2 S^\circ (1-t_1)[(W^u)^2 t_2^2 p(1-p)U_{yy}(y_1)U_{yy}(y_2) + \\ + U_{S^u S^u} E[U_{yy}]] + W^\circ E[U_y][(W^u)^2 E[U_{yy}(1-t_2')^2] + U_{S^u S^u}]\}, \tag{A13}$$

where the first two terms are positive and may be interpreted as income effects, and the last two terms are negative and may be interpreted as substitution effects, hence the entire expression is ambiguous with respect to its sign;

$$\partial S^u/\partial t_1 = (W^\circ W^u/\Delta) \cdot E[U_{yy}(1-t_2')]\{S^\circ U_{S^\circ S^\circ} - W^\circ (1-t_1)E[U_y]\} > 0; \tag{A14}$$

$$\partial S^\circ/\partial t_2 = (1/\Delta) \cdot W^\circ W^u(1-t_1)p\{(W^u)^2 S^u t_2(1-p)U_{yy}(y_1)U_{yy}(y_2) + \\ + S^u U_{S^u S^u} U_{yy}(y_2) - W^u U_y(y_2)E[U_{yy}(1-t_2')]\} > 0; \tag{A15}$$

$$\partial S^u/\partial t_2 = (W^u/\Delta) \cdot p\{U_{yy}(y_2)W^u S^u[(1-t_2)U_{S^\circ S^\circ} - (W^\circ)(1-t_1)^2 \cdot \\ \cdot (1-p)t_2 U_{yy}(y_1)] + U_y(y_2)(W^\circ)^2(1-t_1)^2 E[U_{yy}] + U_y(y_2)U_{S^\circ S^\circ}\}, \tag{A16}$$

which is negative except for very large values of $| (1-t_2)U_{S^u S^u} |$ (this term expresses again some kind of an income effect);

The Consequences of Progressive Income Taxation for the Shadow Economy 171

$$\partial S^o/\partial W^o = -(1/\Delta)\{(1-t_1)E[U_y]\cdot[(W^u)^2E[U_{yy}(1-t_2')^2]+U_{S^uS^u}]+$$
$$+W^oS^o(1-t_1)^2[(W^u)^2t_2^2p(1-p)U_{yy}(y_1)U_{yy}(y_2)+U_{S^uS^u}E[U_{yy}]]\}, \qquad (A17)$$

which also has an indeterminate sign, with the first two terms being positive (expressing substitution effects), and the last two terms being negative (expressing income effects);

$$\partial S^u/\partial W^o = (W^u/\Delta)\cdot(1-t_1)\{W^o(1-t_1)E[U_y]-U_{S^oS^o}S^o\}E[U_{yy}(1-t_2')] < 0; \qquad (A18)$$

$$\partial S^o/\partial W^u = (W^o/\Delta)\cdot(1-t_1)\{W^uE[U_y(1-t_2')]-U_{S^uS^u}S^u\}E[U_{yy}(1-t_2')] < 0; \qquad (A19)$$

$$\partial S^u/\partial W^u = -(1/\Delta)\cdot\{E[U_y(1-t_2')]\cdot[(W^o)^2(1-t_1)^2E[U_{yy}]+U_{S^oS^o}]+$$
$$+W^uS^u[(W^o)^2(1-t_1)^2t_2^2p(1-p)U_{yy}(y_1)U_{yy}(y_2)+U_{S^oS^o}E[U_{yy}(1-t_2')^2]]\}, \qquad (A20)$$

where the first two terms are positive (substitution effects) and the last two terms are negative (income effects), hence the sign remains undetermined.

Appendix 4:
Comparative-Static Effects of Changes in the Model Parameters on Labor Demanded and Goods Supplied in the Official and the Underground Economy

Implicit differentiation of (35) and (36) with respect to the parameters gives:

$$\partial D^o/\partial q = \partial D^u/\partial t = \partial D^o/\partial t_3 = \partial D^u/\partial P^o = \partial D^o/\partial P^u =$$
$$= \partial D^u/\partial W^o = \partial D^o/\partial W^u = 0; \qquad (A21)$$

$$\partial D^u/\partial q = t_3 g_{D^u}/[g_{D^u D^u}(1 - qt_3)] < 0; \qquad (A22)$$

$$\partial D^o/\partial t = f_{D^o}/[f_{D^o D^o}(1 - t)] < 0; \qquad (A23)$$

$$\partial D^u/\partial t_3 = qg_{D^u}/[g_{D^u D^u}(1 - qt_3)] < 0; \qquad (A24)$$

$$\partial D^o/\partial P^o = -f_{D^o}/(f_{D^o D^o}P^o) > 0; \qquad (A25)$$

$$\partial D^u/\partial P^u = -g_{D^u}/(g_{D^u D^u}P^u) > 0; \qquad (A26)$$

$$\partial D^o/\partial W^o = 1/[f_{D^o D^o}P^o(1 - t)] < 0; \qquad (A27)$$

$$\partial D^u/\partial W^u = 1/[g_{D^u D^u}P^u(1 - qt_3)] < 0. \qquad (A28)$$

The effects of a change in any parameter, say ς, on n can be determined from

$$\partial n/\partial \varsigma = (\partial D^u/\partial \varsigma) \cdot (n/D^u) - (\partial D^o/\partial \varsigma) \cdot (n/D^o), \qquad (A29)$$

from which the results given in the text follow in a straightforward way. The supply functions for official and underground goods are given by (28) and (29), with D^o and D^u determined from (35) and (36), respectively. Therefore, it is obvious that the effects of parameter changes on s^o and s^u have the same signs as those on D^o and D^u, respectively. In fact, they are given by

$$\partial s^o/\partial \varsigma = f_{D^o} \cdot (\partial D^o/\partial \varsigma), \ \partial s^u/\partial \varsigma = g_{D^u}(\partial D^u/\partial \varsigma). \qquad (A30)$$

Note that s^o is independent of q, t_3, W^u, P^u and the parameters of g, and that s^u is independent of t, W^o, P^o and the parameters of f.

7. References

Allingham, M.G., and **Sandmo, A.** (1972): "Income Tax Evasion: A Theoretical Analysis." *Journal of Public Economics* 1: 323–338.

Andersen, P. (1977): "Tax Evasion and Labor Supply." *Scandinavian Journal of Economics* 79: 375–383.

Baldry, J.C. (1979): "Tax Evasion and Labour Supply." *Economics Letters* 3: 53–56.

Büchner, H.-J. (1987): "Der Einfluß der Steuerhinterziehung auf direkte und indirekte Steuern." Discussion Paper No. A–100, Sonderforschungsbereich 303, University of Bonn.

Christiansen, V. (1980): "Two Comments on Tax Evasion." *Journal of Public Economics* 13: 389–393.

Clotfelter, Ch.T. (1983): "Tax Evasion and Tax Rates: An Analysis of Individual Returns." *Review of Economics and Statistics* 65: 363–373.

Cowell, F.A. (1981): "Taxation and Labour Supply with Risk Activities." *Economica* 48: 365–379.

Cowell, F.A. (1985): "Tax Evasion with Labour Income." *Journal of Public Economics* 26: 19–34.

Cowell, F.A. (1987): "Honesty is Sometimes the Best Policy." Discussion Paper No. TIDI/107, ESRC Programme, London School of Economics and Political Science.

Cowell, F.A. (1988): "Tax Sheltering and the Cost of Evasion." Discussion Paper No. TIDI/119, ESRC Programme, London School of Economics and Political Science.

Cowell, F.A. (1989): *Cheating the Government. The Economics of Evasion.* Cambridge, Mass.: MIT Press.

Cowell, F.A., and **Gordon, J.P.F.** (1988): "Unwillingness to Pay: Tax Evasion and Public Good Provision." *Journal of Public Economics* 36: 305–321.

Crane, S.E., and **Nourzad, F.** (1985): "Time Value of Money and Income Tax Evasion under Risk-Averse Behavior: Theoretical Analysis and Empirical Evidence." *Public Finance* 40: 381–394.

Crane, S.E., and **Nourzad, F.** (1986): "Inflation and Tax Evasion: An Empirical Analysis." *Review of Economics and Statistics* 68: 217–223.

Crane, S.E., and **Nourzad, F.** (1987): "On the Treatment of Income Tax Rates in Empirical Analysis of Tax Reform." *Kyklos* 40: 338–348.

Cross, R., and **Shaw, G.K.** (1982): "On the Economics of Tax Aversion." *Public Finance* 37: 36–47.

Dubin, J.A., Graetz, M.J., and **Wilde, L.L.** (1987): "Are We a Nation of Tax Cheaters? New Econometric Evidence on Tax Compliance." *American Economic Review, Paper and Proceedings* 77: 240–245.

Frey, B.S., and **Pommerehne, W.W.** (1984): "The Hidden Economy: State and Prospects for Measurement." *Review of Income and Wealth* 30: 1–23.

Friedland, N., Maital, S., and **Rutenberg, A.** (1978): "A Simulation Study of Income Tax Evasion." *Journal of Public Economics* 10: 107–116.

Gaertner, W., and **Wenig, A.** (eds.) (1985): *The Economics of the Shadow Economy*, Heidelberg: Springer-Verlag.

Geeroms, H., and **Wilmots, H.** (1985): "An Empirical Model of Tax Evasion and Tax Avoidance." *Public Finance* 40: 190–209.

Graetz, M.J., Reinganum, J.F., and **Wilde, L.L.** (1986): "The Tax Compliance Game: Toward an Interactive Theory of Law Enforcement." *Journal of Law, Economics and Organization* 2: 1–32.

Greenberg, J. (1984): "Avoiding Tax Avoidance: A (Repeated) Game-Theoretic Approach." *Journal of Economic Theory* 32: 1–13.

Isachsen, A.J., and **Strøm, S.** (1980): "The Hidden Economy: The Labor Market and Tax Evasion." *Scandinavian Journal of Economics* 82: 304–311.

Jacobsson, U. (1976): "On the Measurement of the Degree of Progression." *Journal of Public Economics* 5: 161–168.

Kolm, S.-C. (1973): "A Note on Optimum Tax Evasion." *Journal of Public Economics* 2: 265–270.

Koskela, E. (1983): "On the Shape of Tax Schedules, the Probability of Detection, and the Penalty Schemes as Deterrents to Tax Evasion." *Public Finance* 38: 70–80.

Koskela, E. (1983a): "A Note on Progression, Penalty Schemes and Tax Evasion." *Journal of Public Economics* 22: 127–133.

Lewis, A. (1979): "An Empirical Assessment of Tax Mentality." *Public Finance* 34: 245–257.

McCaleb, T.S. (1976): "Tax Evasion and the Differential Taxation of Labor and Capital Income." *Public Finance* 31: 287–294.

Mork, K.A. (1975): "Income Tax Evasion: Some Empirical Evidence." *Public Finance* 30: 70–76.

Nayak, P.B. (1978): "Optimal Income Tax Evasion and Regressive Taxes." *Public Finance* 33: 358–366.

Nitzan, S., and **Tzur, J.** (1987): "Taxpayers, Auditors and the Government – An Extended Tax Evasion Game." Discussion Paper No. A–105, Sonderforschungsbereich 303, University of Bonn.

Pencavel, J.H. (1979): "A Note on Income Tax Evasion, Labor Supply and Non-linear Tax Schedules." *Journal of Public Economics* 12: 115–124.

Poterba, J.M. (1987): "Tax Evasion and Capital Gains Taxation." *American Economic Review, Papers and Proceedings* 77: 234–239.

Reinganum, J.F., and **Wilde, L.L.** (1985): "Income Tax Compliance in a Principal-Agent Framework." *Journal of Public Economics* 26: 1–18.

Reinganum, J.F., and **Wilde, L.L.** (1986): "Equilibrium Verification and Reporting Policies in a Model of Tax Compliance." *International Economic Review* 27: 739–760.

Sandmo, A. (1981): "Income Tax Evasion, Labour Supply, and the Equity-Efficiency Tradeoff." *Journal of Public Economics* 16: 265–288.

Sandmo, A. (1983): "Progressive Taxation, Redistribution, and Labor Supply." *Scandinavian Journal of Economics* 85: 311–323.

Schneider, F., and **Hofreither, M.F.** (1987): "The Effects of a Changing Shadow Economy on the Official Economy: First Results with a Small Econometric Model." Discussion Paper, University of Linz.

Shoven, J.B., and **Whalley, J.** (1984): "Applied General-Equilibrium Models of Taxation and International Trade: An Introduction and Survey." *Journal of Economic Literature* 22: 1007–1051.

Singh, B. (1973): "Making Honesty the Best Policy." *Journal of Public Economics* 2: 257–263.

Slemrod, J., and **Yitzhaki, S.** (1987): "The Optimal Size of a Tax Collection Agency." *Scandinavian Journal of Economics* 89: 183–192.

Spicer, M.W., and **Hero, R.E.** (1985): "Tax Evasion and Heuristics. A Research Note." *Journal of Public Economics* 26: 263–267.

Spicer, M.W., and **Lundstedt, S.B.** (1976): "Understanding Tax Evasion." *Public Finance* 31: 295–305.

Sproule, R.A. (1985): "Tax Evasion and Labor Supply under Imperfect Information about Individual Parameters of the Tax System." *Public Finance* 40: 441–456.

Sproule, R.A., Komus, D., and **Tsang, E.** (1980): "Optimal Tax Evasion: Risk-Neutral Behaviour under a Negative Income Tax." *Public Finance* 35: 309–317.

Srinivasan, T.N. (1973): "Tax Evasion: A Model." *Journal of Public Economics* 2: 339–346.

Watson, H. (1985): "Tax Evasion and Labor Markets." *Journal of Public Economics* 27: 231–246.

Weck, H., Pommerehne, W.W., and **Frey, B.S.** (1984): *Schattenwirtschaft.* München: Franz Vahlen-Verlag.

Weiss, L. (1976): "The Desirability of Cheating Incentives and Randomness in the Optimal Income Tax." *Journal of Political Economy* 84: 1343–1352.

Wiegard, W. (1984): "Schwarzarbeit und Besteuerung." In *Schattenökonomie,* edited by W. Schäfer. Göttingen: Vandenhoeck & Ruprecht.

Yitzhaki, S. (1974): "A Note on: Income Tax Evasion: A Theoretical Analysis." *Journal of Public Economics* 3: 201–202.

The Consequences of Progressive Income Taxation for the Shadow Economy

Frank A. Cowell, London, UK

The seminal paper of Allingham and Sandmo (1972) characterised the phenomenon of tax evasion as though it were a game of roulette, with the tax loader as an idle gambler and the government – or its tax authority – acting as a rather clumsy croupier. Much of the subsequent literature has been devoted to the development of richer models of the underlying economic problems based on the Allingham–Sandmo insights. The Neck et al. paper in this volume pursues one of the more important themes that have emerged in this literature: and understanding of the role that the underground sector plays in an economy with production is central to many policy questions that are commonly raised in taxation analysis. If we do not know what the linkage is between the public sector and the underground sector, then propositions about the linkages between the public sector and the "official" private sector are likely to be seriously misleading.

The standard approach to this sort of problem is to modify the framework of consumer choice to include decisions about labour supply choice as well as risk-taking: this extension inevitably complicates the formal analysis considerably.

The Neck et al. contribution is to imbed previous analyses of the working tax-evader in a model that has an explicit treatment of the product market as well as the labour market. One might expect that this further development exacerbates the difficulty of deriving interpretable results from an already complicated set-up. Anticipating this, the authors point out, quite rightly, that it has long been recognized that one cannot get very far with comparative static analysis of a combined risk-taking and labour/leisure choice problem without imposing a certain amount of structure on the problem. So, to get specific answers in their more elaborate model, Neck et al. do just that: however, it is appropriate to ask a couple of questions whenever such a step is taken.

First, where does the structure come from? Ideally it should derive from some intrinsically interesting economic feature within the problem rather than from mathematical convenience: it could be that some commonly-observed institutional restriction or an inherent informational complaint imposes patterns of behaviour that conform to a special model structure. Second, what purpose does the structure serve? The simplifications that enable you to tell an elementary "as if" fable clearly may not be the most appropriate for empirical investigation; each

178   Frank A. Cowell

has its role: "as if" tales are often useful in gaining insights on important economic mechanisms and policy questions.

It is my impression that the Neck et al. paper does rather better on the second question than on the first. There are three types of structure in the paper. The first concerns preferences: little can be done without imposing either some sort of separability, or some side condition (such as fixed hours in one of the sectors), although the particular form of separability introduced by the authors seems questionable.[1] The second concerns production in that underground activities constitute almost a distinct sector;[2] this fits many actual situations quite well; working with the firm's equipment on your day off is one example, the Soviet concept of "left-handed" – unofficial – production is another. However it is the third type of structural restriction – which is less explicitly acknowledged by the authors – that I find particularly intriguing.

This restriction concerns the relationship between buyer and seller – a particularly interesting and relatively little explored aspect of the economics of tax evasion. Since many taxes are based upon market transactions, the scope for modifying those transactions through evasion activities is obviously of crucial concern to anyone interested in the effects of taxes. The parties to the transaction may collude; they may strike various types of bargain which share the gains and the risks from evasion; the clandestine nature of the transaction may confer special market power on one or other party. Neck et al. do not go into all this, but one feature of their model – the household demand for goods in the two sectors (d^o, d^u) raised important questions in this area. Let us briefly consider their approach.

Writing the household's utility function for goods demanded as $V[d^o, d^u]$ seems pretty innocuous and unremarkable at first sight. However, why should not the commodities in the two sectors be regarded as perfect substitutes in consumption? After all, a refrigerator is a refrigerator regardless of whether it is bought in the observed or the underground sector. The short answer to this question is that making the commodities perfect substitutes could result in a trivial economic problem. Utility may be written as $v[d^o + d^u]$ and – whether situation 1 or situation 2 obtains (whether he escapes or is caught) – the evader simply buys the commodity from whichever source is cheaper. The more substantial answer acknowledges that physically similar goods or services are not viewed by customers as truly identical across the two sectors.[3] This may be because of a straightforward

---

[1] The third restriction in (18) is especially worrying.
[2] Apart from fixed factors which are "ambidextrous".
[3] See, for example, Cowell and Gordon (1989) who analyse this problem from the producer's point of view.

The Consequences of Progressive Income Taxation for the Shadow Economy 179

quality difference between the sectors – "cowboy" building contractors working for cash, for example. However, to suppose that the source of supply of a commodity automatically alters its quality is not particularly informative or compelling. More interestingly it may be that there is an element of uncertainty which affects the customer, and which is treated in a different way in each sector.

One possibility is that the customer himself may get penalised for receiving "hot" goods. Neck et al. rule this out: the relationship between buyer and seller is such that the seller bears all the risk of the penalties for evasion. Alternatively there may be some risk associated with the product – uncertain quality or reliability for example – which is present regardless of where the product is bought; the point is that this risk is likely to be borne exclusively by the customer if he buys in the underground sector so that apparently identical items bought in different sectors are not treated as perfect substitutes. I may be able to buy the same model of refrigerator in either sector, but if I buy it with an official receipt I am assured that I can take it back should it go wrong. In a trading model of evasion, then, there are two types of risk – product risk and detection risk; one way of interpreting the Neck et al. structure is to say that the relationship between buyers and sellers is such that the seller is assumed to bear all the detection risk, and the buyer bears all the product risk.

The authors hint that their framework may be extended to take account of general equilibrium considerations. This certainly raises interesting issues, but may require that an even more restrictive structure be imposed in order to get worthwhile results. It may actually be more fruitful to develop their insights by considering further one or more of the structural questions which they have already introduced in this paper. In particular it would be interesting to examine in more detail what the consequences of taxation are for the different types of risk-bearing in the shadow economy.

References

Allingham, M.G., and **Sandmo, A.** (1972): "Income Tax Evasion: A Theoretical Analysis." *Journal of Public Economics* 1: 323–338.

Cowell, F.A., and **Gordon, J.P.F.** (1989): "On Becoming a Ghost." TIDI Discussion Paper No. 127, London School of Economics.

The Consequences of a Changing Shadow Economy for the "Official" Economy: Some Empirical Results for Austria

Friedrich Schneider, Markus F. Hofreither, and Reinhard Neck,
Linz, Vienna, Austria[*]

1. Introduction

During the last few years, growing concern about the phenomenon of the shadow (or hidden) economy has arisen; as a consequence, the shadow economy has received increasing attention by the public, politicians, and social scientists.[1] For industrial countries, there are at least two reasons why politicians have become concerned about the growth and size of the shadow economy:

(1) If an increase in the size of the shadow economy is mainly caused by a rising tax burden, any increase in tax rates may lead to a further shift from official to inofficial activities and, hence, to a further decrease in tax revenues.

(2) If – due to the existence of the shadow economy – some individuals have a second source of income and spend at least part of this income in the "official" economy, any change in the size of the shadow economy directly affects the development of the official economy.

The aforementioned concern is reflected in many attempts by economists to measure the size of the shadow economy, and a considerable number of studies have been undertaken which yield quantitative results on the size and development of the shadow economy in the OECD-countries. To measure the shadow economy, the currency-demand and the model approach are the two methods most often used.[2] The results of both approaches indicate that for Austria, Denmark, Norway,

---

[*] We are indebted to the participants of the Vienna conference on the political economy of progressive taxation, and particularly to D. Bös, J. Brunner and J. Falkinger for helpful discussions. Remaining errors and shortcomings are our responsibility.

[1] A useful working definition used in most studies of the shadow economy is: the shadow economy is defined by all those economic activities which contribute to value-added and should be included in national income according to national income accounting conventions but are at present *not registered* by the national measurement agencies. Compare, e.g., Frey and Pommerehne (1984) and Kirchgässner (1984).

[2] These two methods are the most commonly used and are explained in various surveys, which

---

D. Bös and B. Felderer (Eds.)
The Political Economy of Progressive Taxation
© Springer-Verlag Berlin Heidelberg 1989

Germany, Sweden, Switzerland and the USA, for which estimates for the period 1970 – 1980 are available, the unofficial sector grew from 2 to 4 percent of official GNP in 1970 to 5 to 10 percent of official GNP in 1980 – a magnitude which can no longer be neglected.

So far, almost all studies have concentrated either on a theoretical model of why people work in the shadow economy, or they have tried to estimate the size of the shadow economy by applying a variety of methods.[3] As we, too, have pursued a theoretical approach and have analysed some determinants of shadow economy activities of households and firms in the contribution by Neck et al. in this volume, in the present study we make an attempt to go a step further and to empirically analyse the effects of a changing shadow economy on an official economy. For this purpose, a small econometric model for the official Austrian economy has been developed in which the unofficial (shadow) economy is determined endogenously. The goal of our investigation is to study the effects of a change in the size of the Austrian shadow economy on important "official" macroeconomic indicators.[4] To our knowledge, such an attempt has not been made for Austria (or for other OECD-countries). In addition, our interest is in obtaining empirical information about the impact of changes in the tax rates on the underground and "official" economy, not only for theoretical purposes, but also for practical reasons. Regarding the particular economy of Austria, such information is important for the policy debate concerning, for example, tax reform proposals and attempts to reduce the federal budget deficit. For this purpose, we will report several results of some policy simulations which show the impacts of changes in the marginal tax rate of wage earners designed to reduce the incentives to work in the shadow economy and of changes in indirect taxes on the endogenous variables of an econometric model containing an underground sector.

For those readers who are not so familiar with how the size and development of a shadow economy can be measured, we present a short description of one method to calculate the Austrian shadow economy in Section 2. In Section 3, a

---

all report empirical results for OECD-countries and give a detailed description of and a comparison between the different methods; compare the surveys by Weck et al. (1984), Boeschoten and Fage (1984), Frey and Pommerehne (1984) and Schneider and Hofreither (1987).

[3] The methods applied to estimate the size and development of the shadow economy in the individual countries vary considerably – e.g., from direct approaches like tax auditing or other compliance methods to indirect approaches where macroeconomic indicators in the product, labor and financial markets are analysed, which leave some "traces" of the size and development of the shadow economy. Compare, e.g., Schneider and Hofreither (1987).

[4] A similar idea was already developed by Peacock and Shaw (1982). They argue that the effects of shadow economy activities on the official economy can only be analysed within the framework of a fully articulated macroeconomic model endogenizing the shadow economy. Similar arguments are brought forward in Frey (1984) and Kirchgässner and Pommerehne (1985).

The Consequences of a Changing Shadow Economy for the "Official" Economy   183

brief description of the econometric model is provided. In Section 4, various policy simulations are undertaken to show what may happen if the government wants to reduce the size of the shadow economy. Finally, in Section 5, a summary is given and some conclusions are drawn.

2. The Calculation of the Austrian Shadow Economy: A Description of the Currency-Demand Approach

2.1 Previous Studies

In view of the large number of studies measuring the size of the shadow economy in Austria's neighboring countries Germany, Switzerland and Italy, it is somewhat astonishing that only a few attempts have been made to measure the size of the Austrian shadow economy:[5] Frey and Weck–Hannemann (1984) used the technique of the unobserved variables to compute the size of the shadow economy for the OECD-countries and estimate a shadow economy of 8.9 percent (of official GDP) for Austria in 1978. Franz (1985) computed the scope of the shadow economy on the basis of official data, which were available in a very detailed form only for 1976. Comparing the income earned in different occupational sectors where shadow economy activities are possible and very likely with those sectors where it is very difficult to engage in moonlight activities, Franz estimated the size of the shadow economy to be 3.5 percent of official GDP for 1976. Furthermore, he argued that this figure has remained more or less constant until 1982.[6] Apart from these two studies, which only provide results for certain years, only Hofreither and Schneider (1987) have made an attempt to measure the size and the development of the Austrian shadow economy over an extended period of time.

2.2 The Method Applied

The method chosen for estimating the shadow economy in Austria is the currency-

---

[5] This short description is a summary of a much longer study by Hofreither and Schneider (1987). A comprehensive survey concerning all aspects of the Austrian shadow economy is given in Skolka (1985).

[6] Franz reached this conclusion quoting a study by Mooslechner (1985) who tried to apply monetary approaches (including the currency-demand approach) for measuring the shadow economy. Mooslechner argued that, on the basis of financial indicators, it is not likely that the shadow economy has increased significantly in the last decade.

demand approach.[7] It assumes that shadow (or hidden) transactions are undertaken in the form of cash payments in order to leave no written traces for the state authorities. Therefore, an increase in shadow economy activities will raise the demand for currency. In order to isolate this "excess" demand for currency, a currency-demand equation is econometrically estimated, controlling for all conventional factors, like the development of income, payment habits, interest rates, etc. Additionally, variables (like the tax burden) which are assumed to be the major causes why people work in the shadow economy, are included in the estimated equation. The excess increase in currency, i.e., that which is not "explained" by the conventional factors mentioned above, is then attributed to the rising tax burden and regarded as an indicator of the size of the shadow economy.

One of the problems with this approach is in estimating a "normal" currency-demand equation for a country over an extended period of time; another problem is due to the fact that shadow economy activities can be undertaken in the forms of barter or payment by check.[8] Therefore, the figures derived by this method may underestimate the "true" size of the underground economy. Such an underestimation may also be due to the fact that in most studies only one cause (a rising tax burden) of the size of the shadow eonomy is taken into account.[9]

After having introduced the currency-demand approach and having also discussed its major weaknesses, the question may arise as to why we have chosen this approach. Our answer is that (i) we have reliable time-series data for Austria over the period 1958 to 1985 concerning the monetary sector and different measures of the tax burden as the major cause of the shadow economy; and (ii) the currency-demand approach is the most widely used approach. It has been applied to 14 of the 17 OECD-countries, which allows comparisons with other European and North American countries over an extended period (e.g., 10 years). Moreover,

---

[7] This approach was first used by Cagan (1958), who calculated a correlation of the currency demand and the tax pressure for the United States over the period 1919 to 1955. Twenty years later Gutman (1979) used the same approach. He did not apply any statistical procedures, but "only" looked at the ratio between currency and demand deposits over the years 1937 to 1976. Cagan's approach was further developed by Tanzi (1980, 1983) who estimated a currency-demand function for the United States for the period 1929 to 1980 in order to calculate the size of the shadow economy.

[8] A further weakness of this approach is discussed by Garcia and Pak (1979) who point out that the increase in currency-demand deposits may be largely connected to a slowdown in the growth of demand deposits rather than to an increase in currency demand caused by shadow economy activities. The assumption that the velocities of currency are the same in the official and the shadow economy is questionable as well (Frey and Pommerehne, 1984).

[9] Schneider and Pommerehne (1985) introduced more than one hypothesized cause for the size of the shadow economy into the currency-demand equation for the United States. However, besides the tax burden, only the regulation measure seems to have a statistically significant and quantitatively important influence on the currency demand.

the figures for the size of the shadow economy obtained by this method can be compared to the results from other methods.

In applying the currency-demand approach, we follow the procedure developed by Klovland (1984). His basic model relates the stock of currency demanded by the public to the price level, the volume of transactions in the regular economy and the interest rate as a measure of the opportunity costs of holding currency. Furthermore, he employs a marginal tax rate as a causal variable for shadow economy activities. A similar function is estimated in the econometric model for Austria as discussed in Section 3.

2.3 Calculation of the Austrian Shadow Economy

The estimated currency-demand equation (shown in Table 3.4 in the Appendix) is used to calculate the development of the shadow economy in Austria from 1960 to 1985. As in most studies for Austria's neighboring countries, as well as for the Scandinavian countries, it is assumed that there would have been no shadow economy if the marginal tax rate had remained at its historical minimum from 1960 until 1985. Keeping tax rates at the minimum level of the year 1960, the "normal" (without shadow economy) level of currency holdings is calculated by undertaking a dynamic simulation. The difference between the actually observed and the simulated currency holdings is assumed to reflect the amount of currency used for shadow economy transactions. Assuming the same income velocity for currency used in the shadow economy as for legal M 1 in the official economy, the size of the shadow economy is computed and compared to the official GDP.[10]

In the Appendix, in Table 2.1, the results for the development of the Austrian shadow economy over the period from 1961 to 1985 are shown. The Austrian shadow economy increases more or less steadily and reaches a peak value in 1985 with 3.4 percent of official GDP. The computed size of the shadow economy is considerably lower than the one in Hofreither and Schneider (1987). The reason might be that the two tax rates (direct and indirect) are endogenously approximated by the two tax functions in the econometric model and are not exogenously given, as is done in the single-equation estimation in Hofreither and Schneider (1987). The conclusion by Franz (1985) and Mooslechner (1985) that the shadow economy has not grown from 1976 to 1982 is *not* supported by our findings.

---

[10] Because of a complete lack of knowledge about the velocity of money in the shadow economy, this assumption is made here as in most other studies using this approach (e.g., Tanzi, 1980, 1983; Kirchgässner, 1983, 1984; Isachsen and Strøm, 1985; Schneider, 1986).

3. A Small Econometric Model for the Austrian Economy

3.1 The Structure of the Model

In order to study the consequences of changing direct and indirect tax rates on the development of the shadow economy and on the official economy over time, we undertake simulations with an econometric model which captures the basic relations of the Austrian economy. We use a slightly modified version of the model developed by Hofreither (1988), which additionally includes a currency-demand function for calculating the size of the shadow economy as the eleventh behavioral equation (see also Hofreither and Schneider, 1987).

In general, the model developed by Hofreither belongs to some "standard" type of fundamental Keynesian macro models with substantial neoclassical influences. A few special characteristics are worth mentioning:

- For incorporating medium-range aspects, the model includes a production sector, which works as a medium-run equilibrium element. This and the associated factor-demand functions represent neoclassical elements in the model.

- Personal income is split into gross wage and gross profit income. This has been implemented in a similiar way as in the SNA-approach, where profit income is determined as a residual quantity.

- Both income elements constitute the basis for the accompanying tax functions. For simplification, these functions consider all direct tax payments of income earners, including social security contributions.

- Furthermore, this distinction between categories leads to a specific kind of consumption function. Due to the problems of determining a correct allocation of transfer payments, this income element emerges as an independent argument within the consumption function.

The complete model structure is shown in the Appendix, Tables 3.1 to 3.3. Table 3.1 provides the explanation of the abbreviations of the variables. Table 3.2 presents the behavioral equations and Table 3.3 the definitions.

The production sector of the model consists of a single aggregate production function of the Cobb-Douglas-type. This production function relates output to capital stock and labor in long-run equilibrium. If one assumes that decisions on desired factor inputs are made to minimize the costs of the production of expected output, factor-demand equations can be derived from this production function in a very straightforward way (Coen and Hickman, 1970; Schebeck and Thury, 1976). Our attempts in estimating factor-demand equations sequentially were only partially successful.[11] Therefore, we had to drop this way of determining the coefficients of the production function and stepped back to a much simpler procedure, which has been utilized for Austrian data by Breuss (1982).

From the adding-up theorem, it follows that the exponents α and β of the Cobb-Douglas function also represent the functional income distribution. Therefore, they may be approximated a priori by information provided in income statistics. Relating labor income to total net income gives 0.85 over the period 1956–1985. The numerical values of α and β are then 0.85 and 0.15, respectively. For calculating the residual factor of the Cobb-Douglas production function (Φ), actual values of labor and capital input have been applied.

The labor input results from multiplying the number of employed persons (e) by the effective working time (h^e). However, more obstacles must be overcome in determining the amount of capital (k) actually used. Again we follow a procedure suggested by Breuss (1982). Potential capital (k^{pot}) is calculated by the Almon-procedure (Almon et al., 1974) and, therefore, consists of two parts: an "actual" and a "silent" one. Actually used capital is calculated by applying figures provided by a quarterly investment-utilization test.

Due to the difficulties in obtaining reliable factor-demand functions and to the lack of a computer program by which we could estimate nonlinear restrictions within a simultaneous estimation procedure, we had to weaken the theoretical approach provided by Coen and Hickman (1970) substantially. Using linear approximations of the derived factor-demand specifications, the direct theoretical connection to the production function has been eliminated; but the variables which emerge in the linear estimated equations have been derived according to the theoretical considerations.

Instead of the employment volume in hours, the number of employed persons has been chosen (e^w) as the dependent variable of the labor demand equation. Therefore, the effective working time per worker (h^e) has been included as an additional independent variable in this equation. Moreover, some special events influencing the labor market in the last decades have been accounted for by adding a dummy variable. Besides other effects, the employment dummy (d^{ew}) tries to capture the changing employment regulations for foreign workers in the early seventies, changes in income-tax legislation in 1973 affecting the labor market and

---

[11] Possibly that may be caused by a too high aggregation level of the utilized variables; for instance, the employment variable includes agricultural and state employment as well. The same holds for the capital stock.

the lengthening of compulsory school attendance in the mid-sixties.

Unfortunately the first estimation attempts showed the coefficient of the relative price of the production factors obstinately having the wrong sign. Therefore, we finally altered the theoretical concept by assuming that employment-demand decisions are determined by real unit labor cost (Θ) instead of by the cost ratio of the individual production factors. Real shadow economy income (se) is assumed to have a negative impact on the demand for officially employed persons. The number of self-employed persons, as well as the potential labor force, are treated exogenously. Unemployment is determined endogenously and is indirectly influenced by the volume of the shadow economy (see Table 3.2, equation (4)). The supply side of the labor market is treated exogenously.

Effective working time (h^e) is determined by a simple adjustment process to legal working time regulations (h^n). The growth rate of real gross domestic product ($\dot{q}$) is supposed to capture the different speeds of adjustment over a business cycle (see Table 3.2, equation (5)).

To allow for the examination of income-distribution effects, personal income has been split into wage and profit income. This poses no problem in the case of the gross income figures, as the SNA-accounts provide them directly. More difficulties arise, however, when disposable income is split-up into these two components. Here the following procedure has been applied: in general, national income (Y) consists of wage income (Y^w), profit income (Y^p) and "other income" (Y^o) – the income of joint stock companies and government income from property and state enterprises. After ascertaining wage incomes by multiplying the number of employees (e^w) by per capita wages (W), total profit income may be calculated residually by subtracting Y^w from national income. To isolate personal profit income, "other income" has to be deducted as well. Deducting direct taxes from gross income and deflating the resulting figures gives the real disposable income of wage and profit earners after taxes, but without public transfers to private households.

As the tax payments of the two income groups include not only direct wage and profit taxes, respectively, but also a number of accompanying taxation components, no theoretically satisfying tax functions could be constructed. Therefore, a very simple form of ad-hoc plausible estimation equations have been utilized. A quadratic function has been assumed as a basis for per capita taxation (see Table 3.2, equations (9) and (10)). Dummy variables account for some special influences on wage and profit taxation.

Fundamentally, the determination of per capita wages (W) is carried out by combining a Phillips-curve concept with the special way of wage bargaining in Austria (cf. also Wörgötter, 1977). Price predictions being very accurate, the actual price index of domestic demand (p) is used as a regressor instead of a theoretically more plausible expected price index. The second Phillips-curve element in the equation is the three-years average of the number of cyclically unemployed persons (u^{cyc}). Here structural unemployment, which is assumed to amount to approximately 1.5 percent of the labor supply, has been deducted from total unemployment. Until the late-seventies, a third element influenced institutionalized wage bargaining ("Austrian Social Partnership") far more than unemployment: the development of labor productivity (Π). If money wages are assumed to be equal to the nominal marginal product per worker, the estimation equation (6) in Table 3.2 may, in principle, be interpreted as being consistent with the so-called "Benya-formula".[12]

There are four price indices in this model: the price index for gross domestic product (p^q), the price index for domestic demand (p), an import price index (p^{im}) and an export price index (p^x). While the first two are endogenously determined, the remaining two are exogenous. The deflator of GDP at market prices (p^q) is the dependent variable in an estimation function primarily being based on a mark-up approach, where unit labor cost (Θ), user cost of capital (S), and indirect taxation (TQ^{ind}) constitute the basic components. Additionally the price index of imports (p^{im}) has been included. To allow for different situations of demand pressure during the business cycle, the capacity utilization variable (Ω) has been incorporated (see Table 3.2, equation (7)). Given the deflators of exports and imports, the price index of domestic demand, which is the dominant deflator within the model, can easily be derived (see Table 3.3, equation (8)).

The estimation equation for the interest rate on newly issued bonds (R^B) stems from some textbook money-demand function, containing real money supply (m^s), real gross domestic product (q) and the inflation rate $(\dot{p})$. To capture the strong influence of foreign monetary developments, which is in part a consequence of the special Austrian "hard-currency policy", the interest rate of the Euro-Dollar-Market (R^E) has been added (see Table 3.2, equation (8)).

There are four sectors where final demand is pertinent: the consumption, investment, export and import sectors. Only the export sector is treated as exogenous.

---

[12] During the early seventies, which were primarily characterized by a very low rate of unemployment, the sum of the percentage increases of the price level and the labor productivity was widely accepted as some rule of thumb of wage determination, often declared as the "Benya-formula". Compare Hofreiter (1988).

Private consumption (c) is explained by a very conventional theoretical approach, based on Brown's formulation of habit persistence (see, e.g., Klein, 1983). Only slight alterations have been introduced. The consumption function should also account for the different income groups. As consumption is usually determined by "disposable" personal income, the problem of the missing transfer payments in our measure of "disposable" income has to be solved carefully. Due to our unreliable prior knowledge of the personal incidence of transfer payments (z^H), the arbitrariness of splitting this figure into a wage and a profit share has been avoided by including transfer payments as an independent regressor within the consumption function. Here the shadow economy plays a very important role as an additional regressor: income earned in the underground economy is assumed to be positively correlated with private consumption, as some part of this income is spent for purchasing official consumption goods. This may induce slightly lower propensities to consume out of officially earned income. Whether the marginal propensity to consume from shadow economy income is higher than the one from the officially earned sources cannot be determined theoretically and will be examined empirically. Peacock and Shaw (1982) argue that on a priori grounds it seems reasonable to assume a higher marginal propensity to consume for tax evaders over non-evaders, because the acquisition of financial or durable real assets can be easily detected by the fiscal authorities, at least in Great Britain. On the other hand, if the discrepancy between consumption expenditures and official income becomes very large, the fiscal authorities might also detect tax-evading behavior. Therefore, it might well be that in Austria, some part of the shadow economy income is spent abroad or put into a savings account out of the reach of the tax authorities.

All variables entering the consumption equation are measured at constant prices. The consumption dummy (d^c), which is additionally included, captures effects such as the introduction of a special tax on newly bought cars in 1969 or of the VAT in 1973, which changed the time pattern of consumer purchases.

Gross investment is divided into private and public fixed investment and inventory investment. Whilst the last two elements are treated exogenously, the determination of real private gross fixed investment (i) has already been explained above. Investment functions of this type heavily depend on the quality of the data on fixed capital. As this capital series is generated within the model using relatively weak priors, some problems may arise during simulation.

Though exports (x) are exogenously given, the current account balance is determined endogenously by the import function. Imports (im) are simply determined by the level of demand (q) and the relative import prices ($\overset{\approx im}{p}$) (cf. Breuss, 1983). Due to an evident structural break in import behavior in the

The method chosen for estimating the shadow economy in Austria is the currency-demand approach: it assumes that hidden transactions are undertaken exclusively in the form of cash payments. Therefore, an increase in shadow-economy activities – although not directly observable – will raise the demand for currency. Hence, an eleventh equation has been added to the model. This currency-demand equation is required to endogenously determine the size of the shadow economy (see Table 3.2, equation (11)).

mid-seventies, a simple spline mechanism concerning price behavior has been introduced (see Table 3.2, equation (3)). The coefficients of the relative import prices show very clearly that the import price effect, which was complementary before 1973, changed into a substitutional one after this date. Finally, real gross domestic product results from the adequate summation of the components of final demand (see Table 3.3, equation (1)).

The method chosen for estimating the shadow economy in Austria is the currency-demand approach: it assumes that hidden transactions are undertaken exclusively in the form of cash payments. Therefore, an increase in shadow-economy activities – although not directly observable – will raise the demand for currency. Hence, an eleventh equation has been added to the model. This currency-demand equation is required to endogenously determine the size of the shadow economy (see Table 3.2, equation (11)).

The calculation of the size of the shadow economy applying the currency-demand approach is described in detail in Section 2 of this paper. Despite the obvious weaknesses of this approach, it has been utilized within the model because it is one of the very few procedures which produce time-series data of the shadow economy.

One problem of this approach concerns the choice of the adequate tax variables. According to theoretical considerations (see the paper by Neck et al. in this volume), the marginal income tax rate and the indirect tax rate seem to be appropriate. Unfortunately, no marginal tax rate exists in the base model. As a simple remedy for this drawback, an auxiliary function for transforming average tax rates into marginal ones is employed. The average tax rate on wage income, which is endogenous in our model, the wage-tax dummy and both a quadratic and a cubic trend variable serve as regressors to estimate the marginal tax rate of the average income of a wage earner:

$$(TQ^{marg})_t = 8.40 \ + 1.67(t^w/y^w)_t + \ 1.014d^T - \ 0.052t^2 + \ 0.0014t^3.$$
$$(4.35) \quad (8.02) \qquad\qquad (1.55) \qquad (-4.21) \quad (5.22)$$

$$R^2 = 0.979 \quad S.E. = 1.40 \quad DW = 2.32$$

The indirect tax rate (TQ^{ind}) is defined as the percentage ratio of the sum of all indirect taxes to gross domestic production net of taxes.

With these last steps, the theoretical structure of the model has been completed, and it seems to be ready for the first estimation attempts.

3.2 Estimation of the Model

A serious problem arises when one tries to estimate the model system simultaneously: the size of the shadow economy cannot be computed without an estimation of the currency-demand equation. But the size of the shadow economy is needed to estimate the consumption and the employment function. This dilemma has to be overcome by an iterative procedure:

1) At the first iterative step, the system is estimated, including the currency-demand equation, and the consumption and the employment function still enter the system in their basic specification without shadow economy income.

2) With this first estimation of the currency-demand equation, a preliminary size of the shadow economy is computed.

3) The model is re-estimated in its final specification, and a second preliminary shadow economy size is computed.

4) The procedure is repeated several times. During the iterative steps, most of the model parameters remain nearly unchanged. Only the coefficients of the tax rates vary slightly, and so the shadow economy varies slightly, too. The procedure is stopped when the size of the shadow economy and hence the coefficients of the model remain stable. This is actually the case at the fifth iteration step.

All equations in the model are simultaneously estimated by an iterative three-stage least squares procedure over the period 1956 to 1985 using annual data. The estimates of the coefficients of the eleven behavioral equations are shown in the Appendix, Table 3.4. In general, the estimated coefficients have the expected sign and are in most cases statistically significant; Durbin's h-statistic indicates that the estimated residuals are not autocorrelated. If we compare the sizes of the coefficients for the four different marginal propensities to consume, the coefficient for real transfer payments to private households is the greatest with 0.66, followed by those for wage income with 0.56 and for the shadow economy income with 0.42. From this empirical result, we conclude that the income from shadow economy activities, which is spent for official consumption to 60 percent in the long run according to the final form of the consumption function, plays quite an important role and cannot be neglected in an econometric model for the Austrian economy. The marginal propensity to consume from profit income has the lowest value of 0.36. In our case, Peacock's and Shaw's hypothesis of a larger marginal propensity to consume for the inofficial income is not confirmed. The negative sign of the statistically significant coefficient of the shadow economy variable in the employment equation indicates that a rising shadow economy reduces official employment. The estimation of the currency-demand function shows a statistically significant influence of the marginal tax rate on wage incomes and (somewhat less) of the indirect tax rate, apart from "classical" factors like consumption per capita and an interest rate.

3.3 Simulation Properties of the Model

In order to test how well the model predicts the development of the Austrian economy over the period 1966 to 1985, we undertake a dynamic ex-post simulation, where – apart from the exogenous variables – all variables are determined by the model. This simulation shows clearly that there are not too strong deviations of the simulated from the actual values for most of the variables of the model. The results of the simulation and error analysis are shown in the Appendix, Table 3.5.

In Table 3.5 the mean as well as the mean-square-percentage errors for the most important variables are shown. Furthermore, Table 3.5 provides Theil's U2 for these variables, which is additionally decomposed into its systematic and unsystematic components.[13]

In general, the mean absolute deviations are quite small, and only for the very volatile profit income and the related profit taxes the deviations reach unsatisfactorily high values. To summarize, the expanded model seems to be able to predict the development of the Austrian economy over the time period under consideration ex-post sufficiently well to be actually used for simulation purposes.

4. The Effects of a Changing Shadow Economy on the Official Austrian Economy – Some Simulation Results

We start all dynamic simulations in 1975, where the shadow economy has reached a size of 11.0 bill. Austrian Schillings (AS), and continue up to 1985. In all simulations shown below, either the percentage deviations or the first differences from the ex-post simulation (the control solution, using actual values for all exogenous variables as inputs) are computed. We assume that the actual size and development of the shadow economy can be approximated using the currency-demand approach. We assume for the government that it has some idea about the magnitude of the

---

[13] For a detailed explanation, see footnote 5 in Table 3.5.

shadow economy and has the policy goal of reducing the shadow economy in order to improve the tax base and to obtain (hopefully) additional revenues or to correct officially measured – but so far mistaken – indicators (like employment). Some policy options available to the government will now be discussed and the policy simulations of the econometric model will be used to demonstrate the effects on the official and inofficial economy.

4.1 Lowering the Direct Tax Burden

Most studies dealing with the measurement of the shadow economy conclude that a high tax burden is one of the major causes of shadow economy activities (compare Section 2). Hence, the government can lower direct and indirect tax rates and hope that people will reduce their shadow economy activities due to the lower incentive to work in the shadow economy. In the first simulation, the government reduces the wage-earner tax burden by 5 percent every year as compared to the control solution, starting in 1975. The aim of lowering the marginal tax burden to such an extent is to let people have less (more) incentive to work in the shadow (official) economy. According to our model, suppliers of inofficial services will react with a reduction of their shadow economy activities when tax rates are decreased.[14]

The simulation results are shown in the Appendix, Tables 4.1 and 4.2. These results clearly indicate a modest upswing of the economy for the years 1975 – 1985; real GDP (employment) increases by 0.29 (0.40) percent (as compared to the control solution) on average over these 11 years. Real consumption rises by 1.21 percent and prices increase by 0.61 percent on average over the period 1975 – 1985. On the other hand, the shadow economy decreases on average by 8.81 percent over that period, which is quite a considerable amount. In Table 4.2, we address the question of the effects of a tax decrease and, as a consequence, a reduction of the shadow economy in terms of total value-added. We have defined "total value-added" as the sum of the official and the inofficial (= shadow economy) GDP. Table 4.2 shows the first differences in value-added and tax-revenue measures between the simulation results obtained when the shadow economy is changing and those of the ex-post simulation. So a comparison of the overall net effects on total value-added and tax revenue is possible. Considering the same period (1975 – 1985), total value-added increases by 7.53 bill. AS. The simulation clearly indicates that

---

[14] This assumption of such a "symmetric" reaction is implicitly made in the currency-demand approach; it is, however, questionable whether people react to a decrease of their tax burden with a reduction of their shadow economy activities (compare Pommerehne, 1986). Alm (1985) makes such an assumption in his analysis of the welfare cost of the underground economy.

The increase in official GDP is by far larger than the decrease in inofficial GDP (shadow economy). On the tax revenue side, the government gains an additional 4.14 bill. AS in tax revenues over the period 1975 – 1985 – an amount available for reducing the budget deficit or effecting some extra investments. On the whole, a direct-tax reduction seems to be an efficient policy measure for reducing the shadow economy and stimulating the official economy.

4.2   Lowering the Indirect Tax Burden

The high value-added tax rates in Austria are also said to be one major cause of the large shadow economy. In the Appendix, Tables 4.3 and 4.4 show the simulation results that are obtained if the indirect tax rate is permanently decreased by 1 percentage point every year, starting in 1975, as compared to the control solution.

Considering once more the period 1975 – 1985, real GDP increases by only 0.06 percent and employment increases slightly by 0.19 percent on average, as compared with the control solution. The increase achieved is thus much weaker than the result of a direct tax decrease. Moreover, the shadow economy shrinks "only" by an average 6.2 percent compared to 8.81 percent in the case of a direct-tax rate reduction.

If we compare the results in Table 4.4 with the results in Table 4.2, we realize that even with a lower overall reduction of the shadow economy (–12.3 bill. AS compared to –17.1 bill. AS), there is a very modest increase of official GDP by 4.3 bill. AS which leads to a reduction of total value-added of 7.9 bill. AS over the period 1975 – 1985. Also, the loss of indirect tax revenues of 67.0 bill. AS is not compensated by the increase of direct tax revenues of 44.2 bill. AS over the same period. In total, an indirect-tax reduction reduces the shadow economy, too, but the positive stimulating effect on the official economy is not strong enough to compensate for the reduction of the shadow economy. Hence, an indirect-tax rate reduction may not be an effective policy means, especially as the government will lose tax revenues.

Another possibility for the government to reduce the size of the shadow economy may be to raise the wages (*after taxes*) in the official economy. But as illustrated in our model, the size of the shadow economy depends solely on indirect and direct tax rates, consequently an increase in official wages stimulates the shadow economy in our simulation model only through a change in indirect tax rates. Therefore, our model – as it stands now – is not suitable for such simulations.

5. Summary and Conclusions

In this paper we tried to analyse the effects of a changing shadow economy on the development of the official economy. First, we have presented the currency-demand approach in order to demonstrate how the size and development of the shadow economy over time can be computed. After introducing a small econometric model for Austria, in which the shadow economy has been determined endogenously, various policy simulations have been analysed. If the government reduces direct tax rates in order to eliminate some of the incentives to work in the shadow economy, the total effect on the official economy will be positive, and the shadow economy will decline considerably. Hence, easing the direct tax burden can be seen as an efficient policy instrument, especially as compared to a reduction of indirect tax rates, where the positive development of the official economy will be more modest.

In general, these simulations should be seen as a first step in the study of the interactions between the official and the shadow economy. For example, we have demonstrated that the shadow economy is an important factor in official private consumption expenditures. Hence, it may be safe to conclude that the shadow economy has to be integrated into econometric models so that policy simulations can be more realistically evaluated. Tax policy has been shown to be of potential influence on the amount of the hidden economy. In the next step of research, the degree of progression of the total tax system (including direct and indirect taxes) should be introduced as a policy instrument of the government. This will, however, necessitate a great deal of additional theoretical and empirical work.

6. Appendices

Table 2.1:   Size of the Austrian Shadow Economy[1]

Year	Official Gross Domestic Prod. real	Value-added in the Shadow Economy, real	Size of the Shadow Economy in per cent of the "official" GDP
1961	379.68	2.85	0.75
1962	388.93	2.79	0.72
1963	404.45	2.30	0.57
1964	428.60	3.51	0.82
1965	440.95	5.31	1.20
1966	466.20	5.14	1.10
1967	479.98	5.69	1.19
1968	502.18	5.49	1.09
1969	533.44	5.20	0.98
1970	571.25	8.38	1.47
1971	600.31	7.51	1.25
1972	637.69	7.90	1.24
1973	669.29	13.35	1.99
1974	695.79	11.81	1.70
1975	692.84	11.02	1.59
1976	724.75	9.76	1.35
1977	756.12	14.01	1.85
1978	760.23	15.25	2.01
1979	795.96	18.34	2.30
1980	820.03	20.07	2.45
1981	818.58	22.32	2.73
1982	828.62	24.97	3.02
1983	845.54	24.53	2.90
1984	862.66	26.90	3.12
1985	887.39	29.89	3.37

1) Assumptions made for the calculation of the shadow economy:
(i) All transactions in the shadow economy are done in cash.
(ii) Tax pressure is the only reason for working in the shadow economy.
(iii) In 1960 there existed no shadow economy.
(iv) The velocity of currency is the same in the shadow economy and in the official economy and is calculated by dividing total official income by M1.
(v) For the calculation the currency-demand equation from the econometric model in Table 3.4 is used.

Table 3.1: Variables – Abbreviations and Sources

General Remarks: Real variables (all based 1976) are indicated by lower case letters. Capital letters refer to variables at current prices. The data sources are abbreviated in the following manner: V – Volkswirtschaftliche Gesamtrechnung; S – Statistisches Handbuch der Republik Österreich; T – Wirtschafts- und Sozialstatistisches Taschenbuch der AK; M – Mitteilungen des Direktoriums der OeNB; X – Calculated by the authors.

Symbol	Variable (Dimension)	Source
c	Private consumption, real (in bill. of 1976 AS)	V
cur	Currency	M
C^g	Consumption expenditures of public sector (in bill. of AS)	V
d	Dummy variable	–
e	Employment	–
e^w	Demand for employed persons (in 1000)	S
e^s	Self-employed persons (in 1000)	S
h^e	Effective working time per worker (in hours)	S
h^n	Legal working time per worker (in hours)	X
i	Private fixed investment, real (in bill. of 1976 AS)	V
ii	Inventory investment, real (in bill. of 1976 AS)	V
I^g	Fixed investment of public sector (in bill. of AS)	V
im	Total imports, real (in bill. of 1976 AS)	V
k	Stock of capital, real (in bill. of 1976 AS)	X
m^s	Money base, real (in bill. of 1976 AS)	M
p	Price index of domestic demand (1976=100)	S,V
p^q	Price index of gross domestic product (1976=100)	S,V
p^{im}	Price index of imports (1976=100)	S,V
p^x	Price index of exports (1976=100)	S,V
$\overset{\approx}{p}$	Relative price	X
pop	Population	S
q	Gross domestic product, real (in bill. of 1976 AS)	S,V
R^B	Interest rate on bonds (in percent)	M
R^E	Euro-Dollar interest rate (in percent)	M,X

S	User cost of capital	X
se	Shadow economy income	X
SIC	Social insurance contributions	V
t	Time	–
T	Tax volume, current value (in bill. of AS)	S,V,X
TQ	Tax rate (in percent)	V,X
TQ^{marg}	Marginal tax rate on labor income (in percent)	X
TQ^{ind}	Indirect tax rate (in percent)	X
T^p	Taxes on profit income (in bill. of AS)	V
T^w	Taxes on wage income (in bill. of AS)	V
u	Unemployment (in 1000 persons)	S,T
u^{cyc}	Cyclical unemployment (in 1000 persons)	X
u^s	Structural unemployment (in 1000 persons)	X
v	Velocity of money	X
W	Wages per capita, current value (in bill. of AS)	S,X
x	Exports, real (in bill. of 1976 AS)	V
Y	National income, current value (in bill. of AS)	V
Y^w	Total wage income (in bill. of AS)	S,V
Y^p	Total personal profit income (in bill. of AS)	S,V
Y^o	Sum of income of joint stock companies and the public sector income from property and state enterprises (in bill. of AS)	S,V
z^H	Transfers to private households, real (in bill. of AS)	V
δ	Depreciation rate of capital	X

Table 3.2: Behavioral Equations:[1]

(1) Private consumption, real (c):
$$c_t = \tau_{1,1}c_{t-1} + \tau_{1,2}((Y^w - T^w)/p)_t + \tau_{1,3}((Y^p - T^p)/p)_t + \tau_{1,4}z_t^H + \tau_{1,5}d_t^c +$$
$$+\tau_{1,6}se_t + \tau_{1,7}$$

(2) Private fixed investment, real (i):
$$i_t = \tau_{2,1}i_{t-1} + \tau_{2,2}[aq_t + (1-a)q_{t-1}] + \tau_{2,3}(S/W)_t + \tau_{2,4}t + \tau_{2,5}k1_{t-1} +$$
$$+\tau_{2,6}d_t^i; \qquad \text{with } 0 \le a \le 1$$

(3) Imports, real (im):
$$im_t = \tau_{3,1}im_{t-1} + \tau_{3,2}q_t + \tau_{3,3}\overset{\approx im}{p_t} + \tau_{3,4}\overset{\approx 73}{p_t} + \tau_{3,5}d^{im} + \tau_{3,6}$$

(4) Demand for employed persons (e^w):
$$e_t^w = \tau_{4,1}e_{t-1}^w + \tau_{4,2}[aq_t + (1-a)q_{t-1}] + \tau_{4,3}\Theta_t + \tau_{4,4}se_t + \tau_{4,5}h_t^e +$$
$$+\tau_{4,6}t + \tau_{4,7}d_t^e + \tau_{4,8}; \qquad \text{with } 0 \le a \le 1$$

(5) Effective working time (h^e):
$$h_t^e = \tau_{5,1}h_t^n + \tau_{5,2}h_{t-1}^n + \tau_{5,3}h_{t-2}^n + \tau_{5,4}(\dot{q})_t$$

(6) Wages, per capita (W):
$$W_t = exp\{\tau_{6,1}ln(W_{t-1}) + \tau_{6,2}ln(p_t) + \tau_{6,3}ln(\Pi)_t + \tau_{6,4}ln[(\sum_{i=1}^{3}u_{t-1}^{cyc})/3] +$$
$$+\tau_{6,5}\}$$

(7) Price index of gross domestic product (p^q):
$$p_t^q = \tau_{7,1}p_{t-1}^q + \tau_{7,2}\Theta_t + \tau_{7,3}S_t + \tau_{7,4}\Omega_t + \tau_{7,5}p_t^{im} + \tau_{7,6}(TQ^{ind} \cdot p)_t +$$
$$+\tau_{7,7}[(TQ^{ind} \cdot p) \cdot d^{73}]_t + \tau_{7,8}d_t^{73} + \tau_{7,9}$$

(8) Interest rate on bonds (R^B):
$$R_t^B = \tau_{8,1}R_{t-1}^B + \tau_{8,2}m_t^s + \tau_{8,3}q_t + \tau_{8,4}R_t^E + \tau_{8,5}\dot{p}_t + \tau_{8,6}$$

(9) Taxes on wage income, per capita (T^w/e^w):
$$(T^w/e^w)_t = \tau_{9,1}(Y^w/e^w)_t + \tau_{9,2}(Y^w/e^w)_t^2 + \tau_{9,3}d_t^T + \tau_{9,4}d_t^{80} + \tau_{9,5}$$

(10) Taxes on profit income, per capita (T^p/e^s):
$$(T^p/e^s)_t = \tau_{10,1}(T^p/e^s)_{t-1} + \tau_{10,2}(Y^p/e^s)_t + \tau_{10,3}(Y^p/e^s)_t^2 + \tau_{10,4}d^{73} +$$
$$+\tau_{10,5}d_t^T + \tau_{10,6}$$

(11) Currency demand, real, per capita (cur/pop):
$$ln(cur/pop)_t = \tau_{11,1}ln(cur/pop)_{t-1} + \tau_{11,2}ln(c/pop)_t + \tau_{11,3}ln(p)_t +$$
$$+\tau_{11,4}d^{cur} + \tau_{11,5}ln(R^B)_t + \tau_{11,6}ln(TQ^{marg})_t + \tau_{11,7}ln(TQ^{ind})_t + \tau_{11,8}$$

1) In general, nominal rsp. real variables are indicated by capital rsp. lower case letters. The subscript 't' always indicates periods. Superscripts in connection with dummies indicate their affiliation to special variables, whereby numbers always indicate years.

The Consequences of a Changing Shadow Economy for the "Official" Economy 201

Table 3.3: **Definition Equations:**[1)]

(1) Gross domestic product (q):
$$q_t = c_t + (C_t^g + I_t^g)/p_t + i_t + x_t - im_t + ii_t$$

(2) Potential output (q^{pot}):
$$q_t^{pot} = \Phi_t \cdot (k_t^{pot})^{0.15} \cdot (e_t^{pot} \cdot h_t^{pot}/1000)^{0.85}$$

(3) Capacity utilization (Ω):
$$\Omega_t = q_t \cdot 100/q_t^{pot}$$

(4) Potential stock of capital (k^{pot}):
$$k_t^{pot} = k1_t + k2_t,$$
with $k1_t = (1 - \delta)k1_{t-1} + i_t$,
$$k2_t = (1 - \delta)k2_{t-1} + \delta k1_{t-1}$$

(5) Cyclical unemployment (u^{cyc}):
$$u_t^{cyc} = (e_t^{pot} - e_t^s - e_t^w - u^s)$$

(6) Growth rate of gross domestic product $(\dot{q})$:
$$\dot{q}_t = [ln(q_t) - ln(q_{t-1})] \cdot 100$$

(7) Labor productivity (Π):
$$\Pi_t = q_t/e_t^w$$

(8) Price index of domestic demand (p):
$$p_t = (p_t^q q_t - p_t^x x_t + p_t^{im} im_t)/(q_t - x_t + im_t)$$

(9) Inflation rate $(\dot{p})$:
$$\dot{p}_t = [ln(p_t) - ln(p_{t-1})] \cdot 100$$

(10) Gross wage income (Y^w):
$$Y_t^w = e_t^w \cdot W_t$$

(11) Gross profit income (Y^p):
$$Y_t^p = q_t \cdot p_t^q - (Y_t^w + SIC_t + T_t^{ind} + Y_t^o)$$

(12) Unit labor cost (Θ):
$$\Theta_t = (Y_t^w + SIC_t)/q_t$$

(13) User cost of capital (S):
$$S_t = p_t \cdot (R^B + \delta)_t$$

(14) Indirect taxes (T^{ind}):
$$T_t^{ind} = TQ_t^{ind} \cdot (q_t \cdot p_t^q)/100$$

(15) Relative import price $(\overset{\approx im}{p}_t)$:
$$\overset{\approx im}{p}_t = p_t^{im} \cdot 100/[(p_t^q q_t - $$
$$- p_t^x x_t)/(q_t - x_t)]$$

(16) Spline variable in import function $(\overset{\approx 73}{p})$:
$$\overset{\approx 73}{p} = (\overset{\approx im}{p}_t - 0.98916) \cdot d_t^{73}$$

(17) Shadow economy income (se):
$$se_t = (cur(TQ_{act}^{marg})_t - $$
$$- cur(TQ_{min}^{marg})_t) \cdot v_t \cdot pop_t$$

---

1) See explanation of Table 3.1. The meaning of the following not explicitly explained variables within this table is: TQ_{act}^{marg} - actual marginal tax rate on per capita income; TQ_{min}^{marg} - historical minimum of marginal tax rate on per capita income. The superscript "pot" indicates potential values of the individual variables.

Table 3.4: Estimation Results of an Annual Macroeconometric Model for Austria [1]

Equation	Variable	Coeff.
Consumption	Lagged dependent variable	0.299
	Real wage income (after taxes)	0.559
	Real profit income (after taxes)	0.358
	Real transfers to private households	0.659
	Consumption dummy	7.693
	Shadow economy income	0.420
	Intercept	30.940
Investment	Lagged dependent variable	0.094
	Real gross domestic product (weighted)	0.710
	Capital/labor price-ratio	−1.421
	Time trend	−4.821
	Lagged value of capital	−0.134
	Investment dummy	7.692
Imports	Lagged dependent variable	0.461
	Real gross domestic product	0.319
	Relative import price	0.394
	Spline variable (relative import price, 1973)	−1.522
	Import dummy	10.383
	Intercept	−131.160
Employment	Lagged dependent variable	0.818
	Real gross domestic product	1.345
	Real unit labor cost	−312.630
	Effective working time	−0.135
	Shadow economy income	−2.788
	Time trend	−25.072
	Employment dummy	25.560
	Intercept	571.060
Wages (ln)	Lagged dependent variable (ln)	0.559
	Price index of domestic demand (ln)	0.515
	Labor productivity (ln)	0.358
	Cyclical unemployment (ln, 3-years-average)	−0.032
	Intercept	−5.180
Working time (effective)	Legal working time	0.569
	Legal working time (lagged one year)	0.235
	Legal working time (lagged two years)	0.094
	Growth rate of real GDP	5.511

1) All equations are simultaneously estimated by an iterative least-squares procedure using annual data over the period 1956 – 1985. R-Square is the coefficient of determination; Std.Err. shows the standard error of the estimation. Durbins-h is Durbin's h-test against autocorrelation when lagged dependent variables are used as regressors. D.F. stands for the "degrees of freedom". The term "ln" indicates that these variables have been transformed to natural logarithms.

t–Value	R–Square	Std.Err.	RHO (1)	Durbins–h	D.F.
5.37					
12.25					
7.28					
7.99	0.999	2.392	0.159	0.913	23
8.28					
2.16					
5.54					
1.45					
14.53					
−6.47	0.996	2.575	−0.006	−0.036	24
−6.56					
−12.75					
6.92					
9.24					
10.67					
4.59	0.998	3.777	−0.239	−1.359	24
−7.38					
10.11					
−7.07					
24.90					
17.68					
−2.38					
−2.15	0.998	8.413	−0.055	−0.307	23
−4.39					
−15.26					
12.03					
2.85					
13.62					
9.94					
8.76	0.999	0.009	0.094	0.528	25
−13.42					
−10.14					
11.05					
3.57	0.994	11.816	0.322	—	26
1.76					
5.04					

Cont. of Table 3.4

Interest Rate	Lagged dependent variable	0.518
	Real money supply	−0.035
	Real gross domestic product	0.002
	Interest rate for Euro-Dollars	0.161
	Inflation rate	0.151
	Intercept	3.642
GDP-Price Index	Lagged dependent variable	0.647
	Unit labor cost	12.224
	User cost of capital	16.115
	Capacity utilization	0.121
	Price index of imports	0.077
	Indirect tax rate index	1.064
	Indirect tax rate index (before 1973 = 0)	−0.064
	Dummy 1973 (before 1973 = 0)	1.539
	Intercept	−11.050
Wage Income Tax (per capita)	Wage income (per capita)	0.154
	Squared wage income (per capita)	0.704
	Dummy 80 (before 1980 = 0)	0.001
	Income tax dummy	0.001
	Intercept	−0.000
Profit Income Tax (per capita)	Lagged dependent variable	0.581
	Profit income (per capita)	0.137
	Squared profit income (per capita)	−0.072
	Dummy variable 1973 (before 1973 = 0)	0.007
	Income tax dummy variable	0.003
	Intercept	−0.001
Currency Demand (per capita, ln)	Lagged dependent variable (ln)	0.489
	Real consumption per capita (ln)	0.723
	Price index of domestic demand (ln)	−0.400
	Currency demand dummy variable	−0.166
	Interest rate on bonds (ln)	−0.033
	Marginal tax rate on wage income (ln)	0.195
	Indirect tax rate (ln)	0.123
	Intercept	−2.232

6.97					
−3.07					
1.38	0.856	0.389	0.034	0.206	24
6.34					
4.47					
6.64					
21.23					
2.01					
1.23					
1.97	0.999	0.440	−0.069	−0.385	21
2.32					
17.36					
−1.05					
1.64					
−1.84					
17.18					
15.39					
2.81	0.999	0.001	0.267	−	25
5.73					
−1.12					
6.97					
4.89					
−2.95					
4.96	0.998	0.001	−0.022	−0.135	25
6.62					
−1.15					
8.36					
6.84					
−5.02					
−5.09	0.983	0.017	0.266	1.541	24
−4.77					
3.16					
1.34					
−3.14					

Table 3.5: Statistical Characteristics of a Dynamic Ex-Post Simulation of the Basic Macroeconometric Model

Variable	Mean Value	Mean Error[3]	MSP-[4] Error	Theil's U2	Decomposition of U		
					U^m	U^s	U^c
Private Consumption[1]	390.86	0.53	1.35	0.14	0.01	0.03	0.96
Private Investment[1]	147.21	−0.95	3.10	0.46	0.04	0.03	0.93
Imports[1]	233.39	−0.37	1.83	0.08	0.01	0.00	0.99
Gross Domestic Product[1]	697.15	0.15	0.89	0.09	0.00	0.00	1.00
Employed Persons	2613.4	−0.35	0.42	0.06	0.00	0.16	0.84
Effective Working Time	1838.1	0.11	0.65	0.03	0.01	0.09	0.90
Labor Productivity	264.76	−0.07	0.84	0.00	0.01	0.09	0.90
Price Index of GDP	99.04	0.03	0.64	0.01	0.00	0.40	0.60
Wages (per Capita)	120.4	−1.90	2.13	0.03	0.26	0.03	0.71
Unit Labor Cost	0.529	−0.01	2.02	0.05	0.21	0.06	0.73
User Cost of Capital	0.155	0.00	3.22	0.59	0.01	0.07	0.92
Interest Rate on Bonds	8.150	−0.03	5.59	0.39	0.01	0.04	0.95
Total Wage Income	322.67	−4.60	2.42	0.04	0.18	0.06	0.77
Total Profit Income	112.79	4.16	8.13	0.32	0.12	0.21	0.67
After-Tax Wage Income[1]	230.09	−2.84	2.53	0.24	0.16	0.00	0.84
After-Tax Profit Income[1]	78.52	4.58	10.00	0.67	0.23	0.15	0.62
After-Tax Private Inc.[1]	423.75	−0.36	1.51	0.13	0.03	0.11	0.89
Taxes on Wage Income[2]	80.21	−2.31	3.92	0.11	0.27	0.01	0.72
Taxes on Profit Income[2]	31.81	1.05	6.00	0.23	0.28	0.00	0.72
Indirect Taxes	121.65	−0.09	1.12	0.02	0.01	0.10	0.89

1) Real values at prices of 1976
2) Including Social-Security Contributions
3) Defined as simulated minus actual value
4) Mean Square Percentage Error
5) U^m measures the extent to which the average values of the simulated and actual series deviate from each other; U^s indicates the ability of the model to replicate the degree of variability of the series; U^c measures the unsystematic error of the simulation. All three decomposing elements sum up to 1. The ideal distribution of inequality over the three measures would be $U^m = U^s = 0$, $U^c = 1$. (For details see, for example, Pindyck–Rubinfeld, 1981, pp. 365 ff.)

The Consequences of a Changing Shadow Economy for the "Official" Economy   207

Tables 4.1 and 4.2: Lowering the Direct Tax Burden
(The government reduces the wage-earner tax burden by 5 percent every year as compared to the control solution, starting in 1975)

Table 4.1: Simulation of the Austrian Economy Under a Changing Shadow Economy from 1975 to 1985[1]

Year	GDPR[2]	Employ-ment	Price Index	Consump-tion[2]	Private Income[2]	Total Taxes	Shadow Economy
1975	0.26	0.21	0.10	0.53	0.52	−0.90	−15.19
1976	0.51	0.39	0.26	0.97	1.04	−0.18	−15.44
1977	0.64	0.53	0.45	1.28	1.45	0.46	−10.73
1978	0.68	0.63	0.64	1.60	1.71	0.70	−10.54
1979	0.56	0.62	0.80	1.63	1.75	1.12	−7.56
1980	0.38	0.52	0.89	1.59	1.65	1.23	−6.11
1981	0.22	0.37	0.94	1.51	1.54	1.15	−4.73
1982	0.04	0.28	0.89	1.28	1.04	0.28	−5.42
1983	−0.04	0.24	0.76	1.07	0.65	−0.39	−6.58
1984	−0.05	0.28	0.62	0.94	0.34	−0.76	−7.18
1985	0.04	0.40	0.51	0.91	0.24	−0.96	−7.45

[1] All figures represent percentage deviations from the ex-post-simulation.
[2] Real values at prices of 1976.

Table 4.2: Effects of a Changing Direct Tax Rate on Value-Added (= official and inofficial real GDP) and Tax Revenues (in bill. of AS)[1]

Year	Total Value-Added[2]			Tax Revenues		
	GDPR	Shadow-Ec.	Total	Direct	Indirect	Total
1975	1.80	−1.67	0.12	−2.24	0.39	−1.85
1976	3.59	−1.51	2.09	−1.30	0.90	−0.40
1977	4.78	−1.50	3.28	−0.33	1.48	1.15
1978	5.13	−1.61	3.52	0.05	1.84	1.89
1979	4.47	−1.39	3.08	1.23	2.09	3.32
1980	3.13	−1.23	1.91	1.91	2.14	4.04
1981	1.80	−1.06	0.75	2.05	2.10	4.15
1982	0.34	−1.35	−1.02	−0.68	1.73	1.05
1983	−0.35	−1.61	−1.96	−2.95	1.41	−1.53
1984	−0.42	−1.93	−2.35	−4.53	1.26	−3.27
1985	0.34	−2.23	−1.88	−5.66	1.25	−4.41
Total	24.62	−17.08	7.53	−12.45	16.59	4.14

[1] The figures represent absolute differences from the ex-post-simulation in bill. of AS.
[2] Real values at prices of 1976.

Tables 4.3 and 4.4: Lowering the Indirect Tax Burden

(The indirect tax rate is permanently decreased by 1 percentage point every year, starting in 1975, as compared to the control solution)

Table 4.3: **Simulation of the Austrian Economy Under a Changing Shadow Economy from 1975 to 1985[1]**

Year	GDPR[2]	Employment	Price Index	Consumption[2]	Private Income[2]	Total Taxes	Shadow Economy
1975	0.19	0.15	0.14	0.45	1.61	−1.44	−9.97
1976	0.31	0.26	0.29	0.72	1.99	−0.82	−9.99
1977	0.34	0.33	0.42	0.84	2.19	−0.35	−6.71
1978	0.27	0.35	0.53	0.91	2.26	−0.18	−6.39
1979	0.16	0.31	0.62	0.87	2.22	−0.06	−5.27
1980	0.04	0.22	0.67	0.81	2.18	0.03	−4.64
1981	−0.07	0.11	0.69	0.71	2.11	−0.05	−4.16
1982	−0.17	0.06	0.65	0.56	1.83	−0.62	−4.84
1983	−0.19	0.05	0.57	0.46	1.67	−0.97	−5.26
1984	−0.15	0.08	0.50	0.42	1.56	−1.12	−5.15
1985	−0.07	0.16	0.44	0.42	1.57	−1.19	−5.25

[1] All figures represent percentage deviations from the ex-post-simulation.
[2] Real values at prices of 1976.

Table 4.4: **Effects of a Changing Indirect Tax Rate on Value-Added (= official and inofficial real GDP) and Tax Revenues (in bill. of AS)[1]**

Year	Total Value-Added[2]			Tax Revenues		
	GDPR	Shadow-Ec.	Total	Direct	Indirect	Total
1975	1.31	−1.10	0.21	1.21	−4.16	−2.95
1976	2.23	−0.98	1.26	2.49	−4.29	−1.80
1977	2.53	−0.94	1.59	3.58	−4.45	−0.88
1978	2.06	−0.97	1.09	4.27	−4.76	−0.49
1979	1.26	−0.97	0.29	5.17	−5.34	−0.18
1980	0.32	−0.93	−0.61	6.03	−5.94	0.09
1981	−0.57	−0.93	−1.49	6.26	−6.45	−0.19
1982	−1.36	−1.21	−2.57	4.77	−7.11	−2.34
1983	−1.54	−1.29	−2.83	3.80	−7.56	−3.77
1984	−1.28	−1.39	−2.66	3.37	−8.18	−4.82
1985	−0.65	−1.57	−2.22	3.29	−8.72	−5.43
Total	4.33	−12.27	−7.94	44.23	−66.98	−22.75

[1] The figures represent absolute differences from the ex-post-simulation in bill. of AS.
[2] Real values at prices of 1976.

7. References

Alm, J. (1985): "The Welfare Cost of the Underground Economy." *Economic Inquiry* 26: 243–263.

Almon, C., Buckler, M. B., Horwitz, L.M., and **Reimbold, Th. C.** (1974): *Interindustry Forecasts of the American Economy.* Lexington, Mass.: D.C. Heath and Company.

Boeschoten, W.C., and **Fage, M.M.G.** (1984): *The Volume of Payments and the Informal Economy in the Netherlands 1965-1982.* Dordrecht: M. Nijhoff Publishers.

Breuss, F. (1982): "Potential Output und gesamtwirtschaftliche Kapazitätsauslastung." *WIFO-Monatsberichte* 55: 104–118.

Breuss, F. (1983): *Österreichs Außenwirtschaft 1945-1982.* Institut für Angewandte Sozialforschung. Vienna: Signum-Verlag.

Cagan, P. (1958): "The Demand for Currency Relative to the Total Money Supply." *Journal of Political Economy* 66: 302–328.

Coen, R.M., and **Hickman, B.G.** (1970): "Constrained Joint Estimation of Factor Demand and Production Functions." *Review of Economics and Statistics* 52: 280–300.

Franz, A. (1985): "Estimates of the Hidden Economy in Austria on the Basis of Official Statistics." *Review of Income and Wealth* 36: 325–336.

Frey, B.S. (1984): "Schattenwirtschaft und Wirtschaftspolitik." *Kredit und Kapital*: 102–119.

Frey, B.S., and **Pommerehne, W.W.** (1984): "The Hidden Economy: State and Prospects for Measurement." *Review of Income and Wealth* 30: 1–21.

Frey, B.S., and **Weck–Hannemann, H.** (1984): "The Hidden Economy as an 'Unobserved' Variable." *European Economic Review* 26: 33–53.

Gaertner, W., and **Wenig, A.** (eds.) (1985): *The Economics of the Shadow Economy.* Heidelberg: Springer-Verlag.

Garcia, G., and **Pak, S.** (1979): "The Ratio of Currency to Demand Deposits in the United States." *Journal of Finance* 34: 703–715.

Gutman, P.M. (1979): "Statistical Illusions, Mistaken Policies." *Challenge* 22: 21–38.

Hofreither, M.F. (1988): "Modelling the Austrian Economy: A Conventional Approach." *Discussion Paper 8802*. Linz: University of Linz, Department of Economics.

Hofreither, M.F., and **Schneider, F.** (1987): "Die Erfassung der Schattenwirtschaft durch den Bargeldansatz – plausible Ergebnisse mittels unzulässiger Methode?" *Wirtschaftspolitische Blätter* 34: 99–118.

Isachsen, A.J., and **Strøm, S.** (1985): "The Size and Growth of the Hidden Economy in Norway." *Review of Income and Wealth* 31: 21–38.

Kirchgässner, G. (1983): "Size and Development of the West German Shadow Economy, 1955-1980." *Zeitschrift für die gesamte Staatswissenschaft* 139: 197–214.

Kirchgässner, G. (1984): "Verfahren zur Erfassung des in der Schattenwirtschaft erarbeiteten Sozialprodukts." *Allgemeines Statistisches Archiv* 68: 378–405.

Kirchgässner, G., and **Pommerehne, W.W.** (1985): "Schattenwirtschaft: Eine Herausforderung für die Wirtschafts- und Finanzpolitik." *Quartalshefte der Girozentrale Wien* 20: 165–177.

Klein, R.L. (1983): *Lectures in Econometrics, Advanced Textbooks in Economics.* Amsterdam: North-Holland.

Klovland, J. (1984): "Tax Evasion and the Demand for Currency in Norway and Sweden. Is there a Hidden Relationship?" *Scandinavian Journal of Economics* 86: 423–439.

Mooslechner, P. (1985): "Der monetäre Ansatz zur Schattenwirtschaft – Eine empirische Illustration an Hand österreichischer Daten." In *Die andere Wirtschaft. Schwarzarbeit und Do-It-Yourself in Österreich*, edited by J. Skolka. Vienna: 101–119.

Peacock, A., and **Shaw, G.K.** (1982): "Tax Evasion and Tax Revenue Loss." *Public Finance* 37: 269–278.

Pindyck, R.S., and **Rubinfeld, D.L.** (1981): *Econometric Models and Economic Forecasts.* New York: McGraw Hill, 2nd edition.

Pommerehne, W.W. (1986): "Was wissen wir eigentlich über Steuerhinterziehung?" *Rivista Internazionale di Science Economiche e Commerciali* 35: 230–262.

Schebeck, F., and **Thury, G.** (1976): "Gesamtwirtschaftliche Auslastungsmaße." *Empirica* 3: 219–239.

Schneider, F. (1986): "Estimating the Size of the Danish Shadow Economy Using the Currency Demand Approach: An Attempt." *Scandinavian Journal of Economics* 88: 643–668.

Schneider, F., and **Hofreither, M.F.** (1987): "Measuring the Size of the Shadow Economy." *Economic Affairs* 7: 18–23.

Schneider, F., and **Pommerehne, W.W.** (1985): "The Decline of Productivity Growth and the Rise of the Shadow Economy in the U.S." *Working Paper*. Aarhus: University of Aarhus.

Skolka, J. (1985): *Die andere Wirtschaft. Schwarzarbeit und Do-It-Yourself in Österreich.* Vienna.

Tanzi, V. (1980): "The Underground Economy in the United States: Estimates and Implications." *Banca Nazionale del Lavoro Quarterly Journal* 135: 427–453.

Tanzi, V. (1983): "The Underground Economy in the United States: Annual Estimates, 1930–1980." *IMF-Staff Papers* 30: 283–305.

Weck, H., **Pommerehne, W.W.**, and **Frey, B.S.** (1984): *Schattenwirtschaft.* München: Franz Vahlen-Verlag.

Wörgötter, A. (1977): "Lohn- und Preissysteme für Österreich." *Empirica* 4: 127–140.

Notes on Taxes and Tax Evasion in Austria

Gerhard Lehner, Vienna, Austria

The Austrian income tax schedule is highly progressive, with marginal tax rates between 21 percent (for taxable income below 50,000 Austrian Schillings (AS)) and 62 percent (for taxable income above 1.5 million AS). The marginal tax rate for average incomes in Austria is presently as high as 39 percent.[1] If social security contributions are included, an increment in average income is subject to a tax levy of more than 50 percent. The high marginal tax rates are indeed an important factor in the development of the shadow economy.

It would be wrong, nonetheless, to consider progressive taxation to be the only crucial determinant of the shadow economy. Changes in the annual working time and in the value-added tax also play an important role in the development of the hidden economy.

The line of causality between progressive taxation and the shadow economy is reciprocal. Progressivity influences the extent and development of the shadow economy, while the hidden economy affects the financing of public expenditures and the strength of the redistributional effects of the income tax.

This paper begins with a few remarks on the work by Schneider–Hofreither–Neck, in particular on the extent and causes of the shadow economy and the effects of changes in tax rates. It then discusses some peculiarities of the Austrian tax system, expanding on the paper by Schneider–Hofreither–Neck, and finally deals with effects of the hidden economy on redistribution and the financing of the public sector.

1. The Influence of Progressivity on the Extent and Development of the Shadow Economy

The progressive income tax affects the range and extent of goods and services supplied in the shadow economy. Note, however, that the time allocation and the

---

[1] This comment was written before the most recent tax reform in Austria. Commencing January 1, 1989, marginal tax rates vary from 10 percent (for taxable income below 50,000 AS) to 50 percent (for taxable income above 700,000 AS). The marginal tax rate for average incomes is 32 percent.

trend in the standard working time is also of great importance for the supply side. The demand side in the shadow economy is less influenced by the income tax than by the value-added tax.

The shadow economy is not homogeneous. It is necessary to differentiate between two areas, the so-called off-book activities and moonlighting. These two sectors vary strongly in their impact on taxes and public expenditures. The off-book activities are usually carried out with that labor officially employed, which most often does not receive additional recompensation. In this case then, private households (employed individuals) do not receive income from the shadow economy. "Only" the tax on profits and the value-added tax are reduced. Increases in wages and changes in the income tax on wages are unlikely to effect the extent and the development of off-book activities. In the case of moonlighting, activities are carried out between private households without the intervention of the business sector. Here, personal income taxes, social security contributions, and value-added taxes are reduced. It should also be noted that relatively few people work exclusively in the shadow economy. As a rule, people work in the official economy and are active in the shadow economy only outside of regular working hours. They are therefore covered by the social security system and are not disadvantaged in this area. Furthermore, capital intensive activities are not well suited for the shadow economy. The hidden economy is found mainly in labor intensive areas. This applies not only to moonlighting but also to off-book activities.

The effect of the marginal tax rate on the shadow economy might be smaller than is commonly assumed. The strength of the substitution effect is limited by the legally or contractually fixed working time. Overtime, where the substitution effect might play a role, is treated preferentially by the tax system. In Austria, the overtime payment premium is not subject to progressive tax rates. Up to 5,070 AS per month (more than one fourth of average income) premiums are tax-free. Premium payments in excess of this amount are taxed at the proportional rate of 15 percent. Thus, for wage and salary earners, the incentive to engage in off-book activities within firms is very small.

Since the mid-fifties, the average annual time of work has decreased by about one fourth. This reduction was brought about by the reduction in weekly working hours from 48 to 40 hours (in some sectors to even fewer), as well as by the lengthening of the annual vacation time from two to five weeks. With the reduction of the legislated (annual) working hours over the last few decades, the potential for activities in the shadow economy in the form of moonlighting has increased considerably. In the long run, the increase in the marginal tax rate and the reduction in the number of working hours have followed a parallel development, though for very different reasons. Both, however, have contributed to the growth of the hidden economy.

An important determinant of demand for goods and services in the hidden economy is the value-added tax. The former gross sales tax was not listed explicitly on invoices, and consumers did not know what share of the price was comprised by the sales tax. With the introduction of the value-added tax in Austria in 1973, the share of the sales tax in the price is stated. Consumers now realize how much they can save if they shift from the official economy to the shadow economy. Furthermore, the standard rate of the value-added tax was raised from 16 percent (1973) to 18 percent (1976) and finally to 20 percent in 1984.

Schneider–Hofreither–Neck (Table 2.1, p. 197) show that since the early seventies the shadow economy has grown at a considerably faster pace than in the sixties. The marginal rate of the (personal) income tax for average incomes posted, however, about the same increases in the periode 1975/1985 as in the period 1960/1975 (Lehner, 1987, p. 96). The increase in the marginal tax rates, therefore, might not provide a sufficient explanation of the growth of the hidden economy. The reform of the sales tax system and the increases in the sales tax rates, as well as the legislated reduction in the hours of work, might have had as equally strong an influence on the growth of the shadow economy (as calculated by Schneider–Hofreither–Neck) as the rise in the marginal tax rates had.

2. Special Characteristics of the Austrian Tax System

The Austrian system of taxation exhibits high (marginal) tax rates. There are, however, many special provisions. The effective tax rates are therefore substantially lower than the schedule tax rates. The large discrepancy between effective and schedule tax rates is indeed the most outstanding feature of the Austrian tax system. As already mentioned, the schedule marginal tax rate for average incomes is 39 percent, but the effective tax rate is only 16 percent. This gap has increased markedly over the last decade. In the mid-seventies, the schedule marginal tax rate for average incomes was 28 percent; the effective tax rate was 13 percent.

This difference is caused by many factors. Tax reductions in recent years were accomplished through the introduction of or increase in tax credits, while the marginal tax rates remained unchanged. Many special provisions are also responsible for narrowing the tax base. Finally, and most important for the problem at hand, only part of income is subject to a progressive tax. In 1985 only some 62 percent of income was subject to progressivity, in the mid-sixties more than 70 percent. The remainder is free of taxation or is taxed at lower proportional rates.

Because of the high share of income not subject to progressive taxation, the relationship between marginal tax rates and the size of the shadow economy is probably more complex than is often supposed, and the influence of marginal tax rates may be lower. This must be kept in mind when the results obtained by Schneider–Hofreither–Neck on the change in tax rates are evaluated. The surprising conclusion by Schneider–Hofreither–Neck (p. 195) that lower indirect taxes mean less value-added could be very relevant politically. The special characteristics of the Austrian tax system, however, might well call for a substantial modification of the results presented. Changes in the tax system could possibly produce results quite different from those shown in the model. The statement must be viewed, therefore, with great caution.

Schneider–Hofreither–Neck emphasize that information on the effects of the shadow economy is crucial for the current discussion of tax reform in Austria. This tax reform is supposed to appreciably lower the marginal (personal) income tax and to reduce the extent of progressivity. This, it is often claimed, decreases the substitution effect and the incentive to move into the shadow economy. But it is questionable whether these predictions would indeed materialize. It has already been stressed that the progressivity of the income tax is only one factor which determines the size of the shadow economy. Therefore, the effect of the tax reform on the shadow economy should not be overestimated. Add to this the planned abolition of preferential tax treatment of overtime premiums by the tax reform and an incentive to move into the hidden economy is created. Furthermore, the demand for products of the shadow economy remains unchanged because it is not affected by the planned tax measures.

3. Short Summary

The progressivity of the tax system is just one factor in the development of the shadow economy. The number of standard working hours in the official economy and the value-added tax also exert a significant influence on the hidden economy. The substitutability between official and shadow economy is likely to be very complex and cannot easily be captured in an economic model. It is therefore very questionable as to whether a reduction of the value-added tax will actually lead to a loss in social welfare. It is more likely that a shadow economy would lead to a divided economy. That the shadow economy can give rise to a serious social problem is most clearly evident in the financial difficulties of the public sector.

Those who work in the hidden economy do not carry the full share of taxes but shift the burden to those who work exclusively in the official economy. Cuts in government programs as a result of financial problems facing the public sector, however, affect all individuals. It it hoped that these remarks on the economic consequences of the shadow economy will stimulate further work in this area.

Reference

Lehner, G. (1987): *Steuerpolitik in Österreich*. Vienna: Manz.

Addresses of Authors

Prof. Dr. Clemens–August **Andreae**, Institute of Public Economics, University of Innsbruck, Herzog–Friedrich–Straße 3, A–6020 Innsbruck, Austria.

Prof. Dr.Dr. Dieter **Bös**, Institute of Economics, University of Bonn, Adenauer-allee 24–42, D–5300 Bonn 1, West Germany.

Dr. Frank A. **Cowell**, Reader in Economics, London School of Economics, Houghton Street, London WC2A 2AE, United Kingdom.

Prof. Dr. Bernhard **Felderer**, Institute of Economics, University of Cologne, Albertus–Magnus–Platz, D–5000 Cologne 41, West Germany.

Prof. John **Gray**, Jesus College, Oxford, OX1 3DW, United Kingdom.

Prof. Thomas W. **Hazlett**, Department of Agricultural Economics, University of California at Davis, Davis, California 95616, USA.

Dr. Markus F. **Hofreither**, Institute of Economics, Johannes–Kepler–University, A–4040 Linz, Austria.

Dr. Christian **Keuschnigg**, Institute of Public Economics, University of Innsbruck, Herzog–Friedrich–Straße 3, A–6020 Innsbruck, Austria.

Prof. Dr. Christian **Kirchner**, Department of Law, University of Hannover, Hanomagstraße 8, D–3000 Hannover 91, West Germany.

Dr. Gerhard **Lehner**, Institute of Economic Research, P.O.Box 91, A–1103 Vienna, Austria.

Dr. Reinhard **Neck**, Institute of Economics, University of Economics, Augasse 2–6, A–1090 Vienna, Austria.

Prof. William A. **Niskanen**, CATO Institute, 224 Second Street, SE, Washington, D.C. 20003, USA.

Prof. Sir Alan **Peacock**, DSC, FBA, The Estee Fairbairn Research Centre, Heriot-Watt University, Chambers Street, Edinburgh, EH1 1XH, United Kingdom.

Prof. Dr. Friedrich **Schneider**, Institute of Economics, Johannes–Kepler–University, A–4040 Linz, Austria.

Dr. Peter **Steiner**, Institute for Industrial Operations and Finance, University of Graz, Hans–Sachs–Gasse 3/III, A-8010 Graz, Austria.

Prof. Dr. Erich **Streissler**, Institute of Economics, University of Vienna, Dr. Karl–Lueger–Ring 1, A–1010 Vienna, Austria.

Prof. Dr. Peter **Swoboda**, Institute for Industrial Operations and Finance, University of Graz, Hans–Sachs–Gasse 3/III, A–8010 Graz, Austria.

Prof. Dr. Georg **Tillmann**, Department of Economics, University of Groningen, P.O.Box 800, NL–9700 Groningen, The Netherlands.

Prof. Leland B. **Yeager**, Department of Economics, Auburn University, 107 Thach Hall, Auburn, Alabama 36849–3501, USA.

World economic forecast up to year 2000

W. Krelle (Ed.)

The Future of the World Economy

Economy Growth and Structural Change

1989. 704 pp. 124 figs.
ISBN 3-540-50467-2

Economy growth and structural change – the future of the world economy – is analysed in this book. Conditional forecasts are given for the economic development of the most important world market countries till the year 2000. The driving forces of economic growth are identified and forecasted, in connection with collaborating scholars in most of these countries and with international organizations. This information is used in solving a coherent world model. The model consists of linked growth models for each country (or groups of countries). The solutions show that the inequality in international income distribution will further increase and that the CMEA and OECD countries will approximately keep their relative positions, with some changes within these groups.
Structural change is also analysed.
The book closes with chapters on special features of the future economic development: on the international debt problem, on long waves, on structural change in the world trade, on the emergence of service economics and on the comparison of GDP and NMP national accounting.

Springer-Verlag Berlin
Heidelberg New York London
Paris Tokyo Hong Kong

H.-J. Vosgerau (Ed.)

New Institutional Arrangements for the World Economy

1989. 492 pp. 26 figs. (Studies in International Economics and Intitutions).
ISBN 3-540-50480-X

As technical progress in transportation of goods and people, communication and transmission of information proceeds, the economic interdependencies between nations grow stronger and stronger – at least potentially. Whether this intensification of economic transactions can really materialize, depends upon the political, social, legal and economic institutions within which they take place. Existing institutional arrangements have to a large extent to be adapted to changing needs.
These problems are analysed in four areas: exchange stabilization, international financial markets, protectionism and the Uruguay GATT round, and organization of international production.

G. Fels, G. M. von Furstenberg (Eds.)

A Supply-Side Agenda for Germany

Sparks from – the United States
– Great Britain
– European Integration

1989. VI, 439 pp. 7 figs.
ISBN 3-540-50544-X

This book deals with supply-side economics and the needed reorientation it would bring to West German policy. The change would add up to an overall strategy for freeing markets, for removing government-imposed distortions, and for using free-market approaches to correct distortions imposed by pressure groups. It would equip the country to follow the lead of the United States and Great Britain in starting to escape from the tangle in which taxes, regulations, and unemployment have grown in step. The impending completion of the European internal market in 1992 adds urgency to this task.

Welfare – Efficiency – Resources

D. Bös, University of Bonn; **M. Rose,** University of Heidelberg; **C. Seidl,** University of Kiel, FRG (Eds.)

Welfare and Efficiency in Public Economics

1988. XVI, 424 pp. 28 figs. ISBN 3-540-18824-X

Contents: Introduction. – Welfare and Efficiency Measures – General Aspects. – Computing Welfare Effects of Fiscal Policy Programmes in an Applied General Equilibrium Setting. – Welfare and Efficiency of Selected Fiscal Policy Measures. – Addresses of Authors.

M. Faber, University of Heidelberg; **H. Niemes,** Mannheim; **G. Stephan,** University of Heidelberg, FRG

Entropy, Environment and Resources

An Essay in Physico-Economics

With the cooperation of L. Freytag

Translated from the German by I. Pellengahr

1987. XII, 205 pp. 33 figs. ISBN 3-540-18248-9

The special features of the book are that the authors utilize a natural scientific variable, entropy, to relate the economic system and the environment, that environmental protection and resource use are analyzed in combination, and that a replacement of techniques over time is analyzed. A novel aspect is that resource extraction is interpreted as a reversed diffusion process. Thus a relationship between entropy, energy and resource concentration is established.

The authors investigate the use of the environment both as a supplier of resources and as a recipient of pollutants with the help of thermodynamic relationships. The book therefore provides a new set of tools for workers in the field.

R. Pethig, University of Oldenburg; **U. Schlieper,** University of Mannheim, FRG (Eds.)

Efficiency, Institutions, and Economic Policy

Proceedings of a Workshop held by the Sonderforschungsbereich 5 at the University of Mannheim, June 1986

1987. IX, 255 pp. 21 figs. ISBN 3-540-18450-3

This volume addresses the issue of efficiency and institutions from different angles. First, the efficiency of modern welfare states is analyzed on a general level where topics like social justice, redistribution and rent seeking are studied in an environment of pressure groups and self-interested politicians (papers by Streit, Schlieper, Wickström). Second, several papers deal with more specific issues like intergenerational transfers in a social insurance system, the efficiency of law, and contractual arrangements in the labor market (Witt, Rowley and Brough, Monissen and Wenger). Third, allocation procedures for nonexclusive public goods are analyzed (Güth and Hellwig, Pethig).

Springer-Verlag Berlin
Heidelberg New York London
Paris Tokyo Hong Kong

Printed by Books on Demand, Germany